CONTENTS

ANNALS OF
AUSTRALIAN LITERATURE

ANNALS OF AUSTRALIAN LITERATURE

GRAHAME JOHNSTON

MELBOURNE
OXFORD UNIVERSITY PRESS
LONDON   WELLINGTON   NEW YORK
1970

Oxford University Press, Ely House, London, W.1

GLASGOW NEW YORK TORONTO MELBOURNE WELLINGTON
CAPE TOWN SALISBURY IBADAN NAIROBI DAR ES SALAAM LUSAKA ADDIS ABABA
BOMBAY CALCUTTA MADRAS KARACHI LAHORE DACCA
KUALA LUMPUR SINGAPORE HONG KONG TOKYO

Oxford University Press, 7 Bowen Crescent, Melbourne

© Oxford University Press 1970

First published 1970

SBN 19 550315 5

Registered in Australia for transmission by post as a book
PRINTED IN AUSTRALIA BY HALSTEAD PRESS, SYDNEY

INTRODUCTION

In its general design, this book follows the *Annals of English Literature 1475-1950* by J. C. Ghosh & E. Withycombe, revised by R. W. Chapman (Clarendon Press, Oxford, 1961), but the shorter history and rather different character of Australian literature have led me to make several modifications of detail. A fairly full explanation of the book's arrangement and conventions therefore seems advisable.

The first part, the yearly entries, has two columns. In the main column are listed the noteworthy books (and, in a few exceptional instances, other publications) dated in the year specified; these were sometimes published in the preceding or following year, and where this is known to me I have mentioned it. The title of each work (occasionally shortened, by the omission of such phrases as 'and other verses') is followed by an abbreviation indicating its genre, where this is not self-evident. The English *Annals* contented itself with the initials TCDPV for tragedy, comedy, drama, prose and verse, but I have used a more elaborate classification (see 'Abbreviations and Symbols', p. xi). I make, however, the proviso that the abbreviations I use are to be taken rather generally: N means a single long piece of fiction, A a work of autobiographical interest, and so on, not necessarily a novel or an autobiography in the full formal sense.

The method of indicating the author is usually to give the surname alone, followed by the year of birth in parentheses. But if another author of the same surname also appears in the book, a Christian name or initial is added to make the identification clear; and if the work being cited is posthumous, the date in parentheses is the year of death, not birth. Where an author used a pseudonym habitually, this is given instead of his real name, which will be found, however, in the index; where a pseudonym was used casually, or where it is now more common practice to refer to an author by his real name (Furphy, for instance), the latter is given at the beginning of the entry and the pseudonym is added in brackets after the title of the book. Supplementary information of various kinds—that a book belongs to a series, or is a revision of an earlier title, for example—will also be found in brackets after the title.

The yearly entries also have a side column. This lists the authors born in that year (provided that the year of birth is definite), followed by those that died in that year, each list in alphabetical order. Then follows ancillary information: the founding and duration of newspapers and periodicals; visits or books by notable writers from overseas; books written in Australia in languages other than English; some books on non-Australian subjects by authors whose other works are in the main column; books written abroad by authors now settled in Australia; English classics referring to Australia; and so on.

The distribution of material between the two columns of the yearly entries, although both are fully indexed, poses some difficult problems because it implicitly asks what makes an author 'Australian'. In the nineteenth century, a remarkable number of authors made the long journey from Britain to the Australian colonies, either to visit or to settle, and many of the notable books are by people who spent only a short time here, Henry Kingsley for instance; while in the twentieth, by contrast, many writers of Australian birth have lived and worked in Europe and America and published books with no strictly 'Australian' content. I have dealt with each author as seemed most sensible to me; for the colonial period I arrived at a working rule that places in the main column writers who actually lived in Australia, even if only for a few years, and in the side column those who simply passed through.

The second part of the book indexes both the main and side columns of the first part, listing the authors alphabetically, with their dates, pseudonyms, works (cited in chronological order, often by shortened titles), and cross-references to books about them. This index contains some information (e.g. references to occurrences and publications in 1969) not found in the first part. It employs three symbols which need comment. The double obelisk (‡) prefixed to an author's name indicates that he has published a number of other books, perhaps of a different kind, as well as those listed; this symbol is applied particularly to prolific authors here represented by their first, or most typical, book only. The asterisk (*) denotes a non-Australian author who visited Australia, the section mark (§) a non-Australian author who did not set foot here.

In selecting entries for inclusion, I have chosen to interpret the word 'literature' in a broad sense; if one restricts its meaning to poetry, fiction and drama—as seems increasingly fashionable—the record of the Australian experience is unduly narrowed, because many of its finest documents are historical, biographical, or descriptive. I have tried to some extent to compensate for the fact that we lack an up-to-date, comprehensive bibliography of Australian prose and verse, but this book is not itself a bibliography, and its treatment of many fields of writing—particularly specialised fields like local histories and books for children—is impressionistic, not thorough. Books for children are listed in H. Anderson's *The Singing Roads* (1965, 1969) and in H. M. Saxby's *History of Australian Children's Literature*, of which the first volume (1841-1941) appeared while this book was being proved. Some areas, such as religion, philosophy and the sciences, I have not entered except accidentally, when titles are included for their literary quality or personal associations. But I hope that the book provides an accurate paradigm of the growth of Australian literature from its restricted, factual beginnings to its present range and variety.

In compiling these *Annals* I have depended much on previous histories of literature, biographies and bibliographies. Where they are silent or discrepant, I have tried to supplement or correct them, but where they are united in error I may have failed to detect it. For some authors, I regret, the information remains incomplete; it has been particularly difficult to determine whether or not some are still living. For advice, information and corrections I am indebted to numerous authors and friends; and for invaluable help to Mr David Elder and Miss Josephine Swannie of the Oxford University Press, Mr H. J. Gibbney of the Australian Dictionary of Biography, and Miss Vera Blackburn and Miss Mary Gilchrist of the Australian War Memorial.

Duntroon
19 December 1969   G.J.

Abbreviations and Symbols

A	Autobiography (inc. memoirs, reminiscences, travel)
AP	Australian Poets series (Angus & Robertson)
B	Biography
C	Criticism (inc. aesthetics, literary and social commentary)
CAP	Contemporary Australian Plays (University of Queensland Press)
D	Drama
E	Essays
G	Great Australians series (Oxford University Press)
H	History
L	Legends
M	Miscellanies (i.e. containing both prose and verse)
N	Novels
P	Prose (documentary, politics, economics, geography, anthropology, philology)
S	Stories and/or Sketches
V	Verse (inc. verse drama)
W	Australian Writers and their Work series (Oxford University Press, formerly Lansdowne)
X	Australian Explorers series (Oxford University Press)
Y	Books for children
†	indicates that the book has been reprinted in facsimile by the Libraries Board of South Australia
¶	indicates that the book belongs to the series Australia in the War of 1939-1945
★	indicates a non-Australian author who visited Australia
§	indicates a non-Australian author who never set foot in Australia
‡	indicates an Australian author who has published a number of other books (see introduction, p. vii)

1789

Anon. (ed.): †The Voyage of Governor Phillip to Botany Bay

Tench (1758?): †A Narrative of the Expedition to Botany Bay [cf. 1793]

William Bland b.
P. M. Cunningham b.
Erasmus Darwin, 'A Visit of Hope to Sydney Cove near Botany Bay' [in The Voyage of Governor Phillip]

1790

White, John (1756?): Journal of a Voyage to New South Wales [later ed. by A. H. Chisholm 1962, with intro. by R. Rienits]

W. C. Wentworth b.

1791

P. P. King b.
Henry Savery b.

1792

William Howitt b.
T. L. Mitchell b.

1793

Hunter (1737): †An Historical Journal of the Transactions at Port Jackson and Norfolk Island [later ed. by J. Bach 1968]

Tench (1758?): †A Complete Account of the Settlement at Port Jackson [later ed., with 1789 vol., by L. F. Fitzhardinge 1961, rev. 1964, as Sydney's First Four Years]

1794

Johnson, Richard (1753): †An Address to the Inhabitants of the Colonies, established in New South Wales and Norfolk Island

James Backhouse b.

1795

Charles Sturt b.

1796

1797

George Loveless b.
P. E. de Strzelecki b.

1798

Collins, David (1756): †An Account of the English Colony in New South Wales [vol. i; vol. ii 1802; later ed. by James Collier 1910]

James Macarthur b.
Barzellai Quaife b.
Charles Rowcroft b.

1799

John Dunmore Lang b.
'Henry Melville' b.

1800

John Lhotsky b.
Roger Therry b.

1801

James Busby b.

1802

R. H. Horne b.
New South Wales General Standing Orders [*first book printed in Australia*]

1803

W. Smith O'Brien b.
Sydney Gazette *1803-42 [facsimile reprints of vols 1-7 (1803-09) issued 1963, '65, '66, '68, '69]*

1804

George Bennett b.
J. W. Bull b.
Georgiana McCrae b.
G. C. Mundy b.
Charles Whitehead b.

1805

Tuckey (1776): †An Account of a Voyage to Establish a Colony at Port Phillip in Bass's Strait

Alexander Harris b.

1806

W. B. Ullathorne b.

1807

B. T. Finniss b.
Charles Tompson b.

2

1808

Richard Birnie b.
Anna Maria Bunn b.
Martin Cash b.
Caroline Chisholm b.
W. H. Christie b.
James Tucker b.

1809

J. F. Mortlock b.
John West b.

1810

Robinson, Michael Massey (1744): Odes [in the *Sydney Gazette* 1810-21; later ed. by G. Mackaness 1946]

C. T. Knowles b.
David Collins d.
Derwent Star and Van Diemen's Land Intelligencer

1811

Mann, David Dickenson (1775?): The Present Picture of New South Wales   P

Henry Halloran b.
E. W. Landor b.
Robert Lowe b.

1812

George Grey b.
Louisa Anne Meredith b.

1813

Charles Badham b.
Charles Harpur b.
Joseph Hawdon b.
Ludwig Leichhardt b.
P. E. Warburton b.

1814

Flinders (1774): †A Voyage to Terra Australis

William Woolls b.
Matthew Flinders d.
Van Diemen's Land Gazette and General Advertiser

1815

Samuel Bennett b.
E. J. Eyre b.
John Mitchel b.
Henry Parkes b.
John McDouall Stuart b.
Alexander Tolmer b.
Mary T. Vidal b.
W. Westgarth b.

3

| 1816 | *Annie Maria Dawbin b.*
Charles Gavan Duffy b.
John George Lang b.
J. H. Tuckey d.
Hobart Town Gazette
1816-25 |

| 1817 | *James Bonwick b.* |

1818

Wells, Thomas (1782): Michael Howe, the Last and Worst of the Bushrangers of Van Diemen's Land B [anon.; facsimile reprint 1966]

William Forster b.
C. A. D. Pasco b.

1819

Field (1786): First Fruits of Australian Poetry [2nd edn, enlarged, 1823; later ed. by R. Edwards 1941]

Vaux (1782): Memoirs of James Hardy Vaux A [later ed. by N. McLachlan 1964]

Wentworth (1790): A Statistical, Historical and Political Description of the Colony of New South Wales and its Dependent Settlements in Van Diemen's Land

Edmund Finn b.
James Fenton b.
A. C. Gregory b.
G. W. Rusden b.

1820

Oxley (1785?): †Journals of Two Expeditions into the Interior of New South Wales

David Blair b.
Raffaello Carboni b.
E. M. Curr b.
James Martin b.
James Smith b.
Sir Joseph Banks d.

| 1821 | *F. T. Gregory b.*
S. P. Hill b.
Alfred Joyce b.
John Hunter d.
Australian Magazine
1821-22 |

1822

J. R. Houlding b.
George French Angas b.
J. T. Bigge, †The State of the Colony of New South Wales

1823

Blaxland (1778): A Journal of a Tour of Discovery Across the Blue Mountains [later ed. by G. Mackaness 1950 q.v.]
Wentworth (1790): Australasia V

W. B. Withers b.
J. T. Bigge, †The Judicial Establishments of New South Wales and Van Diemen's Land and †The State of Agriculture and Trade in New South Wales

1824

J. L. Michael b.
The Australian 1824-48

1825

Busby (1801): A Treatise on the Culture of the Vine and the Art of Making Wine
Field (1786) (ed.): Geographical Memoirs on New South Wales

William Landsborough b.
Catherine Spence b.
Colonial Times (Hobart) 1825-57

1826

King, P. P. (1791): †Narrative of a Survey of the Intertropical and Western Coasts of Australia
Tompson (1807): Wild Notes, from the Lyre of a Native Minstrel V

Annabella Boswell b.
T. A. Browne ('Rolf Boldrewood') b.
W. E. Hearn b.
Rachel Henning b.
Joseph Holt d.
Michael Massey Robinson d.
Monitor (Sydney) 1826-41

1827

Cunningham (1789): †Two Years in New South Wales [later ed. by D. S. Macmillan 1966]
'Pindar Juvenal': The Van Diemen's Land Warriors V

Caroline Leakey b.
George Ranken b.
David Syme b.
Richard Johnson d.
South Asian Register 1827-28

5

1828

D. H. Deniehy b.
Roderick Flanagan b.
Richard Rowe b.
William Walker b.
John Oxley d.

1829

Savery (1791): The Hermit in Van Diemen's Land S ['by Simon Stukeley' in the *Colonial Times*, Hobart; anon. as book, dated 1829, publd 1830; later ed. by C. Hadgraft & M. Roe 1964]

David Burn, The Bushrangers *produced in Edinburgh*
Edward Gibbon Wakefield, †A Letter from Sydney
Hobart Town Almanack *1829-37*

1830

Busby (1801): A Manual of Directions for Planting and Cultivating Vineyards and for Making Wine in New South Wales
Dawson, Robert (1782): The Present State of Australia P
Savery (1791): Quintus Servinton N [anon. 1830-31; later ed. by C. Hadgraft 1962]

A. W. Howitt b.
Henry Kingsley b.
C. H. Pearson b.
J. J. Shillinglaw b.
Frederick Sinnett b.
W. T. Moncrieff, Van Diemen's Land D
Fremantle Journal and General Advertiser
Western Australian Gazette

1831

Bland (1789) (ed.): †Journey of Discovery to Port Phillip, New South Wales, in 1824-5 by Messrs W. H. Hovell and Hamilton Hume

Thomas Petrie b.
Robert Sealy b.
Charles Thatcher b.
H. G. Turner b.
Sydney Herald *begins* [*daily since 1840, named* Sydney Morning Herald *since 1842*]
Fremantle Observer
Western Australian Chronicle and Perth Gazette

6

1832

Woolls (1814): The Voyage   V [anon.]

Lorimer Fison b.
J. E. Tenison-Woods b.
John White d.

1833

Sturt (1795): †Two Expeditions into the Interior of Southern Australia
Woolls (1814): Australia   V [anon.]

Frank Fowler b.
Adam Lindsay Gordon b.
G. G. McCrae b.
Watkin Tench d.
Thomas Wells d.
Hobart Town Magazine *1833-34*
Perth Gazette and Western Australian Journal *1833-47* [*cf. 1847*]

1834

Bennett, George (1804): †Wanderings in New South Wales A
Lang, John Dunmore (1799): An Historical and Statistical Account of New South Wales
Martin, R. M. (c. 1803): History of the British Colonies
'Melville, Henry' (1799): The Bushrangers   D [in *Hobart Town Magazine*, April; produced May]

Caroline Atkinson b.
J. A. Macartney b.
W. J. Wills b.

1835

Jorgenson (1780): A Shred of Autobiography [part i; part ii 1838; in *Hobart Town Almanack*; cf. Hogan 1891, Clune & Stephensen 1954]
Lhotsky (1800): A Journey from Sydney to the Australian Alps
'Melville, Henry' (1799): †The History of the Island of Van Diemen's Land [later ed. by G. Mackaness 1965]
Thomas (1801?): The Bandit of the Rhine   D

Ernest Giles b.
Simpson Newland b.
James Brunton Stephens b.
N. W. Swan b.
Colonist, *ed. by J. D. Lang, 1835-40*

7

1836

Martin, R. M. (c. 1803): History of Australasia

G. B. Barton b.
Charles Darwin in
Australia [see Journals
(*1839*, *1891*) and
Diary, ed. by Nora
Barlow (*1933*); see
also Alan Moorehead
1969]
South Australian
Gazette and Colonial
Register *1836-39; as*
Register *1839-1931*

1837

Lang, John Dunmore (1799): Transportation and Colonisation P

Loveless (1797): The Victims of Whiggery P

Macarthur (1798): New South Wales: its Present State and Future Prospects [written by Edward Edwards, q.v., from material supplied by Macarthur]

Mudie, James (1779): The Felonry of New South Wales [later ed. by W. Stone 1964]

Ullathorne (1806): †The Catholic Mission in Australasia

C. Fetherstonhaugh b.
E. H. Thomas d.

1838

Bunn (1808): The Guardian N ['by an Australian']

Holt, Joseph (d. 1826): Memoirs [ed. by T. C. Croker]

Maconochie (1787): †Thoughts on Convict Management

Martin, James (1820): The Australian Sketch Book E

Mitchell, T. L. (1792): †Three Expeditions into the Interior of Eastern Australia

Ullathorne (1806): The Horrors of Transportation Briefly Unfolded

Woolls (1814): Miscellanies in Prose and Verse

J. H. Nicholson b.
Melbourne Advertiser
[*cf. 1839*]
Port Phillip Gazette
1838-51
Southern Australian
1838-52

1839

Light (1786): †A Brief Journal of the Proceedings of William Light   A

Henry Kendall b.
W. L. Ranken b.
H. J. Wrixon b.
William Light d.
Port Phillip Patriot and Melbourne Advertiser *1839-51*

1840

Hill, Fidelia (1790?): Poems and Recollections of the Past
Ullathorne (1806): A Reply to Judge Burton on the State of Religion in the Colony

F. P. Labillière b.
Port Phillip Herald *1840-49 [cf. 1849]*

1841

Christie (1808): A Love Story   N ['by A Bushman']
Grey (1812): †Journals of Two Expeditions of Discovery in North-West and Western Australia

J. Jorgenson d.
A Mother's Offering to Her Children, '*by a Lady Long Resident in N.S.W.*' [*first children's book, prob. by Lady Gordon Bremer*]
South Australian Magazine *1841-43*

1842

Burn (1799?): Plays and Fugitive Pieces
Chisholm, Caroline (1808): Female Immigration
Knowles (1810): Salathiel   D
Parkes (1815): Stolen Moments   V

Robert Barton b.
John Lewis b.
Henry Savery d.

1843

Backhouse (1794): A Narrative of a Visit to the Australian Colonies [repr. 1967]
Hill, S. P. (1821): Tarquin the Proud   D
Rowcroft (1798): Tales of the Colonies   N

Joseph Furphy b.
A. C. Grant b.
John Stanley James b.
Patrick Moloney b.
E. E. Morris b.
Garnet Walch b.
Port Phillip Magazine
Adelaide Observer *1843-1931*

1844

Meredith, Louisa A. (1812): Notes and Sketches of New South Wales

Woolls (1814): A Short Account of the Character and Labours of the Rev. Samuel Marsden B

Ada Cambridge b.
J. B. O'Reilly b.
C. T. Knowles d.
Atlas, ed. by Robert Lowe, 1844-48

1845

Eyre (1815): †Journals of Expeditions of Discovery into Central Australia and Overland from Adelaide to King George's Sound

Franklin, John (1786): Narrative of Some Passages in the History of Van Diemen's Land [facsimile reprint 1967]

Harpur (1813): Thoughts: a Series of Sonnets

McCombie (1813?): Arabin, or the Adventures of a Colonist in New South Wales N

Strzelecki (1797): †Physical Description of New South Wales and Van Diemen's Land P

Vidal (1815): Tales for the Bush S

E. Favenc b.
R. L. Jack b.
George Reid b.
T. E. Spencer b.
Richard Cobbold, The History of Margaret Catchpole [cf. Barton 1924]

1846

Rowcroft (1798): The Bushranger of Van Diemen's Land N

Marcus Clarke b.
James Collier b.
Mary Hannay Foott b.
G. H. Gibson ('Ironbark') b.
W. G. Spence b.
Barron Field d.
Argus (*Melbourne*) *1846-1957*
Moreton Bay Courier *1846-1933; as* Courier *1861-* [cf. *1933*]

1847

Angas (1822): †Savage Life and Scenes in Australia and New Zealand [repr. with note by C. R. H. Taylor 1969]

Harris, Alexander (1805): Settlers and Convicts N ['by an Emigrant Mechanic'; later ed. by C. M. H. Clark 1953, rev. 1964]

Landor (1811): The Bushman, or Life in a New Country A

Leichhardt (1813): †Journal of an Overland Expedition in Australia

John Forrest b.
Catherine Martin b.
A. Montgomery b.
Sir John Franklin d.
T. H. Huxley in Australia 1847-49 [see Diary, ed. by Julian Huxley 1935; see also M. Bassett 1966]
Heads of the People *1847-48*
Perth Gazette *1847-64*

1848

Cozens ( ): Adventures of a Guardsman A

Harris, Alexander (1805): Testimony to the Truth; or, The Autobiography of an Atheist [anon.; 4th edn 1852 titled A Converted Atheist's Testimony ... being the Autobiography of Alex. Harris, author of Settlers and Convicts, The Emigrant Family etc.]

Mitchell, T. L. (1792): †Journal of an Expedition into the Interior of Tropical Australia

Westgarth (1815): Australia Felix P

'Tasma' b.

1849

Harris, Alexander (1805): The Emigrant Family N ['by the Author of Settlers and Convicts'; 2nd edn 1852 titled Martin Beck; later ed. by W. S. Ramson 1967]

Sturt (1795): †Narrative of an Expedition into Central Australia

Alexander Forrest b.
P. Holdsworth b.
Charles Dickens, David Copperfield (1849-50)
Port Phillip Herald *becomes Melbourne Morning Herald [cf. 1869]*

1850

Vidal (1815): Cabramatta, and Woodleigh Farm
  S [contains 'The Cabramatta Store']

J. A. Barry b.
S. M. Caffyn b.
Robert Richardson b.
Samuel Shumack b.
Empire, conducted by
  Henry Parkes, 1850–
  58 [cf. 1859]
Thomas Arnold in
  Australia 1850–56
  [see Passages in a
  Wandering Life
  1900; cf. P. A.
  Howell 1964]
Bulwer Lytton, The
  Caxtons

1851

Julian Ashton b.
J. L. Cuthbertson b.
John Farrell b.
A. Patchett Martin b.
Mrs Campbell Praed b.

1852

Lang, John Dunmore (1799): Freedom and
  Independence for the Golden Lands of
  Australia P
Meredith, Louisa A. (1812): My Home in
  Tasmania P
Morgan (1792?): The Life and Adventures of
  William Buckley B [later ed. by C. E.
  Sayers 1967]
Mundy (1804): Our Antipodes P
West, John (1809): †The History of Tasmania

E. J. Banfield b.
Kathleen Mannington
  Caffyn ('Iota') b.
A. Sutherland b.
James Mudie d.
Lord Robert Cecil, Gold
  Fields Diary [ed. by
  E. Scott 1935]
Samuel Sidney, The
  Three Colonies of
  Australia

1853

Harpur (1813): The Bushrangers [D] and Other
  Poems
Westgarth (1815): Victoria: Late Australia
  Felix P

Gregory Blaxland d.

12

1854

Howitt, William (1792): A Boy's Adventures
in the Wilds of Australia   Y
Mitchel (1815): Jail Journal   A
Spence, Catherine (1825): Clara Morison   N
[anon.]

E. H. Sugden b.
H. A. Tardent b.
Fidelia Hill d.
The Age (*Melbourne*)
   begins
W. S. Jevons in Aus-
   tralia, 1854-59 [*see J.
   A. La Nauze*, Politi-
   cal Economy in Aus-
   tralia *1949*]
T. L. Mitchell, The
   Lusiad of Luis de
   Camoens,   closely
   translated
Hobarton Mercury
   (*later* Mercury) *begins*

1855

Carboni (1820): †The Eureka Stockade   P
[repr. 1942 intro. by H. V. Evatt; 1947
intro. by B. Fitzpatrick; 1963 intro. by
A. G. Serle]
Howitt, William (1792): Land, Labour and
Gold   P
Lang, John George (1816): The Forger's Wife
N   [other edns with various titles]

William   Astley ('*Price
   Warung*') *b.*
Louis Becke b.
F. J. Gillen b.
J. F. Hogan b.
George Sutherland b.
Sir Thomas Mitchell d.
Punch (*Melbourne*)
   1855-1925

1856

Bonwick (1817): The Discovery and Settlement
of Port Phillip   H
William Buckley   B
O'Brien, W. Smith (1803): Principles of
Government   P
Sinnett (1830): The Fiction Fields of Australia
[in the *Journal of Australasia*; later ed. by
C. Hadgraft 1966 and inc. in J. Barnes,
The Writer in Australia 1969]
Spence, Catherine (1825): Tender and True
N   [anon.]

J. F. Archibald b.
T. A. Coghlan b.
Alfred Deakin b.
S. G. Fielding b.
R. Spencer-Browne b.
P. P. King d.
Charles Rowcroft d.
Charles Reade, It is
   Never Too Late to
   Mend
Journal of Australasia
   1856-58
My Note Book *1856-
   59*

13

1857

Atkinson, Caroline (1834): Gertrude the Emigrant N ['by an Australian Lady']
Howitt, William (1792): Tallangetta, the Squatter's Home N
Michael (1824): Songs Without Music V
Thatcher (1831): Colonial Songster V

H. E. Barff b.
James Hebblethwaite b.
J. H. Ross b.
The Month *1857–58*

1858

Harris, Alexander (1805): Religio Christi A [in the *Saturday Evening Post* (Philadelphia); abridged edn as The Secrets of Alexander Harris 1961]
McCombie (1813?): The History of the Colony of Victoria
Michael (1824): Sir Archibald Yelverton V [in *The Month*]
Rowe (1828): Peter Possum's Portfolio M
Whitehead (1804): Emma Latham N [in *My Note Book*]

Victor Daley b.
Thomas Welsby b.
B. R. Wise b.
South Australian Advertiser *begins*

1859

Atkinson, Caroline (1834): Cowanda N ['By the Author of Gertrude'; cf. 1857]
Fowler (1833): Southern Lights and Shadows P
Horne, R. H. (1802): Australian Facts and Prospects P
Kingsley (1830): The Recollections of Geoffry Hamlyn N
Lang, John George (1816): Botany Bay S
Leakey (1827): The Broad Arrow N ['by Oliné Keese']
Sealy (1831): Scraps V ['by Menippus']
Whitehead (1804): The Spanish Marriage D [in the *Victorian Monthly Magazine*]

James Edmond b.
Fergus Hume b.
T. G. Tucker b.
Empire (*new management*) *1859–75*

1860

Deniehy (1828): How I Became Attorney-General of New Barataria S
Michael (1824): John Cumberland V
Vidal (1815): Bengala N

J. P. Bourke ('Bluebush') b.
F. J. Broomfield b.
A. A. G. Hales b.
Jack Moses b.
W. B. Spencer b.
Alexander Maconochie d.
G. C. Mundy d.
Charles Dickens, Great Expectations (1860-61)
Sydney Mail 1860-1938

1861

McCombie (1813?): Australian Sketches
Westgarth (1815): Australia P

Kate Baker b.
Daisy Bates b.
W. J. Jeffrey b.
Edward Jenks b.
William Lane b.
Hubert Murray b.
G. B. Philip b.
Roderick Flanagan d.
S. P. Hill d.
Robert Sealy d.
W. J. Wills d.

1862

Flanagan (d. 1861): The History of New South Wales
Harpur (1813): A Poet's Home V
Kendall (1839): Poems and Songs
Landsborough (1825): †Journal of Expedition from Carpentaria, in search of Burke and Wills

Francis Adams b.
Barbara Baynton b.
W. T. Goodge b.
T. W. Heney b.
J. B. O'Hara b.
A. B. Piddington b.
Charles Whitehead d.

15

1863

Hearn (1826): Plutology P

Therry (1800): Reminiscences of Thirty Years' Residence in New South Wales and Victoria

Wills (d. 1861): A Successful Exploration through the Interior of Australia [ed. from the Journals and Letters of W. J. Wills, d. 1861, by his father William Wills]

G. E. Evans b.
R. W. Giblin b.
A. W. Jose b.
F. Penn-Smith b.
John Sandes b.
E. A. Vidler b.
Frank Fowler d.
Express (Adelaide), later Express and Telegraph, 1863-1951

1864

Gordon (1833): The Feud V ['by A. Lindsay'; later edn with notes by H. Anderson 1965]

Horne, R. H. (1802): Prometheus the Fire-Bringer V

Mortlock (1809): Experiences of a Convict A [anon., 1864-65; later ed. by G. A. Wilkes & A. G. Mitchell 1965]

Stuart, J. McD. (1815): Explorations in Australia [ed. by W. Hardman]

Thatcher (1831): Colonial Minstrel V

Walker, William (1828): Australian Literature C

W. M. Hughes b.
S. W. Jephcott b.
Laura Palmer-Archer b.
A.B. ('Banjo') Paterson b.
C. H. Souter b.
P. M. Cunningham d.
John George Lang d.
W. Smith O'Brien d.
The Australasian 1864-1946
Perth Gazette and Western Australian Times 1864-74

1865

Harpur (1813): The Tower of the Dream V

Howitt, William (1792): The History of Discovery in Australia and New Zealand

Kingsley (1830): The Hillyars and the Burtons N

Spence, Catherine (1825): Mr Hogarth's Will N

Tenison-Woods (1832): A History of the Discovery and Exploration of Australia

A. A. Bayldon b.
Carlton Dawe b.
E. G. Dyson b.
William Gay b.
Mary Gilmore b.
H. H. ('Breaker') Morant b.
Dowell O'Reilly b.
A. G. Stephens b.
A. G. Steven b.
F. S. Williamson b.
G. A. Wood b.
D. H. Deniehy d.
Australian Journal 1865-1958

1866

Barton, G. B. (1836): The Poets and Prose Writers of New South Wales
Literature in New South Wales
Horne, R. H. (1802): The South Sea Sisters D

Barcroft Boake b.
Gilbert Murray b.
Bernard O'Dowd b.
Robert Dawson d.
John Morgan d.
Frederick Sinnett d.
John McDouall Stuart d.

1867

Bennett, Samuel (1815): History of Australian Discovery and Colonisation
Bonwick (1817): John Batman, Founder of Victoria B
Gordon (1833): Sea Spray and Smoke Drift V
Ashtaroth D
Hearn (1825): The Government of England P
Houlding (1822): Australian Capers N ['by Old Boomerang']
McCrae,G.G. (1833): Mämba V
The Story of Balladeädro V

Guy Boothby b.
Herbert Brookes b.
Robert Garran b.
Louis Lavater b.
Henry Lawson b.
Roderic Quinn b.
Ernest Scott b.
James Macarthur d.
Colonial Monthly, ed.
   by Marcus Clarke,
   1867-70
Evening News
   (*Sydney*) *1867-1931*

1868

McCombie (1813?): Frank Henly, or Honest Industry Will Conquer N
Spence, Catherine (1825): The Author's Daughter N

Randolph Bedford b.
H. E. Boote b.
Jennings Carmichael b.
R. J. Crawford b.
A. H. Davis ('Steele Rudd') b.
Mary Fullerton ('E') b.
Fred Johns b.
William Moore b.
William Bland d.
Charles Harpur d.
R. M. Martin d.
J. L. Michael d.

1869

Clarke, Marcus (1846): The Peripatetic Philosopher E
Long Odds N [part written by G. A. Walstab; see S. R. Simmonds, Marcus Clarke and the Writing of Long Odds 1946]
Kendall (1839): Leaves From Australian Forests V
Kingsley (1830): Tales of Old Travel Renarrated
Meredith, Louisa A. (1812): Phoebe's Mother N [in the *Australasian* 1866 titled 'Ebba']
Rowe (1828): The Boy in the Bush Y

G. S. Beeby b.
E. J. Brady b.
R. H. Croll b.
Frank Morton b.
W. H. Ogilvie b.
Marie Pitt b.
A. F. M. Robb b.
E. S. Sorenson b.
Paul Wenz b.
David McKee Wright b.
James Backhouse d.
Thomas McCombie d.
Charles Sturt d.
Mary T. Vidal d.
Melbourne Herald
  changes to afternoon
Daily Telegraph
  (*Melbourne*) *1869-92*

1870

Cash (1808): The Adventures of Martin Cash A [ed. by J. L. Burke]
Clarke, Marcus (1846): His Natural Life N [in the *Australian Journal* 1870-2; cf. 1874, 1885]
Gordon (1833): Bush Ballads and Galloping Rhymes
Houlding (1822): Rural and City Life N ['by Old Boomerang']
Withers (1823): The History of Ballarat

C. J. Brennan b.
M. M. Grover b.
Mrs Æneas Gunn b.
G. C. Henderson b.
W. G. Henderson b.
G. F. Pearce b.
'*Henry Handel Richardson*' *b.*
Adam Lindsay Gordon d.
B. L. Farjeon, Grif: A Story of Australian Life

1871

Clarke, Marcus (1846): Old Tales of a Young Country
Kingsley (1830): Hetty and Other Stories [contains 'The Two Cadets']
Stephens, James Brunton (1835): Convict Once V

J. S. Battye b.
J. Le Gay Brereton b.
D. W. Carnegie b.
A. Dorrington b.
Percival Serle b.
Louis Stone b.
James Busby d.

1871 (contd)

Joseph Hawdon d.
Anthony Trollope, first
visit to Australia
1871-72

1872

Kingsley (1830): Hornby Mills and Other Stories [contains 'Eyre's March' and 'The March of Charles Sturt']
Lang, John Dunmore (1799): Poems Sacred and Secular
Quaife (1798): The Intellectual Sciences P
Walch (1843): Trookulentos D

A. H. Adams b.
Lala Fisher b.
Mabel Forrest b.
Arthur Gask b.
C. A. W. Monckton b.
Shaw Neilson b.
E. E. Pescott b.
Bertram Stevens b.
G. A. Taylor b.
Ethel Turner b.
G. F. Young b.
Caroline Atkinson (Mrs Calvert) d.
W. C. Wentworth d.
Telegraph (Brisbane) begins

1873

Bonwick (1817): The Tasmanian Lily N
Clarke, Marcus (1846): Holiday Peak S
Dawbin (1816): Memories of the Past A ['by a Lady in Australia']
McCrae, G. G. (1833): The Man in the Iron Mask V
O'Reilly, J. B. (1844): Songs from the Southern Seas V
Stephens, James Brunton (1835): The Godolphin Arabian V

Erle Cox b.
W. H. Christie d.
'Henry Melville' d.
Barzellai Quaife d.
Sir Paul Strzelecki d.
John West d.
Anthony Trollope, Australia and New Zealand ['Australia' later ed. by P. D. Edwards & R. B. Joyce 1967; sels. as Trollope's Australia ed. by H. Dow 1966]
Anthony Trollope, Harry Heathcote of Gangoil [repr. 1963 with intro. by M. Muir]

1874

Angas (1822): The Wreck of the Admella V
Clarke, Marcus (1846): His Natural Life N [as book; cf. 1870, 1885]
Kingsley (1830): Reginald Hetherege N
Martin, Catherine (1847): The Explorers V ['by M.C.']
Ranken, W. L. (1839): The Dominion of Australia P
Spencer-Browne (1856): Shadow and Shine V

J. H. M. Abbott b.
A. J. Buchanan b.
J. F. Dwyer b.
Frank Fox b.
'Jim Grahame' b.
Lionel Lindsay b.
R. H. Long b.
Louise Mack b.
Walter Murdoch b.
Ambrose Pratt b.
Nathan Spielvogel b.
Alexander Harris d.
George Loveless d.
Sir Roger Therry d.
Western Australian
    Times *1874-79*

1875

Cambridge (1884): The Manor House V Up the Murray N [in the *Australasian*]
Clarke, Marcus (1846): 'Twixt Shadow and Shine N
Deakin (1856): Quentin Massys D
Forrest, John (1847): †Explorations in Australia
Spencer-Browne (1856): The Last Ride V
Swan (1835): Tales of Australian Life
Warburton (1813): †Journey Across the Western Interior of Australia

C. H. Bertie b.
F. W. Eggleston b.
William Gosse Hay b.
Edward Sweetman b.
James Tyrrell b.
David Burn d.
Raffaello Carboni d.
John Mitchel d.
Havelock Ellis in Australia 1875-79 [see Kanga Creek *1922*, My Life *1940*]
Anthony Trollope, second visit [see The Tireless Traveller, ed. by B. A. Booth, *1941*]
Athenaeum (*Sydney*) *1875-76*

1876

Forster (1818): The Weirwolf D

J. B. Dalley b.
C. J. Dennis b.
Lance Fallaw b.
May Gibbs b.

1876 (contd)

Stephens, James Brunton (1835): A Hundred Pounds N

Syme (1827): Outlines of an Industrial Science P

Bertha Lawson (née Bredt) b.
Will Lawson b.
Hugh McCrae b.
W. S. Robinson b.
A. T. Strong b.
Jeanne Young b.
Henry Kingsley d.
William Sharp ('Fiona McLeod') in Australia [see The Human Inheritance 1882]
Melbourne Review *1876-85*

1877

Clarke, Marcus (1846): Four Stories High S
The Future Australian Race E

Forster (1818): The Brothers D

James (1843): The Vagabond Papers [Series 1-4; Series 5, 1878; sel. edn by M. Cannon 1969]

James (1843) (ed.): The Vagabond Annual M

Sutherland, A. (1852) & **G.** (1855): The History of Australia

W. A. Morrison b.
M. L. Skinner b.
Martin Cash d.
Caroline Chisholm d.

1878

Blair (1820): The History of Australasia

'Boldrewood, Rolf' (1826): Ups and Downs N [cf. 1890]

Bull (1804): Early Experiences of Colonial Life in South Australia A [enlarged edn 1884]

Farrell (1851): Ephemera: an Iliad of Albury V

Gibson, G. H. (1846): Southerly Busters V ['by Ironbark']

Labillière (1840): Early History of the Colony of Victoria [1878-79]

Ranken, George (1827): Windabyne N [in the *Australian* 1878-79; as book 1895]

Mary Grant Bruce b.
H. S. Gullett b.
Lewis Lett b.
Samuel Bennett d.
E. W. Landor d.
John Dunmore Lang d.
Charles Thatcher d.

1879

Birnie (1808): Essays: Social, Moral and Political

Hamilton (c. 1812): Experiences of a Colonist Forty Years Ago A

Martin, A. Patchett (1851) (ed.): An Easter Omelette of Prose and Verse

Moloney (1843): Sonnets ad Innuptam [included in Martin]

O'Reilly, J. B. (1844): Moondyne N

Shillinglaw (1830) (ed.): Historical Records of Port Phillip

L. H. Allen b.
C. E. W. Bean b.
Louis Esson b.
Miles Franklin b.
Norman Lindsay b.
'John O'Brien' b.
W. F. Whyte b.
J. L. Burke d.
William Howitt d.
Richard Rowe d.
Daily Telegraph (*Sydney*) *begins* [*cf. 1930*]
Victorian Review *1879-86*
West Australian *1879-* [*cf. 1847, '64, '74*]
Anthony Trollope, John Caldigate
Joseph Conrad in Australia 1879, '80, '87, '92, '93 [*see* The Mirror of the Sea *1906*]

1880

Finn (1819): The 'Garryowen' Sketches [anon.]

Forrest, Alexander (1849): Journal of Expedition from De Grey to Darwin

Howitt, A. W. (1830) & **Fison** (1832): Kamilaroi and Kurnai P [repr. 1967]

Kendall (1839): Songs from the Mountains V

Praed (1851): An Australian Heroine N

Rowe (d. 1879): Roughing It in Van Diemen's Land Y

R. J. Cassidy ('Gilrooney') *b.*
J. H. L. Cumpston b.
Earle Page b.
T. Griffith Taylor b.
Bulletin *begins*

1881

Clarke, Marcus (1846): The Conscientious Stranger N
  The Mystery of Major Molineux and Human Repetends S

Grant (1843): Bush Life in Queensland N

Kendall (1839): Orara V

E. J. R. Atkinson b.
G. H. Cowling b.
Kathleen Dalziel b.
J. A. Ferguson b.
H. M. Green b.
H. A. Kellow b.

1881 (contd)

Praed (1851): Policy and Passion N [another edn titled Longleat of Kooralbyn 1887]

Spence, Catherine (1825): Gathered In N [in the *Adelaide Observer* 1881-82]

Syme (1827): Representative Government in England P

Rose Lindsay b.
E. Morris Miller b.
E. F. O'Ferrall ('Kodak') b.
Marion Phillips b.
Oswald Pryor b.
Archer Russell b.
Frank Wilmot ('Furnley Maurice') b.
Marcus Clarke d.
Caroline Leakey d.
Sydney University Review *1881-83*

1882

'Boldrewood, Rolf' (1826): Robbery Under Arms N [in the *Sydney Mail* 1882-83; as book 1888; later edn 1949 intro. by Thomas Wood; another 1968 intro. by Alan Brissenden]

Farrell (1851): Two Stories V

Martin, A. Patchett (1851): Fernshawe M [inc. 'Two Australian Poets', on Gordon and Brunton Stephens]

Meredith, Louisa A. (1812): Nellie, or Seeking Goodly Pearls N

Nicholson (1838): The Adventures of Halek N

O'Reilly, J. B. (1844): Songs, Legends and Ballads

Tolmer (1815): Reminiscences of an Adventurous and Chequered Career A

Ruth Bedford b.
Enid Derham b.
George Mackaness b.
Frederic Manning b.
Douglas Mawson b.
Tarlton Rayment b.
'Brian Vrepont' b.
William Forster d.
Henry Kendall d.
J. F. Mortlock d.
Daily News (*Perth*) *begins*

1883

Curr (1820): †Recollections of Squatting in Victoria [abridged edn 1965 by H. W. Forster]

Harpur (d. 1868): Poems [ed. by H. M. Martin]

McCrae, G. G. (1833): A Rosebud from the Garden of the Taj V [in the *Melbourne Review*]

Rusden (1819): History of Australia

Ethel Anderson b.
William Blocksidge ('Baylebridge') b.
W. J. Dakin b.
S. S. Mackenzie b.
G. V. Portus b.
K. S. Prichard b.
George Hamilton d.
Charles Tompson d.
Sydney Quarterly Magazine *1883-92*

1884

'**Boldrewood, Rolf**' (1826): Old Melbourne Memories H [later ed. by C. E. Sayers 1969]

Clarke, Marcus (d. 1881): The Marcus Clarke Memorial Volume [ed. by H. Mackinnon]

Deniehy (d. 1865): Life and Speeches [ed. by E. A. Martin]

Fenton, James (1819): A History of Tasmania

Forster (d. 1882): Midas D

Gregory, A. C. (1819) & **F. T.** (1821): †Journals of Australian Explorations

Bernard Cronin b.
H. E. Riemann b.
E. O. G. Shann b.
Sydney Tomholt b.
Charles Badham d.
R. H. Horne d.
N. W. Swan d.

1885

Clarke, Marcus (d. 1881): For The Term of His Natural Life [first edn to be so titled of the work publd 1870, 1874 qq. v.; later edns inc. 1899 intro. by A. B. Paterson, 1952 intro. by L. H. Allen, 1968 intro. by F. H. Mares]

Foott (1846): Where the Pelican Builds V

Holdsworth (1849): Station Hunting on the Warrego V

Lowe, Robert (1811): Poems of a Life

Praed (1851): The Head Station N Australian Life A

Roy Bridges b.
H. G. Lamond b.
Dorothea Mackellar b.
Nettie Palmer b.
Vance Palmer b.

1886

Adams, Francis (1862): Australian Essays

Clarke, Marcus (d. 1881): Sensational Tales

Curr (1820): The Australian Race [4 vols 1886–87]

Finniss (1807): The Constitutional History of South Australia

Hume (1859): The Mystery of a Hansom Cab N

Kendall (d. 1882): Poems [ed. by A. Sutherland]

Praed (1851): Miss Jacobsen's Chance N

C. L. A. Abbott b.
F. M. Cutlack b.
R. C. Mills b.
Les. Robinson b.
E. J. Rule b.
A. H. Spencer b.
H. P. Tritton b.
George French Angas d.
J. W. Bull d.
William Landsborough d.
Sir James Martin d.
J. A. Froude, Oceana
J. F. Archibald ed. of Bulletin 1886–1902

1887

Adams, Francis (1862): Poetical Works
Cambridge (1844): Unspoken Thoughts V [anon.]
Farrell (1851): How He Died and Other Poems
Halloran (1811): Poems, Odes, Songs
O'Reilly, J. B. (1844): The Golden Secret N [anon.]

F. T. Macartney b.
Jack McLaren b.
Boomerang, *ed.*
William Lane,
1887-92
Australian Star *(Sydney) 1887-90; as* Star *1890-1910*

1888

Adams, Francis (1862): Songs of the Army of the Night V
Favenc (1845): †History of Australian Exploration [repr. 1967]
Finn (1819): The Chronicles of Early Melbourne ['by Garryowen'; sel. edn by M. Weidenhofer 1967 as Garryowen's Melbourne]
Jose (1863): Sun and Cloud on River and Sea V ['by Ishmael Dare']
Martin, A. Patchett (1851) (ed.): Oak-Bough and Wattle-Blossom S
Ross, J. H. (1857): The Laureate of the Centaurs B [of Adam Lindsay Gordon]
Smith, James (1820): From Melbourne to Melrose A

A. R. Chisholm b.
Hal Gye b.
A. C. V. Melbourne b.
Lionel Shave b.
Myrtle Rose White b.
Richard Birnie d.
F. T. Gregory d.
W. E. Hearn d.
Douglas Sladen (ed.)
Australian Ballads and Rhymes; A Century of Australian Song; Australian Poets 1788-1888
Centennial Magazine *1888-90*

1889

Barton, G. B. (1836): The History of New South Wales from the Records [vol. i]
Caffyn, S. M. (1850): Miss Milne and I N
Giles (1835): Australia Twice Traversed
Kennedy, Edward (   ): Blacks and Bushrangers Y
Mennell (   ) (ed.): In Australian Wilds S
Praed (1851): The Romance of a Station N
'Tasma' (1848): Uncle Piper of Piper's Hill N [later ed. by C. Hadgraft & R. Beilby 1969]
Westgarth (1815): Half a Century of Australasian Progress H

Marnie Bassett b.
E. T. Brown b.
Marjory R. Casson b.
'Sydney de Loghe' b.
Eric Lowe b.
C. T. Madigan b.
Harley Matthews b.
Mary P. Mayo b.
W. J. Turner b.
H. R. Williams b.
Anna Maria Bunn d.
E. M. Curr d.
J. E. Tenison-Woods d.
W. B. Ullathorne d.
P. E. Warburton d.
W. Westgarth d.

Archibald (1856) & **Broomfield** (1860) (sel.):
A Golden Shanty: Prose and Verse by
Bulletin Writers

Badham (d. 1884): Speeches and Lectures

'Boldrewood, Rolf' (1826): A Colonial
Reformer N
The Miner's Right N
The Squatter's Dream N [new version of
Ups and Downs 1878]

Caffyn, S. M. (1850): Poppy's Tears N

Cambridge (1844): A Marked Man N

Clarke, Marcus (d. 1881): The Austral Edition
[ed. by H. Mackinnon]

Foott (1846): Morna Lee and Other Poems

Hales (1860): The Wanderings of a Simple Child
S ['by Smiler']

Halloran (1811): A Few Love Rhymes of a
Married Life
In Memoriam V

Heney, T. W. (1862): In Middle Harbour V

Martin, Catherine (1847): An Australian Girl
N [anon.]

Spencer-Browne (1856): Romances of the
Goldfield and Bush S

Syme (1827): On the Modification of Organisms
P

'Tasma' (1848): In Her Earliest Youth N
A Sydney Sovereign S

Tucker, T.G. (1859): Things Worth Thinking
About E

Nancy Adams b.
R. G. Casey b.
A. H. Chisholm b.
Zora Cross b.
C. H. Currey b.
Dulcie Deamer b.
James Devaney b.
M. H. Ellis b.
Randolph Hughes b.
W. R. Humphries b.
Frank Hurley b.
Ion Idriess b.
Daryl Lindsay b.
C. P. Mountford b.
Georgiana McCrae d.
J. B. O'Reilly d.
Alexander Tolmer d.
Robert Louis Stevenson
in Australia 1890,'91,
'93; Open Letter to
Dr Hyde wrtn Syd-
ney 1890 [see G.
Mackaness, R. L.
Stevenson: His
Associations with
Australia 1935]
E. W. Hornung, A
Bride from the Bush

'Boldrewood, Rolf' (1826): A Sydney-side
Saxon N

Cambridge (1844): The Three Miss Kings N

Dawe, Carlton (1865): The Golden Lake N

Evans (1863): The Repentance of Magdalen
Despar V

Hogan (1855): The Convict King B [of J.
Jorgenson; cf. 1835]

Jenks (1861): The Government of Victoria P

'Tasma' (1848): The Penance of Portia James N

A. P. Elkin b.
E. Gerard ['Trooper
Gerardy'] b.
Lesbia Harford b.
Peter Hopegood b.
J. P. McKinney b.
Paquita Mawson b.
H. W. Pryce b.
Charles Rodda b.
Australian Worker
begins

1891 (contd)

Ullathorne (d. 1889): Autobiography [abridged; in full as From Cabin-Boy to Archbishop; ed. by S. Leslie 1941]

Nat Gould, The Double Event
Rudyard Kipling in Australia [*see* Something of Myself *1937*]
Edwin Hodder, George Fife Angas

1892

Adams, Francis (1862): Australian Life S
'Boldrewood, Rolf' (1826): Nevermore N
Cambridge (1844): Not All in Vain N
Jephcott (1864): The Secrets of the South V
Lane (1861): The Working Man's Paradise N ['by John Miller']
Martin, Catherine (1847): The Silent Sea N ['by Mrs Alick McLeod']
Mennell (   ) (ed.): The Dictionary of Australasian Biography
Parkes (1815): Fifty Years in the Making of Australian History
'Tasma' (1848): A Knight of the White Feather N
'Warung, Price' (1855): Tales of the Convict System

J. A. Alexander b.
V. G. Childe b.
Leon Gellert b.
'William Hatfield' b.
'Brian James' b.
Leslie Meller b.
Mary Mitchell b.
A. G. Price b.
Arthur Upfield b.
Barcroft Boake d.
Robert Lowe, Viscount Sherbrooke, d.

1893

Adams, Francis (1862): The Australians C
Barry, J. A. (1850): Steve Brown's Bunyip S
Clarke, Marcus (d. 1881): Chidiock Tichbourne N
Favenc (1845): The Last of Six S
Gibson, G. H. (1846): Ironbark Chips and Stockwhip Cracks V
Hogan (1855): Robert Lowe, Viscount Sherbrooke B
Martin, A. Patchett (1851): Life and Letters of ... Robert Lowe, Viscount Sherbrooke
Newland (1835): Paving the Way N
Pearson (1830): National Life and Character C
Praed (1851): Outlaw and Lawmaker N
Richardson, Robert (1850) Willow and Wattle V

Alec Bagot b.
Martin Boyd b.
Frank Clune b.
Frank Dalby Davison b.
Alan Gross b.
Esther Landolt b.
J. K. Moir b.
Myra Morris b.
Francis Adams d.
George Bennett d.
B. T. Finniss d.
Henry Halloran d.
William Woolls d.
Edwin Hodder, The History of South Australia

27

1894

Becke (1855): By Reef and Palm S
Boothby (1867): In Strange Company N
Caffyn, K. M. (1852): A Yellow Aster N
['by Iota']
Gaunt (c. 1862): Dave's Sweetheart N
Lawson, Henry (1867): Short Stories in Prose and Verse
Neilson (1872): The Tales We Never Hear V
Stephens, A. G. (1865): A Queenslander's Travel-Notes A
Turner, Ethel (1872): Seven Little Australians Y
'Warung, Price' (1855): Tales of the Early Days

Mabel Brookes b.
D. B. Copland b.
Jean Devanny b.
H. V. Evatt b.
Paul Grano b.
J. J. Hardie b.
C. R. Jury b.
R. G. Menzies b.
G. D. Mitchell b.
Eric Partridge b.
Lynette Young b.
C. H. Pearson d.

1895

Becke (1855) & **Jeffery** (1861): A First Fleet Family N
'Boldrewood, Rolf' (1826): The Sphinx of Eaglehawk N
Cambridge (1844): Fidelis N
Carmichael (1868): Poems
Favenc (1845): The Secret of the Australian Desert Y
Jenks (1861): The History of the Australasian Colonies
Morris, E. E. (1843): A Memoir of George Higinbotham B
Paterson (1864): The Man From Snowy River V
Praed (1851): Mrs Tregaskiss N
'Tasma' (1848): Not Counting the Cost N

'Capel Boake' b.
Max Dunn b.
H. H. Finlayson b.
Hudson Fysh b.
G. Hermon Gill b.
W. E. Harney b.
Victor Kennedy b.
Leonard Mann b.
Eris O'Brien b.
E. V. Timms b.
F. P. Labillière d.
Louisa Anne Meredith d.
George Ranken d.
'Mark Twain' in Australia [see Following the Equator 1897]

1896

Brereton (1871): The Song of Brotherhood V
Perdita V
Byrne (   ): Australian Writers C
Dyson (1865): Rhymes from the Mines V
Favenc (1845): Marooned on Australia Y
The Moccasins of Silence N

Keast Burke b.
H. F. Chaplin b.
Roy Connolly b.
E. P. Harrington b.
Joan Lindsay b.
Cecil Mann b.

1896 (contd)

Lawson, Henry (1867): While the Billy Boils S
In the Days When the World was Wide V
Parker (1855?): Australian Legendary Tales
[cf. Drake-Brockman 1953]
Pearson (d. 1894): Reviews and Critical Essays
[ed. by H. A. Strong]

S. M. Caffyn d.
John Stanley James d.
Sir Henry Parkes d.
A. G. Stephens ed. of
Bulletin Red Page
1896-1906

1897

Boake (d. 1892): Where the Dead Men Lie V
[ed. by A. G. Stephens]
Brennan, C. J. (1870): XVIII Poems
XXI Poems (1893-1897): Towards the
Source
Brereton (1871): Sweetheart Mine V
Cambridge (1844): At Midnight S
Farrell (1851): Australia to England V
Lee (c. 1875): The Bush Fire and Other Verses
Mack, Louise (1874): Teens Y
Montgomery (1847): Five Skull Island S
Pasco (1818): A Roving Commission A
Praed (1851): Nulma N
Quinn, Roderic (1867): Mostyn Stayne N
'Tasma' (1848): A Fiery Ordeal N
'Warung, Price' (1855): Tales of the Old
Regime

Marjorie Barnard b.
Flora Eldershaw b.
C. H. Hannaford b.
R. S. Porteous
('Standby') b.
Arnold Shore b.
Helen Simpson b.
J. W. Truran b.
Ruth C. Williams b.
William Gay d.
Ernest Giles d.
'Tasma' d.

1898

Becke (1855) & **Jeffery** (1861): The Mutineer N
'Boldrewood, Rolf' (1826): A Romance of
Canvas Town S
Plain Living N
Bonwick (1817): Australia's First Preacher B
[of Richard Johnson, q. v.]
Cambridge (1844): Materfamilias N
Carnegie (1871): Spinifex and Sand A
Daley (1858): At Dawn and Dusk V
Duffy (1816): My Life in Two Hemispheres A

W. K. Hancock b.
J. H. Hornibrook b.
C. E. T. Newman b.
J. Normington-Rawling
b.
Erle Wilson b.
Edmund Finn d.
Sir George Grey d.
C. A. D. Pasco d.
Ethel Pedley d.

29

1898 (contd)

Dyson (1865): Below and On Top S
Evans (1863): Loraine and Other Verses
Martin, A. Patchett (1851): The Beginnings
    of an Australian Literature C
Morris, E. E. (1843): Austral English P
Ogilvie (1869): Fair Girls and Gray Horses V
Parker (1855?): More Australian Legendary
    Tales [cf. Drake-Brockman 1953]
Sandes (1863): Rhymes of the Times
Turner, H.G. (1831) & Sutherland, A. (1852):
    The Development of Australian Literature C
'Warung, Price' (1855): Tales of the Isle of
    Death
    Half-Crown Bob and Tales of the Riverine

Barrier Truth *begins;*
   daily since 1908
Sidney & Beatrice Webb
   in Australia [*see* The
   Webbs' Australian
   Diary, *ed. by A. G.*
   Austin, 1965]

1899

Brady (1869): The Ways of Many Waters V
Brereton (1871): Landlopers N
Favenc (1845): My Only Murder S
Goodge (1862): Hits! Skits! and Jingles! V
Jose (1863): A Short History of Australasia
Pedley (d. 1898): Dot and the Kangaroo Y
Quinn, Roderic (1867): The Hidden Tide V
'Rudd, Steele' (1868): On Our Selection S
Spencer, W. B. (1860) & Gillen (1855): The
    Native Tribes of Central Australia

F. Alexander b.
H. E. Badham b.
R. S. Byrnes b.
Chester Cobb b.
J. A. Collins b.
F. R. Farmer b.
Douglas Gillison b.
Ernestine Hill b.
Catherine Mackerras b.
John Reynolds b.
Lionel Wigmore b.
David Blair d.
Australian Magazine
The Bookfellow, *1899–*
   1925, founded by A.
   G. Stephens
E. W. Hornung, The
   Amateur Cracksman
   [*Raffles*]

1900

'Boldrewood, Rolf' (1826): The Babes in the
    Bush N
Dorrington (1871): Castro's Last Sacrament S

Bertha Lawson b.
Nan Chauncy b.
H. A. Lindsay b.

Lawson, Henry (1867): On the Track S
  Over the Sliprails S
  Verses, Popular and Humorous
Newland (1835): Blood Tracks of the Bush N
Sandes (1863): Ballads of Battle V

Jack Lindsay b.
E. G. Moll b.
A. A. Phillips b.
Lucille M. Quinlan b.
Charles Shaw b.
N. B. Tindale b.
Malcolm Uren b.
Mona Stuart Webster b.
D. W. Carnegie d.

1901

'Boldrewood, Rolf' (1826): In Bad Company
  S
Dyson (1865): The Gold Stealers N
Franklin, Miles (1879): My Brilliant Career N
Hay (1875): Stifled Laughter N
Lawson, Henry (1867): Joe Wilson and His
  Mates S
Mack, Louise (1874): Dreams in Flower V
Quinn, Roderic (1867): The Circling Hearths V
Stephens, A. G. (1865) (ed.): The *Bulletin* Story
  Book
  The *Bulletin* Reciter

Eleanor Dark b.
Henrietta Drake-
  Brockman b.
Clyde Fenton b.
Xavier Herbert b.
Bertram Higgins b.
Gavin Long b.
T. Inglis Moore b.
G. C. Morphett b.
S. H. Roberts b.
Lloyd Ross b.
C. E. Sayers b.
Kenneth Slessor b.
P. R. Stephensen b.
A. K. Thomson b.
G. B. Barton d.
E. J. Eyre d.
James Fenton d.
Alexander Forrest d.
Alfred Joyce d.
Robert Richardson d.
Commonwealth
  1901–03

1902

Abbott, J. H. M. (1874): Tommy Cornstalk A
Barff (1857): A Short Historical Account of the
  University of Sydney
Baynton (1862): Bush Studies S [later edn
  1965 with memoir by H. B. Gullett and
  intro. by A. A. Phillips]

Dorothy Cottrell b.
R. D. FitzGerald b.
Edward Ford b.
J. M. Harcourt b.
F. S. Hibble b.
V. W. Hyde b.

1902 (contd)

'Boldrewood, Rolf' (1826): The Ghost Camp N

Bonwick (1817): An Octogenarian's Reminiscences A

Brady (1869): The Earthen Floor V

Brereton (1871): Oithona V

Fielding (1856): The New Vicar of Wakefield N

Fox (1874): Bushman and Buccaneer: Harry Morant, his Ventures and Verses ['by Frank Renar'; inc. Morant's verse]

Lawson, Henry (1867): Children of the Bush S

Paterson (1864): Rio Grande's Last Race V

Praed (1851): Dwellers by the River S
My Australian Girlhood A

Stephens, A. G. (1865): Oblation V

Stephens, James Brunton (1835): Poetical Works
My Chinee Cook and Other Humorous Verses

Tucker, T. G. (1859): The Cultivation of Literature in Australia

Alan Marshall b.
T. T. Reed b.
Christina Stead b.
P. Holdsworth d.
A. Patchett Martin d.
H. H. ('Breaker') Morant d.
E. E. Morris d.
W. L. Ranken d.
James Brunton Stephens d.
A. Sutherland d.

1903

Abbott, J. H. M. (1874): Plain and Veldt S

Bedford, Randolph (1868): True Eyes and the Whirlwind N

Cambridge (1844): Thirty Years in Australia A

Furphy (1843): Such is Life: Being Certain Extracts from the Diary of Tom Collins N [later edn 1968 with intro. by J. Barnes]

O'Dowd (1866): Dawnward? V

Ogilvie (1869): Hearts of Gold V

Praed (1851): Fugitive Anne N

'Rudd, Steele' (1868): Our New Selection S

Wilmot, Frank (1881): Some Verses

Wrixon (1839): Jacob Shumate N [cf. 1912]

W. V. Aughterson b.
J. V. Barry b.
Charles Bateson b.
Robert Close b.
Cecil Edwards b.
Lennie Lower b.
Raymond McGrath b.
Paul McGuire b.
D. P. Mellor b.
'Betty Roland' b.
F. B. Vickers b.
Alan Villiers b.
Sir Charles Gavan Duffy d.
G. W. Rusden d.
Daily Mail (Brisbane) 1903-33 [cf. 1933]

1904

Adams, A. H. (1872): Tussock Land N
Crawford, R. J. (1868): Lyric Moods V
Farrell (d. 1904): My Sundowner and Other Poems [ed. by Bertram Stevens]
Forrest, Mabel (1872): The Rose of Forgiveness S
Howitt, A. W. (1830): †The Native Tribes of South-East Australia
Nicholson (1838): Almoni N
Palmer-Archer (1864): A Bush Honeymoon S
Petrie (1831): Tom Petrie's Reminiscences of Early Queensland [dictated to, written and publd by Constance Petrie]
'Rudd, Steele' (1868): Sandy's Selection S
Spencer, W. B. (1860) & Gillen (1855): The Northern Tribes of Central Australia
Stephens, A. G. (1865): The Red Pagan E
Turner, H. G. (1831): A History of the Colony of Victoria
Wilmot, Frank (1881): Some More Verses

P. L. Brown b.
I. F. Champion b.
Dymphna Cusack b.
G. L. Dann b.
J. K. Ewers b.
C. Hadgraft b.
Edgar Holt b.
Frederick Howard b.
Florence James b.
J. A. R. McKellar b.
Enid Moodie Heddle b.
John Morrison b.
Brian Penton b.
F. N. Ratcliffe b.
Jennings Carmichael d.
John Farrell d.
Patrick Moloney d.

1905

Bedford, Randolph (1868): The Snare of Strength N
'Boldrewood, Rolf'(1826): The Last Chance N
Favenc (1845): Voices of the Desert V
Furphy (1843): Rigby's Romance N ['by Tom Collins'; in the Barrier Truth 1905-06; as book, abridged 1921, in full 1946]
Gunn, Mrs Æneas (1870): The Little Black Princess Y
Lawson, Henry (1867): When I Was King V
Moore, William (1868): City Sketches S
Paterson (1864) (ed.): Old Bush Songs
Praed (1851): The Maid of the River N
Spielvogel (1874): A Gumsucker on the Tramp S
Stephens, A. G. (1865): Victor Daley C

Mena Calthorpe b.
Norma Davis b.
Don Edwards b.
Brian Fitzpatrick b.
Kathleen Fitzpatrick b.
Paul Hasluck b.
Donald McLean b.
R. B. Madgwick b.
Leslie Rees b.
Winifred Shaw b.
Guy Boothby d.
Victor Daley d.
Annie Maria Dawbin d.
Sir Augustus Gregory d.
P. Mennell d.
J. J. Shillinglaw d.
George Sutherland d.
R. Jebb, Studies in Colonial Nationalism
'Paul Warrego', A l'autre Bout du Monde

1906

Adams, A. H. (1872): London Streets V
Atkinson, E. J. R. (1881): The Shrine of Desire V
Dyson (1865): Fact'ry 'Ands S
In the Roaring Fifties N
Evans (1863): The Secret Key and Other Verses
Martin, Catherine (1847): The Old Roof-Tree N [anon.]
Moore, William (1868): Studio Sketches S
O'Dowd (1866): The Silent Land V
Paterson (1864): An Outback Marriage N
Praed (1851): The Lost Earl of Ellan N
'Rudd, Steele' (1868): Back at Our Selection S
Spencer, T. E. (1845): How McDougall Topped the Score M
Stevens (1872) (ed.): An Anthology of Australian Verse

Max Afford b.
Godfrey Blunden b.
Jean Campbell b.
R. M. Crawford b.
E. J. Donath b.
Mary Finnin b.
J. G. Hides b.
R. G. Howarth b.
Frank Legg b.
Philip Lindsay b.
Raymond Paull b.
Cyril Pearl b.
James Picot b.
E. O. Schlunke b.
Clive Turnbull b.
James Bonwick d.
A. H. Adams ed. of Bulletin *Red Page 1906-09*
Johns's Notable Australians *1906-21*

1907

Baynton (1862): Human Toll N
Buchanan (1874): The Real Australia C
Hay (1875): Herridge of Reality Swamp N
Henderson, G. C. (1870): Sir George Grey B
Henderson, W.G. (1870): Midnight's Daughter S
Murdoch (1874): The Enemies of Literature C
O'Dowd (1866): Dominions of the Boundary V
Praed (1851): The Luck of the Leura S
Spielvogel (1874): The Cocky Farmer S

Gavin Casey b.
Donovan Clarke b.
Arthur Davies b.
Ralph De Boissiere b.
R. M. Hague b.
Helen Heney b.
Morton Herman b.
John Hetherington b.
A. D. Hope b.
John O'Grady ('Nino Culotta') b.
T. M. Ronan b.
John Thompson b.
Ian Tilbrook b.
Alexander Turner b.
Lorimer Fison d.
Lone Hand *1907-21*
Melbourne University Magazine *begins*

1908

Banfield (1852): The Confessions of a Beach-comber A [later edn 1968 with intro. by A. H. Chisholm]
Blocksidge (1883): Songs o' the South V
Brereton (1871): Sea and Sky V
Daley (1858): Poems
Dorrington (1871): And the Day Came N
Favenc (1845): The Explorers of Australia H
Fullerton (1868): Moods and Melodies V
Gunn, Mrs Æneas (1870): We of the Never Never A
Murphy, E. G. (1867?): Jarrahland Jingles ['by Dryblower']
Ogilvie (1869): My Life in the Open A
Pratt (1874): David Syme B
'Richardson, Henry Handel' (1870): Maurice Guest N
Sorenson (1869): The Squatter's Ward N
Spencer, T. E. (1845): Budgeree Ballads
Stevens (1872) (ed.): Bush Ballads
Turner, H.G. (1831): Alexander Sutherland B
Wenz (1869): Diary of a New Chum S ['by Paul Warrego']

David Adams b.
K. M. Bowden b.
L. F. Fitzhardinge b.
Alexandra Hasluck b.
G. C. Ingleton b.
Eric Irvin b.
Eve Langley b.
Ronald McCuaig b.
Douglas Pike b.
Colin Simpson b.
Clifford Tolchard b.
H. G. Wells b.
E. Favenc d.
A. W. Howitt d.
David Syme d.
William Walker d.
Commonwealth Literary Fund founded [see Helping Literature in Australia 1967]

1909

Blocksidge (1883): Australia to England V
Bridges (1885): The Barb of an Arrow N
Collier (1846): Sir George Grey B
Deamer (1890): In the Beginning S
Dorrington (1871) & **Stephens, A.G.** (1865): The Lady Calphurnia Royal N
Forrest, Mabel (1872): Alpha Centauri V
Franklin, Miles (1879): Some Everyday Folk and Dawn N
'Kirmess, C. H.' ( ): The Australian Crisis N
Macartney, J. A. (1834): Reminiscences of a Pioneer A
McCrae, Hugh (1876): Satyrs and Sunlight: Silvarum Libri V

J. J. Auchmuty b.
Beatrice Davis b.
Allan Edwards b.
W. D. Forsyth b.
Geoffrey Hutton b.
Ronald McKie b.
Lex McLennan b.
Elizabeth Riddell b.
Rex Rienits b.
G. E. Evans d.
W. T. Goode d.

35

O'Dowd (1866): The Seven Deadly Sins   V
Poetry Militant   C
Phillips, Marion (1881): A Colonial Autocracy
H
Praed (1851): A Summer Wreath   S
'Rudd, Steele' (1868): Stocking Our Selection
S
Spence, W. G. (1846): Australia's Awakening:
Thirty Years in the Life of an Australian
Agitator   A
Stevens (1872) (ed.): The Golden Treasury of
Australian Verse
Wise (1858): The Commonwealth of Australia
H

1910

Adams, A. H. (1872): Galahad Jones   N
Bean (1879): On The Wool Track   H
Blocksidge (1883): Moreton Miles   V
Southern Songs   V
A Northern Trail   V
The New Life   V
Brady (1869): Bushland Ballads
Brereton (1871): To-morrow   D
Bruce (1878): A Little Bush Maid   Y
Esson (1879): Bells and Bees   V
Gilmore (1865): Marri'd   V
Lawson, Henry (1867): The Rising of the
Court   S
Mack, Amy Eleanor (c.1877): Bushland Stories
Y
Murdoch (1874): Loose Leaves   E
Praed (1851): Opal Fire   N
'Richardson, Henry Handel' (1870): The
Getting of Wisdom   N [later edn 1968
with intro. by L. Kramer]
Sandes (1863): Love and the Aeroplane   N
Spence, Catherine (d. 1910): An Autobiography
[completed by Jeanne Young, q.v.]

John Béchervaise b.
S. J. Butlin b.
Ross Campbell b.
Eric Dunlop b.
Brian Elliott b.
Alan Moorehead b.
R. D. Murphy b.
Ray Parkin b.
'Denton Prout' b.
Walter Stone b.
J. L. Cuthbertson d.
Thomas Petrie d.
James Smith d.
Catherine Spence d.
Mitchell Library opened
*'G. B. Lancaster', Jim of
the Ranges*
*Paul Wenz, Sous la
Croix du Sud*
Sun (Sydney) begins

1911

Adams, A. H. (1872): A Touch of Fantasy N
Banfield (1852): My Tropic Isle A
Bean (1879): The Dreadnought of the Darling H
Bedford, Randolph (1868): Billy Pagan, Mining Engineer N
Brady (1869): Bells and Hobbles V
Buchanan (1874): Where Day Begins N [based on the life of H. H. Morant, q.v.]
Cassidy (1880): Land of the Starry Cross V ['by Gilrooney']
Collier (1846): The Pastoral Age in Australasia H
Daley (d. 1905): Wine and Roses V [ed. by Bertram Stevens]
Dorrington (1871): Our Lady of the Leopards N Children of the Cloven Hoof N
Dyson (1865): Benno and Some of the Push S
Gay (d. 1897): Complete Poetical Works
Lawson, Henry (1867): Mateship S
Stephens, A. G. (1865): The Pearl and the Octopus M
Steven, A.G. (1865): The Witchery of Earth V
Stone, Louis (1871): Jonah N [later edn 1965 with intro. by Ronald McCuaig]
Strong (1876): Peradventure C

K. A. Austin b.
Robert Clark b.
Renée Erdos b.
George Farwell b.
Eunice Hanger b.
William Hart-Smith b.
J. A. La Nauze b.
Dudley McCarthy b.
A. J. Marshall b.
A. G. Mitchell b.
Ian Mudie b.
Hal Porter b.
Colin Roderick b.
Olaf Ruhen b.
Dal Stivens b.
Celia Syred b.
Judah Waten b.
A. K. Weatherburn b.
Chester Wilmot b.
William Astley ('Price Warung') d.
J. A. Barry d.
T. E. Spencer d.
E. M. Clowes, On the Wallaby Through Victoria

1912

Bertie (1875): Stories of Old Sydney H
Cambridge (1844): The Retrospect A
Cuthbertson (d. 1910): Barwon Ballads and School Verses
Derham (1882): The Mountain Road V
Esson (1879): Red Gums V
The Time is Not Yet Ripe D
Three Short Plays ['The Woman Tamer', 'Dead Timber', 'The Sacred Place']
Gibson, G. H. (1846): Ironbark Splinters from the Australian Bush V
Gordon (d. 1870): Poems [ed. by F. M. Robb]
Hay (1875): Captain Quadring N

S. J. Baker b.
C. B. Christesen b.
Russell Drysdale b.
G. F. James b.
George Johnston b.
P. G. Law b.
Graham McInnes b.
Ian McLaren b.
Barton Maughan b.
J. H. O'Dwyer b.
Joan Phipson b.
J. M. D. Pringle b.
Roland Robinson b.
Kylie Tennant b.

37

D

1912 (*contd*)

Jephcott (1864): Penetralia   V
Macartney, F. T. (1887): Dewed Petals   V
Matthews, Harley (1889): Under the Open Sky   V
Murray, Hubert (1861): Papua or British New Guinea   P
O'Dowd (1866): The Bush   V
Souter, C. H. (1864): Irish Lords   V
Williamson (1865): Purple and Gold   V [enlarged, corrected edn 1940]
Wrixon (1839): Edward Fairlie Frankfort   N [revised version of Jacob Shumate 1903]

Patrick White b.
Joseph Furphy d.
F. J. Gillen d.
Edith Humphris & D. Sladen, Adam Lindsay Gordon and His Friends

1913

Adams, A. H. (1872): Collected Verses
Allen (1879): Gods and Wood Things   M
Brennan, C. J. (1870): Poems [publd 1914]
Brennan, C. J. (1870) & **Brereton** (1871): A Mask   D
Cambridge (1844): The Hand in the Dark   V
Dennis (1876): Backblock Ballads
Edmond (1859): A Journalist and Two Bears   S
Lawson, Henry (1867): Triangles of Life   S
Lindsay, Norman (1879): A Curate in Bohemia   N
Macartney, F. T. (1887): Earthen Vessels   V
O'Reilly, Dowell (1865): Tears and Triumph   N
Prichard (1883): Clovelly Verses
Stephens, A. G. (1865): Bill's Idees   S
Stevens (1872) & **Mackaness** (1882) (edd.): Selections from the Australian Poets
Tardent (1854): The Life and Poetry of George Essex Evans
Wilmot, Frank (1881): Unconditioned Songs [anon.]
Wise (1858): The Making of the Australian Commonwealth   H

L. J. Blake b.
John Blight b.
Robert Crossland b.
Mary Durack b.
Lawson Glassop b.
P. R. Heydon b.
Flexmore Hudson b.
Rex Ingamells b.
Mungo MacCallum b.
Kenneth Mackenzie b.
Elyne Mitchell b.
'Elizabeth O'Conner' b.
Nancy Phelan b.
Douglas Stewart b.
Donald Stuart b.
Louis Becke d.
Garnet Walch d.
W. B. Withers d.
Sir Henry Wrixon d.

1914

Adams, A. H. (1872): Three Plays for the Australian Stage ['The Wasters', 'Galahad Jones' (cf. 1910), 'Mrs Pretty and the Premier']

Blocksidge (1883): Life's Testament V

Dyson (1865): Spat's Fact'ry S

Grover (1870): The Minus Quantity D

Mackellar (1885): The Witch Maid V

Palmer, Nettie (1885): The South Wind V

Scott, Ernest (1867): Life of Matthew Flinders

Spencer, W. B. (1860): The Native Tribes of the Northern Territory [repr. 1966]

Steven, A. G. (1865): Wind on the Wold V

Tucker, T.G. (1859): Platform Monologues E

John Cobley b.
J. M. Couper b.
Peter Cowan b.
Lynn Foster b.
Donald Friend b.
Margaret Kiddle b.
Clement Semmler b.
Margaret Trist b.
Russel Ward b.
J. P. Bourke ('Bluebush') d.
Rachel Henning d.
A. J. Dawson, The Record of Nicholas Freydon [anon.]
Grant Watson, Where Bonds Are Loosed

1915

Adams, A. H. (1872): Grocer Greatheart N

Boote (1868): A Fool's Talk E

Bourke (d. 1914): Off the Bluebush V [ed. by A. G. Stephens]

Dennis (1876): The Songs of a Sentimental Bloke V

Lavater (1867): Blue Days and Grey Days V

McCrae, G. G. (1833): The Fleet and Convoy V

Mawson, Douglas (1882): The Home of the Blizzard A

Mills (1886): The Colonisation of Australia H [repr. 1968]

Palmer, Nettie (1885): Shadowy Paths V

Palmer, Vance (1885): The Forerunners V
The World of Men S

Praed (1851): Lady Bridget in the Never Never Land N

Prichard (1883): The Pioneers N

Stone, Louis (1871): Betty Wayside N

Strong (1876): Sonnets of the Empire

Dorothy Auchterlounie b.
Maurice Biggs b.
David Campbell b.
D. E. Charlwood b.
C. M. H. Clark b.
T. A. G. Hungerford b.
John Manifold b.
David Martin b.
Aileen Palmer b.
John Quinn b.
Michael Thwaites b.
Bill Wannan b.
Judith Wright b.
T. A. Browne ('Rolf Boldrewood') d.
Triad publd in Sydney 1915-27

1916

Blocksidge (1883): Seven Tales M
  A Wreath V
Dennis (1876): The Moods of Ginger Mick V
Furphy (d. 1912): Poems [ed. by Kate Baker]
'Loghe, Sydney de' (1889): The Straits Impregnable N
Morton (1869): Verses for Marjorie
Neilson (1872): Old Granny Sullivan V
Ogilvie (1869): The Australian V
Piddington (1862): Spanish Sketches S
Praed (1851): Sister Sorrow N
Prichard (1883): Windlestraws N
Scott, Ernest (1867): A Short History of Australia

R. M. Berndt b.
D. H. Borchardt b.
Paul Brickhill b.
Hume Dow b.
John Herington b.
Margaret Irvin b.
S. C. McCulloch b.
G. J. Odgers b.
Shawn O'Leary b.
H. J. Oliver b.
A. G. L. Shaw b.
Bernard Smith b.
Harold Stewart b.
George R. Turner b.
Val Vallis b.
Morris West b.
Annabella Boswell d.
B. R. Wise d.
Art in Australia
  1916-42
Birth *1916-22*

1917

Barton, Robert (1842): Reminiscences of an Australian Pioneer A
Baynton (1862): Cobbers S
Bedford, Randolph (1868): The Silver Star N
'Boake, Capel' (1895): Painted Clay N
Cross (1890): Songs of Love and Life V
Dennis (1876): Doreen V
  The Glugs of Gosh V
Gellert (1892): Songs of a Campaign V
Gilmore (1865): The Tale of Tiddley Winks Y
Lavater (1867): A Lover's Ephemeris V
'Loghe, Sydney de' (1889): Pelican Pool N
Long, R. H. (1874): Verses
Macartney, F. T. (1887): Commercium V
'Maurice, Furnley' (1881): To God: From the Weary Nations V [repr. in Eyes of Vigilance 1920 as To God: From the Warring Nations]
  The Bay and Padie Book Y

Nancy Cato b.
Jon Cleary b.
L. F. Crisp b.
David Dexter b.
Frank Hardy b.
John Iggulden b.
Sumner Locke(-)
  Elliott b.
James McAuley b.
David Mossenson b.
D'Arcy Niland b.
Rohan Rivett b.
Ron Tullipan b.
William Lane d.
J. A. Macartney d.

Paterson (1864): Saltbush Bill, J.P. V
Three Elephant Power S
Reid (1845): My Reminiscences
'Richardson, Henry Handel' (1870): Australia
Felix N [cf. 1930]
Souter, C. H. (1864): To Many Ladies and
Others V

1918

Banfield (1852): Tropic Days A
Brennan, C. J. (1870): A Chant of Doom V
Coghlan (1856): Labour and Industry in
Australia H
Cronin (1884): The Coastlanders N
Cross (1890): The Lilt of Life V
The City of Riddle-me-ree V
Dennis (1876): Digger Smith V
Fetherstonhaugh (1837): After Many Days A
Fisher (1872): Earth Spiritual V
Gerard (1891): The Road to Palestine V
['by Trooper Gerardy']
Gibbs (1876): Snugglepot and Cuddlepie Y
Gilmore (1865): The Passionate Heart V
Lindsay, Norman (1879): The Magic Pudding
Y
Macartney, F. T. (1887): In War Time V
McCrae, G. G. (1833): John Rous N
Matthews, Harley (1889): Saints and Soldiers S
Morris, Myra (1893): England and Other Verses
Murdoch (1874) (ed.): The Oxford Book of
Australasian Verse
O'Hara (1862): Poems
Steven, A.G. (1865): Poems
Stow, Catherine (1855?): The Walkabouts of
Wur-run-nah L [cf. Drake-Brockman
1953]
Strong (1876): Poems
Taylor,G. A. (1872): Those Were The Days A
Wright, David McKee (1869): An Irish Heart V

James Aldridge b.
A. G. Austin b.
Niall Brennan b.
W. S. Fairbridge b.
Michael Keon b.
Douglas Lockwood b.
'Esther Roland' b.
Mary Hannay Foott d.
Sir John Forrest d.
J. R. Houlding d.
Sir George Reid d.
Grant Watson, The
Mainland

1919

Atkinson, E. J. R. (1881): A Nocturne D

Bedford, Randolph (1868): Aladdin and the Boss Cockie N

Blocksidge (1883): Selected Poems

Brady (1869): The House of the Winds V

Brereton (1871): The Burning Marl V

Dennis (1876): Jim of the Hills V

Gellert (1892): The Isle of San V

Gerard (1891): Australian Light Horse Ballads and Rhymes ['by Trooper Gerardy']

Hay (1875): The Escape of the Notorious Sir William Heans N [later edn 1955, intros. by R. G. Howarth and E. Morris Miller]

Morton (1867): The Secret Spring V

Neilson (1872): Heart of Spring V

Rodda (1891): The Fortunes of Geoffrey Mayne N

Steven, A.G. (1865): Revolt V

Robin Boyd b.
Zelman Cowen b.
Nene Gare b.
Fayette Gosse b.
Marcie Muir b.
Thea Rienits b.
B. H. Travers b.
J. M. Ward b.
J. F. Archibald d.
Alfred Deakin d.
A. F. M. Robb d.
Paul Wenz, Le Pays de leurs Pères

1920

Adams, A. H. (1872): The Australians N

Allen (1879): Billy Bubbles Y

Boyd, Martin (1893): Retrospect V

Bridges (1885): From Silver to Steel H

Esson (1879): Dead Timber D [contains 'The Drovers' and the three plays of the 1912 vol., q.v.]

Harrington (1896): Songs of War and Peace V

Hebblethwaite (1857): Poems

Kendall (d. 1882): Poems [ed. by Bertram Stevens]

Lindsay, Lionel (1874): Conrad Martens B

Lindsay, Norman (1879): Creative Effort C

Macartney, F. T. (1887): Poems

McCrae, Hugh (1876): Colombine V

'Maurice, Furnley' (1881): Eyes of Vigilance V
Ways and Means V

Rosemary Dobson b.
Gwyneth M. Dow b.
Gwen Harwood b.
H. G. Kippax b.
Jane Lindsay b.
John Meredith b.
Geoff. Taylor b.
Colin Thiele b.
Kath Walker b.
H. G. Turner d.

O'Reilly, Dowell (1865): Five Corners   S
Palmer, Vance (1885): The Camp   V
    The Shantykeeper's Daughter   N   ['by Rann
    Daly']
Quinn, Roderic (1867): Poems
Shaw, Winifred (1905): The Aspen Tree   V
Wright, David McKee (1869): Gallipoli   V
    [in the *Bulletin*]

1921

Allen (1879): Phaedra   V
Bayldon (1865): The Eagles   V
Bean (1879): The Story of Anzac   H   [vol. I;
    vol. II 1924; first 2 volumes of the Official
    History of Australia in the War of 1914-
    1918]
Blocksidge (1883): An Anzac Muster   S   [cf.
    'Baylebridge' 1962]
Crawford, R. J. (1868): The Leafy Bliss   V
Cross (1890): Elegy on an Australian Schoolboy
    V
Dennis (1876): A Book for Kids
Fullerton (1868): The Breaking Furrow   V
    Bark House Days   N
Hay (1875): An Australian Rip Van Winkle   E
Hebblethwaite (1867): New Poems
Jack (1845): Northmost Australia   P
'Maurice, Furnley' (1881): Arrows of Longing
    V
Monckton (1872): Some Experiences of a New
    Guinea Resident Magistrate   A
'O'Brien, John' (1879): Around the Boree
    Log   V
O'Dowd (1866): Alma Venus!   V
O'Ferrall (1881): Bodger and the Boarders   S
Paterson (1864): Collected Verse
Prichard (1883): Black Opal   N

Lex Banning b.
Russell Braddon b.
Max Harris b.
Donald Horne b.
Alister Kershaw b.
Eric Lambert b.
Ray Lawler b.
Nan McDonald b.
Peter Miles b.
Ivan Southall b.
George W. Turner b.
Joan Woodberry b.
Patricia Wrightson b.
*G. H. Gibson ('Iron-
    bark') d.*
James Hebblethwaite d.
R. L. Jack d.

1922

Bertie (1875): Isaac Nathan   B

Cronin (1884) & **'Boake, Capel'** (1895): Kangaroo Rhymes   V

Cross (1890): Introduction to the Study of Australian Literature

Gask (1872): The Mystery of the Sandhills   N

Gilmore (1865): Hound of the Road   E

Lavater (1867): This Green Mortality   V

Lewis (1842): Fought and Won   A

Macartney, F. T. (1887): Something for Tokens   V

McCrae, Hugh (1876): Idyllia   V

'Maurice, Furnley' (1881): Romance   E

Monckton (1872): Last Days in New Guinea   A

Morris, Myra (1893): Us Five   Y

Palmer, Vance (1885): The Boss of Killara   N ['by Rann Daly']

Shaw, Winifred (1905): The Yellow Cloak   V

Wood, G. A. (1865): The Discovery of Australia [repr. 1969]

Clive Barry b.
Peter Bladen b.
H. F. Brinsmead b.
Geoffrey Dutton b.
Frank Kellaway b.
Gwen Kelly b.
David Mattingley b.
Stephen Murray-Smith b.
A. G. Serle b.
'Neilma Sidney' b.
W. J. Jeffery d.
Henry Lawson d.
A. Montgomery d.
Bertram Stevens d.
Who's Who in Australia *1922–*
Sun News-Pictorial (*Melbourne*) *begins*

1923

Beeby (1869): Concerning Ordinary People   D

'Boake, Capel' (1895): The Romany Mark   N

Childe (1892): How Labour Governs   P [later ed. by F. B. Smith 1964]

Cutlack (1886): The Australian Flying Corps in the Western and Eastern Theatres of War   H [vol. VIII of the Official History of Australia in the War of 1914-1918]

Durack, Mary (1913): Little Poems of Sunshine ['by An Australian Child']

Gullett (1878): The Australian Imperial Force in Sinai and Palestine   H [vol. VII of the Official History of Australia in the War of 1914-1918]

Humphries (1890): Patrolling in Papua   A

Ray Aitchison b.
J. Bach b.
Charmian Clift b.
Alex. Craig b.
V. Cunnington b.
Thelma Forshaw b.
G. M. Glaskin b.
Dorothy Hewett b.
Nancy Keesing b.
Harry Marks b.
G. H. Nadel b.
Eric Rolls b.
P. A. Ryan b.
W. N. Scott b.
E. J. Banfield d.
John Lewis d.

1923 (contd)

Lindsay, Jack (1900) & **Slessor** (1901) (edd.): Poetry in Australia

Martin, Catherine (1847): The Incredible Journey N

Moses (1860): Beyond the City Gates M

Murdoch (1874): Alfred Deakin B

Neilson (1872): Ballad and Lyrical Poems

Palmer, Vance (1885): The Enchanted Island N ['by Rann Daly']

Souter, C. H. (1864): The Mallee Fire V

Steven, A.G. (1865): Lures V

Frank Morton d.
J. H. Nicholson d.
Dowell O'Reilly d.
A. G. Steven d.
Vision *1923-24*
D. H. Lawrence,
  Kangaroo
Grant Watson, The
  Desert Horizon
Paul Wenz, L'Homme
  du Soleil Couchant
News *(Adelaide) begins*

1924

Allen (1879): Araby V

Barton, G. B. (d. 1901): The True Story of Margaret Catchpole H [cf. R. Cobbold 1845]

Battye (1871): Western Australia H

Brereton (1871): The Carillon Poem

Dennis (1876): Rose of Spadgers V

Lindsay, Jack (1900): Fauns and Ladies V

McGrath (1903): Seven Songs of Meadow Lane V

O'Reilly, Dowell (d. 1923): Prose and Verse

Palmer, Nettie (1885): Modern Australian Literature C

Palmer, Vance (1885): Cronulla N
  The Black Horse D
  The Outpost N ['by Rann Daly'; cf. 1935]

Price (1892): The Foundation and Settlement of South Australia H

Riemann (1884): Nor' West o' West S

Roberts (1901): History of Australian Land Settlement [repr. 1968]

Shaw, Winifred (1905): Babylon V

Slessor (1901): Thief of the Moon V

Weston Bate b.
F. K. Crowley b.
A. F. Davies b.
'David Forrest' b.
R. B. Joyce b.
Leonie Kramer b.
David Rowbotham b.
Robert Barton d.
J. F. Hogan d.
The Spinner *1924-27*
D. H. Lawrence & M.
  L. Skinner, The Boy
  in the Bush
Grant Watson, Innocent Desires

45

1925

Banfield (d. 1923): Last Leaves from Dunk Island A [ed. by A. H. Chisholm]

Boyd, Martin (1893): Love Gods N ['by Martin Mills']

Cobb (1899): Mr Moffatt N

Cox (1873): Out of the Silence N

Gilmore (1865): The Tilted Cart V

Jose (1863) (ed.): Australian Encyclopedia [1925-26; ed. with H. J. Carter]

Lawson, Henry (d. 1922): Poetical Works

Lee (c. 1875): Early Explorers in Australia H

Murray, Hubert (1861): Papua of Today P

Penn-Smith (1863): Hang! S

Pitt (1869): Poems

'Richardson, Henry Handel' (1870): The Way Home N [cf. 1930]

Serle, P. (1871): Bibliography of Australasian Poetry and Verse

Skinner (1877): Black Swans N

Steven, A. G. (d. 1923): Collected Poems [intro. by Hugh McCrae]

Sweetman (1875): Australian Constitutional Development H

Timms (1895): The Hills of Hate N

Thea Astley b.
Hugh Atkinson b.
Vincent Buckley b.
Robert Burns b.
Laurence Collinson b.
John Gunn b.
D. S. Macmillan b.
J. R. Rowland b.
Lesley Rowlands b.
R. B. Walker b.
Francis Webb b.
Rosemary Wighton b.
H. E. Barff d.
James Collier d.
C. Fetherstonhaugh d.
Simpson Newland d.
E. F. O'Ferrall ('Kodak') d.
Grant Watson, Daimon

1926

Boyd, Martin (1893): Brangane N ['by Martin Mills']

Cobb (1899): Days of Disillusion N

Fallaw (1876): Unending Ways V

Lavater (1867) (ed.): The Sonnet in Australasia [rev. ed. by F. T. Macartney 1956]

McLaren, Jack (1887): My Crowded Solitude A

Newland (d. 1925): Memoirs

Prichard (1883): Working Bullocks N

Pryce (1891): Your Old Battalion V

Shann (1884): Cattle Chosen B

Slessor (1901): Earth-Visitors V [publd 1927]

Vidler (1863) (ed.): The Adam Lindsay Gordon Memorial Volume

Jack Beasley b.
L. H. Evers b.
Noel Macainsh b.
B. E. Mansfield b.
Patsy Adam Smith b.
Kathleen Mannington Caffyn ('Iota') d.
Ada Cambridge d.
Sir Timothy Coghlan d.
W. G. Spence d.
Canberra Times *begins; daily since 1928*

46

1927

Bennett, M. M. ( ): Christison of Lammermoor B
Devaney (1890): The Currency Lass N
FitzGerald (1902): The Greater Apollo V
Idriess (1890): Madman's Island P
Mackenzie, S. S. (1883): The Australians at Rabaul H [vol. X of the Official History of Australia in the War of 1914-1918]
Moll (1900): Sedge Fire V
Neilson (1872): New Poems
Serle, P. (1871) (ed.): An Australasian Anthology V
Spencer, W. B. (1860) & **Gillen** (d. 1912): The Arunta [repr. 1966]
Spencer-Browne (1856): A Journalist's Memories A

Hugh Anderson b.
Lyndsay Gardiner b.
David Ireland b.
J. P. Matthews b.
Charles Osborne b.
T. M. Perry b.
Alan Seymour b.
F. J. West b.
G. A. Wilkes b.
Lesbia Harford d.
G. G. McCrae d.
J. B. O'Hara d.

1928

Alexander, J. A. (1892): The Life of George Chaffey B
Boote (1868): Tea With the Devil E
Boyd, Martin (1893): The Montforts N ['by Martin Mills']
Brereton (1871): Swags Up! V
The Temple on the Hill D
Cottrell (1902): The Singing Gold N
Dalley (1876): No Armour N
Evans (d. 1909): Collected Verse
Franklin, Miles (1879): Up the Country N ['by Brent of Bin Bin']
Gellert (1892): Desperate Measures V
Giblin (1863): The Early History of Tasmania [vol. i; vol. ii 1939]
Howard (1904): The Emigrant N
Jose (1863): The Royal Australian Navy H [vol. IX of the Official History of Australia in the War of 1914-1918]
Builders and Pioneers of Australia B
Lindsay, Norman (1879): Hyperborea C
McCrae, Hugh (1876): Satyrs and Sunlight V
Mackaness (1882) (ed.): Australian Short Stories
Palmer, Nettie (1885) (ed.): An Australian Story Book

Alan Barnard b.
Bruce Beaver b.
Richard Beynon b.
James Birrell b.
R. F. Brissenden b.
Peter Coleman b.
Elizabeth Harrower b.
Donald Kennedy b.
A. L. McLeod b.
A. W. Martin b.
B. W. Muirden b.
Criena Rohan b.
J. P. Sinclair b.
Eleanor Spence b.
T. W. Heney d.
G. A. Taylor d.
G. A. Wood d.
David McKee Wright d.
All About Books
1928-38
London Aphrodite, ed. by Jack Lindsay & P. R. Stephensen, *1928-29*

1928 (contd)

Palmer, Vance (1885): The Man Hamilton   N
Price (1892): Founders and Pioneers of South Australia   B
Prichard (1883): The Wild Oats of Han   Y [rev. edn 1968]
Spencer, W. B. (1860): Wanderings in Wild Australia   A
Stephens, A.G. (1865): Henry Kendall   C
Upfield (1892): The House of Cain   N

1929

Adams, A. H. (1872): A Man's Life   N
Bean (1879): The Australian Imperial Force in France   H [further vols 1933, 1937, 1942; vols III-VI of the Official History of Australia in the War of 1914-1918]
Dalley (1876): Max Flambard   N
Dyson (1865): The Golden Shanty   S [repr. 1963 intro. by N. Lindsay]
'Eldershaw, M. Barnard': A House is Built   N
Ewers (1904): Boy and Silver   V
FitzGerald (1902): To Meet the Sun   V
Hay (1875): Strabane of the Mulberry Hills   N
Jury (1894): Love and the Virgins   D
Lindsay, Norman (1879): Madam Life's Lovers   C
Macartney, F. T. (1887): A Sweep of Lute Strings   V
'Maurice, Furnley' (1881): The Gully and Other Verses
Morris, Myra (1893): White Magic   V
Piddington (1862): Worshipful Masters   E
Prichard (1883): Coonardoo   N
'Richardson, Henry Handel' (1870): Ultima Thule   N [cf. 1930]
Scott, Ernest (1867) (ed.): Australian Discovery   H [repr. 1966]
Stephensen (1901): The Bushwhackers   S

Michael Cannon b.
Catherine Gaskin b.
Louis Green b.
K. S. Inglis b.
Grahame Johnston b.
W. S. McPheat b.
Ray Mathew b.
Peter Porter b.
Kap Pothan b.
R. A. Simpson b.
Gavin Souter b.
Barbara Baynton d.
Lala Fisher d.
Laura Palmer-Archer d.
Sir Walter Spencer d.
H. A. Tardent d.
Australian Quarterly *begins*
Desiderata *1929-39*
Verse, *ed. by L. Lavater, 1929-33*
The Middle Parts of Fortune: Somme and Ancre, *by 'Private 19022' i.e. Frederic Manning* [abridged edn *1930* titled Ḥer Privates We]
C. Hartley Grattan, Australian Literature
Paul Wenz, Le Jardin des Coraux

1930

Brereton (1871): Knocking Round E
Broomfield (1860): Henry Lawson and His
  Critics C
Dalley (1876): Only the Morning N
Franklin, Miles (1879): Ten Creeks Run N
  ['by Brent of Bin Bin']
Gilmore (1865): The Wild Swan V
Green, H. M. (1881): An Outline of Australian
  Literature C
Hancock (1898): Australia H
Kellow (1881): Queensland Poets C
Lindsay, Norman (1879): Redheap N
Lower (1903): Here's Luck N
Murdoch (1874): Speaking Personally E [cf.
  Roderick 1945]
Palmer, Vance (1885): Men Are Human N
  The Passage N
Prichard (1883): Haxby's Circus N
'Richardson, Henry Handel' (1870): The
  Fortunes of Richard Mahony N [con-
  tains the trilogy publd in 1917, 1925, 1929;
  later edn 1968 with intro. by G. A. Wilkes]
Shann (1884): Economic History of Australia
Spielvogel (1874): Old Eko's Note Book S
Stow, Catherine (1855?): Woggheeguy L [cf.
  Drake-Brockman 1953]

Mena Abdullah b.
Geoffrey Blainey b.
Bruce Dawe b.
Jean Prest b.
R. J. Crawford d.
S. G. Fielding d.
A. C. Grant d.
Sir Archibald Strong d.
Daily Telegraph (Syd-
  ney) called Daily
  Pictorial Feb. 1930–
  Feb. 1931
Geoffrey Rawson, Bligh
  of the 'Bounty'

1931

Brereton (1871): So Long, Mick D
Davison (1893): Forever Morning N
  Man-Shy N
'Eldershaw, M. Barnard': Green Memory N
Franklin, Miles (1883): Old Blastus of Bandi-
  coot ,N
  Back to Bool Bool N ['by Brent of Bin
  Bin']
Gilmore (1865): The Rue Tree V
Gray ( ): Red Dust A ['by Donald Black']

John Barnes b.
G. C. Bolton b.
P. D. Edwards b.
Shirley Hazzard b.
H. P. Heseltine b.
Charles Higham b.
Evan Jones b.
Peter Mathers b.
Gerald O'Collins b.
L. L. Robson b.
Michael Roe b.

1931 (contd)

'Hatfield, William' (1892): Sheepmates N
Idriess (1890): Lasseter's Last Ride P
Lawson, Bertha (1900) & Brereton (1871) (edd.): Henry Lawson, by His Mates
Mackaness (1882): The Life of Vice-Admiral William Bligh
Moll (1900): Native Moments V
Murdoch (1874): Saturday Mornings E
Palmer, Nettie (1885): Henry Bournes Higgins B
Palmer, Vance (1885): Separate Lives S
Slessor (1901), Matthews, Harley (1889) & Simpson, Colin (1908): Trio V [contains 'Five Visions of Captain Cook', 'Two Brothers' and 'Infidelities', respectively]
Sugden (1854) & Eggleston (1875): George Swinburne B

J. M. Tregenza b.
E. G. Dyson d.
Manuscripts 1931-35 Stream
Paul Wenz, L'Écharde

1932

Bayldon (1865): Collected Poems
Champion (1904): Across New Guinea A
Dark (1901): Slow Dawning N
Eggleston (1875): State Socialism in Victoria P
Ercole ( ): No Escape N
Gilmore (1865): Under the Wilgas V
Holt, Edgar (1904): Lilacs out of the Dead Land V
Hopegood (1891): Austral Pan V
Idriess (1890): Flynn of the Inland B
The Desert Column H
Lindsay, Norman (1879): Miracles by Arrangement N
The Cautious Amorist N
McKellar (1904): Twenty-six V [with biog. note by K. Slessor]
Mann, Leonard (1895): Flesh in Armour N
Meller (1892): Quartette N
Murdoch (1874): Moreover E
Palmer, Nettie (1885): Talking It Over E
Palmer, Vance (1885): Daybreak N

Alan Brissenden b.
Keith Harrison b.
Christopher Koch b.
Sylvia Lawson b.
C. J. Brennan d.
Fergus Hume d.
Fred Johns d.
J. A. R. McKellar d.
Marion Phillips d.

50

1932 *(contd)*

Prichard (1883): Kiss on the Lips S
  The Earth Lover V
Simpson, Helen (1897): Boomerang N
Slessor (1901): Cuckooz Contrey V
Truran (1897): Green Mallee N
White, M. R. (1888): No Roads Go By A

1933

Brady (1869): Wardens of the Seas V
Campbell, Jean (1906): Brass and Cymbals N
Clune (1893): Try Anything Once A
Davison (1893): The Wells of Beersheba N
Ewers (1904): Money Street N
Franklin, Miles (1879): Bring the Monkey N
Harcourt (1902): The Pearlers N
Higgins (1901): Mordecaius' Overture V
Jose (1863): The Romantic Nineties E
Lindsay, Norman (1879): Saturdee N
Macartney, F. T. (1887): Hard Light V
Meller (1892): A Leaf of Laurel N
O'Ferrall (d. 1925): Stories ['by Kodak']
Paterson (1864): The Animals Noah Forgot Y
Penn-Smith (1863): The Unexpected A
Robinson, Les. (1886): The Giraffe's Uncle S
  [intro. by K. Slessor]
Rule (1886): Jacka's Mob A
Simpson, Helen (1897): The Woman on the
  Beast S
Slessor (1901): Darlinghurst Nights V
  Funny Farmyard Y
Stephens, A. G. (1865): Chris. Brennan C
  [later inc. in J. Barnes, The Writer in
  Australia 1969]
Strong (d. 1930): Four Studies C [with
  memoir by R. C. Bald]
Truran (1897): Where the Plain Begins N
Turnbull (1906): Outside Looking In V
White, M. R. (1888): For Those That Love
  It N
Williams (1889): The Gallant Company A

Hugh Edwards b.
J. P. Fogarty b.
Craig McGregor b.
W. S. Ramson b.
Vivian Smith b.
Margaret Steven b.
J. Le Gay Brereton d.
James Edmond d.
A. G. Stephens d.
E. Scott (ed.), Cam-
  bridge History of the
  British Empire,
  VII.i
'G. B. Lancaster',
  Pageant
Grant Watson, The
  Partners ['by John
  Lovegood']
Edith Humphris, Life of
  Adam Lindsay
  Gordon
Courier-Mail (Bris-
  bane), formed by
  merger of Courier and
  Daily Mail, 1933-

'Baylebridge, William' (1883): Love Re-
deemed V [first book under this pseudonym; earlier vols under own name]

Boyd, Martin (1893): Scandal of Spring N

Dakin (1883): Whalemen Adventurers H

Dark (1901): Prelude to Christopher N

Drake-Brockman (1901): Blue North N

Ercole ( ): Dark Windows N

Farmer (1899): Thirsty Earth N

Fysh (1895): Taming the North H

Gilmore (1865): Old Days: Old Ways H

Harcourt (1902): Upsurge N

Hibble (1902): Karangi N

Hughes, Randolph (1890): C. J. Brennan: An
Essay in Values C

Johns (d. 1932): An Australian Biographical
Dictionary

Lamond (1885): Tooth and Talon S

Lindsay, Norman (1879): Pan in the Parlour N

McCrae, Hugh (1876) (ed.): Georgiana's Journal
[journal of Georgiana McCrae q.v.]

'Maurice, Furnley' (1881): Melbourne Odes

Melbourne (1888): William Charles Wentworth
B
Early Constitutional Development in
Australia: New South Wales 1788-1856
[later ed. 1963 by R. B. Joyce, adding
Queensland 1859-1922]

Mitchell, Mary (1892): A Warning to Wantons
N

Monckton (1872): New Guinea Recollections A

Moore, William (1868): The Story of Australian Art H

Murdoch (1874): The Wild Planet E

Neilson (1872): Collected Poems [ed. by R. H.
Croll]

Palmer, Vance (1885): The Swayne Family N
Sea and Spinifex S

Paterson (1864): Happy Dispatches A

Penton (1904): Landtakers N

David Malouf b.
Chris. Wallace-Crabbe b.
Derek Whitelock b.
A. W. Jose d.
Douglas Sladen (ed.),
Adam Lindsay
Gordon
Thomas Wood, Cobbers
'Leslie Parker', Trooper
to the Southern
Cross [by Angela
Thirkell]

'**Richardson, Henry Handel**' (1870): The End of a Childhood S

'**Rudd, Steele**' (1868): Green Grey Homestead N

Stead (1902): The Salzburg Tales S
Seven Poor Men of Sydney N

1935

Blunden (1906): No More Reality N

Boyd, Martin (1893): The Lemon Farm N

Brown, E. T. (1889): Excursions and Enquiries E

Brown, P. L. (1904) (ed.): The Narrative of George Russell of Golf Hill A

Copland (1894): W. E. Hearn B

Cowling (1881) & '**Maurice, Furnley**' (1881) (edd.): Australian Essays

Croll (1869): Tom Roberts B

Dennis (1876): The Singing Garden M

Durack, Mary (1913): All-About S [text; illustrations by E. Durack]

Ewers (1904): Fire on the Wind N

Finlayson (1895): The Red Centre P

Forsyth (1909): Governor Arthur's Convict System H

Gilmore (1865): More Recollections A

Hides (1906): Through Wildest Papua A

Hopegood (1891): Peter Lecky By Himself A

Ingamells (1913): Gumtops V

McCrae, Hugh (1876): My Father and My Father's Friends B [repr. in Story Book Only 1948]

McKinney (1891): Crucible N

Mann, Leonard (1895): Human Drift N

Moll (1900): Blue Interval V

Moore, T. Inglis (1901): The Half Way Sun N

Palmer, Vance (1885): Hurricane N [revision of The Outpost 1924 q.v.]

Ann Blainey b.
Rodney Hall b.
Thomas Keneally b.
Thomas Shapcott b.
Jan Smith b.
Randolph Stow b.
J. B. Dalley d.
A. H. Davis ('*Steele Rudd*') *d.*
Carlton Dawe d.
Mabel Forrest d.
H. A. Kellow d.
Louise Mack d.
Frederic Manning d.
Mrs Campbell Praed d.
E. O. G. Shann d.
Louis Stone d.
E. H. Sugden d.
Australian Mercury
W. J. Turner, Blow for Balloons
Grant Watson, The Nun and the Bandit

1935 *(contd)*

Roberts (1901): The Squatting Age in Australia H

Souter, C. H. (1864): The Lonely Rose V

Spielvogel (1874): The History of Ballarat

Tennant (1912): Tiburon N

Thompson, John (1907): Three Dawns Ago V

White, Patrick (1912): The Ploughman and Other Poems

Williams (1889): Comrades of the Great Adventure A

1936

Afford (1906): The Founder D

'Boake, Capel' (1895): The Dark Thread N

Boyd, Martin (1893): The Painted Princess Y

Cusack (1904): Jungfrau N

Dark (1901): Return to Coolami N

Davison (1893): Children of the Dark People Y

Devanny (1894): Sugar Heaven N

Drake-Brockman (1901): Sheba Lane N

Durack, Mary (1913): Chunuma S [text; illustrations by E. Durack]

'Eldershaw, M. Barnard': The Glasshouse N

Ferguson (1881) & **Green, H. M.** (1881): The Howes and their Press H [with Mrs A. G. Foster]

Franklin, Miles (1879): All That Swagger N

Harrington (1896): Boundary Bend V

Hides (1906): Papuan Wonderland A

Idriess (1890): The Cattle King B

Ingamells (1913): Forgotten People V

Lawson, Will (1876): When Cobb and Co. Was King N

Lindsay, Norman (1879): The Flyaway Highway Y

Mackaness (1882): Sir Joseph Banks B

Madigan (1889): Central Australia P

Morphett, G. C. (1901): The Life and Letters of Sir John Morphett

R. K. Forward b.
Judith Green b.
Wendy Sutherland b.
Norman Talbot b.
A. H. Adams d.
R. W. Giblin d.
A. A. G. Hales d.
C. A. W. Monckton d.
F. S. Williamson d.
Annual Catalogue of Australian Publications (*National Library*) *1936-60*
Douglas Stewart, Green Lions *V* [*in N.Z.*]

1936 (contd)

Murdoch (1874): Lucid Intervals E
Paterson (1864): The Shearer's Colt N
Penton (1904): Inheritors N
Scott, Ernest (1867): Australia During the War H [vol. XI of the Official History of Australia in the War of 1914-1918]
A History of the University of Melbourne
Stead (1902): The Beauties and Furies N
Stephensen (1901): The Foundations of Culture in Australia C [later inc. in J. Barnes, The Writer in Australia 1969]
Stivens (1911): The Tramp S
Tomholt (1884): Bleak Dawn D

1937

Boyd, Martin (1893): The Picnic N
Dark (1901): Sun Across the Sky N
Drake-Brockman (1901): Younger Sons N
Durack, Mary (1913): Son of Djaro S [text; illustrations by E. Durack]
'Eldershaw, M. Barnard': Plaque With Laurel N
Harcourt (1902): It Never Fails N
Hay (1875): The Mystery of Alfred Doubt N
Hill, Ernestine (1899): The Great Australian Loneliness P
Water into Gold P
Mackaness (1882): Admiral Arthur Phillip B
Mackenzie, Kenneth (1913): Our Earth V
The Young Desire It N ['by Seaforth Mackenzie']
Madgwick (1905): Immigration into Eastern Australia H [repr. 1969]
Mann, Leonard (1895): A Murder in Sydney N
Mayo (1889): The Life and Letters of Colonel William Light
Mitchell, G. D. (1894): Backs to the Wall A
The Awakening N
Moodie Heddle (1904): Solitude V
Moore, T. Inglis (1901): The Third Spring N

William Dick b.
Don Maynard b.
Catherine Martin d.
William Moore d.
Venture, *ed. by Rex Ingamells, 1937-40*
'Elinor Mordaunt', Sinabada

Moore, William (1868) & **Moore, T. Inglis** (1901) (edd.): Best Australian One-Act Plays

O'Brien, Eris (1895): The Foundation of Australia H

Palmer, Vance (1885): Legend for Sanderson N

Prichard (1883): Intimate Strangers N

Rayment (1882): The Valley of the Sky N

Ross, Lloyd (1901): William Lane and the Australian Labour Movement B

Simpson, Helen (1897): Under Capricorn N

Turner, Alexander (1907): Hester Siding D

Young, Jeanne (1876): Catherine Helen Spence B

1938

Bates (1861): The Passing of the Aborigines A

Boyd, Martin (1893): Night of the Party N

Brennan, C. J. (d. 1932): Twenty-three Poems

Coombes ( ): Some Australian Poets C

Dark (1901): Waterway N

Drake-Brockman (1901): Men Without Wives D [cf. 1955]

'Eldershaw, M. Barnard': Phillip of Australia H

    Essays in Australian Fiction C

Elkin (1891): The Australian Aborigines

Evatt (1894): Rum Rebellion H

Finnin (1906): A Beggar's Opera V

FitzGerald (1902): Moonlight Acre V

Herbert (1901): Capricornia N

Hides (1906): Savages in Serge A

Ingamells (1913): Sun-Freedom V

Ingamells (1913) & **Tilbrook** (1907): Conditional Culture C [later inc. in J. Barnes, The Writer in Australia 1969]

Lindsay, Norman (1879): Age of Consent N

Lowe, Eric (1889): Salute to Freedom N

P. A. Howell b.
Colin Johnson b.
Morris Lurie b.
Les. Murray b.
Tony Morphett b.
B. Thompson b.
C. J. Dennis d.
J. G. Hides d.
John Sandes d.
Jindyworobak Anthology *1938-53*
Geoffrey Rawson, The Strange Case of Mary Bryant

McCrae, Hugh (1876): The Mimshi Maiden   V
McCuaig (1908): Vaudeville   V
Mackenzie, Kenneth (1913): Chosen People
   N   ['by Seaforth Mackenzie']
Mann, Leonard (1895): The Plumed Voice   V
Matthews, Harley (1889): Vintage   V
Moore, T. Inglis (1901): Adagio in Blue   V
Morris, Myra (1893): The Wind on the Water
   N
Moses (1860): Nine Miles From Gundagai   V
Murdoch (1874): Collected Essays
Neilson (1872): Beauty Imposes   V
Pescott (1872): The Life Story of Joseph Furphy
Ratcliffe (1904): Flying Fox and Drifting Sand
   P
Stead (1902): House of All Nations   N
Tilbrook (1907): Torn Edges   V

1939

'Baylebridge, William' (1883): Sextains   V
   This Vital Flesh   V   [cf. 1961]
Boyd, Martin (1893): A Single Flame   A
Cox (1873): Fools' Harvest   N
Crawford, R. M. (1906): The Study of History
   P
Croll (1869): I Recall   A
'Eldershaw, M. Barnard': My Australia   H
   The Life and Times of Captain John Piper   H
Fallaw (1876): Hostage and Survival   V
Finnin (1906): Look Down, Olympians   V
Fitzpatrick, Brian (1905): British Imperialism
   and Australia   H
Franklin, Miles (1879) & **Cusack** (1904):
   Pioneers on Parade   N
Gilmore (1865): Battlefields   V
Green, H. M. (1881): Christopher Brennan   C

Edward Jenks d.
Amy Eleanor Mack d.
E. G. Murphy ('Dry-
   blower') d.
Sir Ernest Scott d.
E. S. Sorenson d.
Paul Wenz d.
Southerly begins [ed. by
   R. G. Howarth 1939-
   56, with A. G.
   Mitchell 1939-44; by
   K. Slessor 1956-61;
   by W. Stone 1962;
   by G. A. Wilkes
   1963-]
Douglas Stewart, The
   White Cry   V
   [written N.Z., publd
   London]

1939 (contd)

Hardie (1894): Pastoral Symphony   N
Hasluck, Paul (1905): Into the Desert   V
Hides (d. 1938): Beyond the Kubea   A
Jury (1894): Galahad, Selenemia and Poems
McCrae, Hugh (1876): Poems
Mann, Leonard (1895): Mountain Flat   N
Morris, Myra (1893): Dark Tumult   N
Murdoch (1874): The Spur of the Moment   E
Pescott (1872): James Bonwick   B
Philip (1861): Sixty Years' Recollections   A
'Richardson, Henry Handel' (1870): The Young Cosima   N
Slessor (1901): Five Bells   V
Tennant (1912): Foveaux   N
White, Patrick (1912): Happy Valley   N

Douglas Sladen, My Long Life

1940

Auchterlounie (1915): Kaleidoscope   V
Bassett (1889): The Governor's Lady   B   [of Mrs Philip Gidley King]
Boyd, Martin (1893): Nuns in Jeopardy   N
Clarke, Donovan (1907): Ritual Dance   V
Connolly (1896): Southern Saga   N
Davison (1893): The Woman at the Mill   S
Durack, Mary (1913): Piccaninnies   Y   [text; illustrations by E. Durack]
Evatt (1894): Australian Labour Leader   B
Finnin (1906): Poems
Fitzpatrick, Brian (1905): A Short History of the Australian Labour Movement [reprinted 1969 with intro. by Ian Turner]
Harrington (1896): My Old Black Billy   V
Harris, Max (1921): The Gift of Blood   V
Hopegood (1891): Thirteen from Oahu   V
Ingamells (1913): Memory of Hills   V
Lowe, Eric (1889): Framed in Hardwood   N
Matthews, Harley (1889): The Breaking of the Drought   V

Geoffrey Lehmann b.
Craig Powell b.
Sir Henry Gullett d.
Sir Hubert Murray d.
G. B. Philip d.
Mrs Catherine Stow (formerly Langloh Parker) d.
Samuel Shumack d.
Helen Simpson d.
Arnold Haskell, Waltzing Matilda
Commonwealth Literary Fund lectures begin
A Comment *1940-47*
Angry Penguins, ed. by Max Harris et al., *1940-46*
Meanjin, ed. by C. B. Christesen, begins [titled Meanjin Papers *1940-46*, Meanjin *1947-60*, Meanjin Quarterly *1961-*]

1940 (contd)

Miller (1881): Australian Literature [biblio.]
Moll (1900): Cut From Mulga V
Morrison, W. A. (1877): The Moon Turned Round V
Mudie, Ian (1911): Corroboree to the Sun V
Neilson (1872): To the Men of the Roads V
Palmer, Vance (1885): National Portraits B [enlarged edn 1954]
Prichard (1883): Brumby Innes D
Riddell (1909): The Untrammelled V
Stead (1902): The Man Who Loved Children N [later edn 1966 with intro. by Randall Jarrell]
Stephensen (1901): The Life and Works of A. G. Stephens
Stewart, Douglas (1913): Elegy for an Airman V

1941

Allen (1879): Patria V
Ashton (1851): Now Came Still Evening On A
Barnard, Marjorie (1897): Macquarie's World H
Brown, P. L. (1904) (ed.): Clyde Company Papers [vol. i; ii, 1952; iii, 1958; iv, 1959; v, 1963; vi, 1968]
Chisholm, A. H. (1890): Strange New World B [about John Gilbert and Ludwig Leichhardt, q.v.; revised edn 1955]
Crawford, R. M. (1906): Ourselves and the Pacific H
Dalziel (1881): Known and Not Held V
Dark (1901): The Timeless Land N
Ferguson (1881): Bibliography of Australia i [1784-1830]
Finnin (1906): Royal V
Fitzpatrick, Brian (1905): The British Empire in Australia H [rev. 1949, repr. 1969]
Gilmore (1865): The Disinherited V
Harford (d. 1927): Poems

Randolph Bedford d.
F. J. Broomfield d.
A. J. Buchanan d.
Enid Derham d.
A.B.('Banjo') Paterson d.
Thomas Welsby d.
Douglas Stewart, ed. of Bulletin *Red Page 1941-61*
Poetry, ed. by F. Hudson et al., 1941-47
Australian Poetry begins
Coast to Coast begins
'Sarah Campion', Mo Burdekin
Charles Nordhoff & James Hall, Botany Bay
Daily Mirror (Sydney) begins

Hill, Ernestine (1899): My Love Must Wait N
[about Matthew Flinders, q.v.]

Kennedy, Victor (1895): Flaunted Banners C

Lindsay, Philip (1906): I'd Live the Same Life
Over A

Macartney, F. T. (1887): Preferences V

McCuaig (1908): The Wanton Goldfish V

Manifold (1915): The Death of Ned Kelly V

Mann, Leonard (1895): Poems from the Mask

Moore, T. Inglis (1901): Emu Parade V

Mudie, Ian (1911): This is Australia V

O'Dowd (1866): Poems

O'Dwyer (1912): Poems

O'Leary (1916): Spikenard and Bayonet V

Palmer, Vance (1885): A. G. Stephens, His Life
and Work

Prichard (1883): Moon of Desire N

Stewart, Douglas (1913): Sonnets to the
Unknown Soldier

Tennant (1912): The Battlers N

Uren (1900): Waterless Horizons H [with
Robert Stephens]

White, Patrick (1912): The Living and the
Dead N

1942

Aldridge (1918): Signed With Their Honour N

Anderson, Ethel (1883): Squatter's Luck V

Casey, Gavin (1907): It's Harder for Girls S

Clarke, Donovan (1907): Blue Prints V

Dunn (1895): Random Elements V

Fullerton (1868): Moles Do So Little With
Their Privacy V ['by E']

Harris, Max (1921): Dramas from the Sky V

Hasluck, Paul (1905): Black Australians P

Ingamells (1913): News of the Sun V

Joyce, Alfred (d. 1901): A Homestead History
[ed. by G. F. James; enlarged edn 1969]

Janette Finch b.
Julian Ashton d.
Sir George Beeby d.
*William 'Baylebridge'
(Blocksidge) d.*
Mary Gaunt d.
Shaw Neilson d.
E. A. Vidler d.
*Frank Wilmot ('Furnley
Maurice') d.*
*David Martin, Battle-
fields and Girls V
[in U.K.]*

1942 (contd)

Langley (1908): The Pea Pickers N
Locke-Elliott (1917): Interval D
McKie (1909): This Was Singapore H
Mann, Leonard (1885): The Go-Getter N
Moir (1893) (ed.): Shaw Neilson: A Memorial [editor anon.]
Moore, T. Inglis (1901): Six Australian Poets C
O'Dowd (1866): Fantasies E
Palmer, Vance (1885): Frank Wilmot (Furnley Maurice) C [later inc. in J. Barnes, The Writer in Australia 1969]
Porter, Hal (1911): Short Stories
'Roland, Betty' (1903): The Touch of Silk D
Southall (1921): Out of the Dawn S

C. Hartley Grattan, Introducing Australia
'Sarah Campion', Bonanza
Esther Landolt, Ewige Herde
Karl Shapiro in Australia [see The Place of Love *1942*, V-Letter *1944*]

1943

Barnard, Marjorie (1897): The Persimmon Tree S
Casey, Gavin (1907): Birds of a Feather S
Christesen (1912): North Coast V
Dann (1904): Caroline Chisholm D
Davis (1905): Earth Cry V
Harris, Max (1921): The Vegetative Eye N
Hart-Smith (1911): Columbus Goes West V
Hetherington (1907): Airborne Invasion P
The Australian Soldier P [publd 1944]
Ingamells (1913): Content Are the Quiet Ranges V
Unknown Land V
Kershaw (1921): The Lonely Verge V
Lawson, Bertha (1876): My Henry Lawson B [ed. by Will Lawson, q.v.]
McLennan (1909): The Spirit of the West V
Mudie, Ian (1911): The Australian Dream V
Their Seven Stars Unseen V
Neilson (1872): Lines Written in Memory of Adam Lindsay Gordon V
Shaw, Charles (1900): The Warrambungle Mare V
Outback Occupations S

Elizabeth J. Gunton b.
Chester Cobb d.
Louis Esson d.
M. M. Grover d.
Esther Landolt d.
Ida Lee d.
A. C. V. Melbourne d.
R. Spencer-Browne d.
Australian New Writing *1943-46*
Barjai *1943-47*

1943 (contd)

Stewart, Douglas (1913): Ned Kelly D [cf. 1958; also repr. 1963 in Three Australian Plays, intro. H. G. Kippax]
Tennant (1912): Ride on Stranger N
Time Enough Later N
Thwaites (1915): The Jervis Bay V
Trist (1914): In the Sun S
'Vrepont, Brian' (1882): Beyond the Claw V

1944

Afford (1906): Lady in Danger D
Anderson, Ethel (1883): Adventures in Appleshire E
Bayldon (1865): Apollo in Australia and Bush Verses V
Bedford, Randolph (d. 1941): Naught to Thirty-three A
Christesen (1912): South Coast V
Cowan (1914): Drift S
Dann (1904): Fountains Beyond D
Davis (1905): I, the Thief V
Deakin (d. 1919): The Federal Story H [ed. by Herbert Brookes, q.v.; later ed. by J. A. La Nauze 1963]
Devaney (1890): Shaw Neilson B
Dobson (1920): In a Convex Mirror V
Dunn (1895): No Asterisks V
Durack, Mary (1913): The Way of the Whirlwind Y [text; illustrations by E. Durack]
Dutton (1922): Night Flight and Sunrise V
Edwards, Don (1905): High Hill at Midnight S
Elliott (1910): James Hardy Vaux B
Esson (d. 1943) et al.: Six Australian One-Act Plays
Ewers (1904): Tell the People C
Tales from the Dead Heart L
Franklin, Miles (1879) & **Baker, Kate** (1861): Joseph Furphy C
Glassop (1913): We Were the Rats N
Green, H. M. (1881): Fourteen Minutes C

Suzanne Holly Jones b.
'Capel Boake' d.
G. C. Henderson d.
James Picot d.
Ambrose Pratt d.
C. H. Souter d.
'Sarah Campion', The Pommy Cow

Harrington (1896): The Kerrigan Boys V
Howarth (1906): Spright and Geist V ['by R.G.H.']
Hudson (1913): As Iron Hills V
Ingamells (1913): Selected Poems
Ingleton (1908): Charting a Continent H
'James, Brian' (1892): First Furrow S
Kershaw (1921): Excellent Stranger V
Lawson, Will (1876): Bill the Whaler V
Lawson, Will (1876) (ed.): Australian Bush Songs and Ballads
Macartney, F. T. (1887): Ode of Our Times
McCrae, Hugh (1876): Forests of Pan V [sel. by R. G. Howarth]
McCuaig (1908): Tales out of Bed S
Mackenzie, Kenneth (1913): The Moonlit Doorway V
'Malley, Ern': The Darkening Ecliptic V [cf. M. Harris 1961]
Manifold (1915): Trident V [with Martin, David, q.v., and H. Nicholson]
Mann, Leonard (1895): The Delectable Mountains V
Marshall, Alan (1902): These Are My People A
'Maurice, Furnley' (d. 1942): Poems [sel. by P. Serle]
Mudie, Ian (1911) (ed.): Poets at War
O'Dwyer (1912): The Turning Year V
Prichard (1883): Potch and Colour S
Quinn, John (1915): Battle Stations V
Robinson, Roland (1912): Beyond the Grass-Tree Spears V
Shaw, A. G. L. (1916): The Economic Development of Australia H
Shaw, Charles (1900): A Sheaf of Shorts S
Slessor (1901): One Hundred Poems
Stead (1902): For Love Alone N
Stewart, Douglas (1913): A Girl With Red Hair S
The Fire on the Snow and The Golden Lover D [cf. 1958]

1944 (contd)

Thompson, John (1907): Sesame V
Turnbull (1906): Fourteen Poems
Turner, Alexander (1907): Australian Stages D
   Royal Mail D
Wilmot, Chester (1911): Tobruk H

1945

Anderson, Ethel (1883): Timeless Garden E
Baker, S. J. (1912): The Australian Language P
   [rev. edn 1966]
Biggs (1915): Poems of War and Peace
Bladen (1922): Selected Poems
Blight (1913): The Old Pianist V
Casey, Gavin (1907): Downhill is Easier N
Christesen (1912): Dirge and Lyrics V
Close (1903): Love Me Sailor N
Crawford, R. M. (1906): The Renaissance and
   Other Essays
Dark (1901): The Little Company N
Davies, Arthur (1907): The Fiddlers of
   Drummond N
Ewers (1904): Creative Writing in Australia
   [rev. edns 1956, 1962, 1966]
Ferguson (1881): Bibliography of Australia ii
   [1831-38]
Foster (1914): There is no Armour D
Gilmore (1865): Pro Patria Australia V
Grano (1894): Poems New and Old
Hart-Smith (1911): Harvest V
Ingamells (1913): Yera V
Irvin, Eric (1908): A Soldier's Miscellany V
Kiddle (1914): Moonbeam Stairs Y
Lindsay, Jane (1920): Kurrajong N
Lindsay, Norman (1879): The Cousin from
   Fiji N
McCrae, Hugh (1876): Voice of the Forest V
Mann, Cecil (1896): The River S
Miles (1921): Pacific Moon V

Patricia O'Brien b.
Norma Davis d.
William Gosse Hay d.
Jack Moses d.
A. B. Piddington d.

1945 (contd)

Moll (1900): Brief Waters V
Moore, T. Inglis (1901): We're Going Through
D
Mudie, Ian (1911): Poems 1934-1944
Porteous (1897): Little Known of these Waters
S ['by Standby']
Roderick (1911): A Companion to Speaking
Personally [cf. Murdoch 1930]
Roderick (1911) (ed.): The Australian Novel C
Ronan (1907): Strangers on the Ophir N
Smith, Bernard (1916): Place, Taste and
Tradition C
Thiele (1920): Progress to Denial V
Splinters and Shards V
Tilbrook (1907): Time-Shadows V
Trist (1914): Now That We're Laughing N
Turnbull (1906): Mulberry Leaves B [of
Charles Whitehead, q.v.; cf. 1965]
Bluestone B [of James Stephens; cf. 1965]
West, Morris (1916): Moon in My Pocket N
['by Julian Morris']

1946

Bean (1897): Anzac to Amiens H
'Boake, Capel' (d. 1944): The Twig is Bent N
Boyd, Martin (1893): Lucinda Brayford N
Brickhill (1916): Escape to Danger A [with
Conrad Norton]
Chisholm, A. H. (1890): The Making of a
Sentimental Bloke B [of C. J. Dennis,
q.v.]
Chisholm, A. R. (1888): Christopher Brennan
C
Cleary (1917): These Small Glories S
Davison (1893): Dusty N
Durack, Mary (1913): The Magic Trumpet Y
[text; illustrations by E. Durack]
Elliott (1910): Leviathan's Inch N
Esson (d. 1943): The Southern Cross D
Ewers (1904): Men Against the Earth [publd
1947]

G. H. Cowling d.
Mary Fullerton ('E') d.
'Henry Handel
Richardson' d.
T. G. Tucker d.
W. J. Turner d.
David Martin, Tiger
Bay *N*; The Shep-
herd and the Hunter
D [*in U. K.*]
'Sarah Campion', Dr
Golightly

Fitzpatrick, Brian (1905): The Australian
People H

Franklin, Miles (1879): My Career Goes
Bung N

Fullerton (1868): The Wonder and the Apple
V ['by E']

Gaskin (1929): This Other Eden N

Green, H. M. (1881) (ed.): Modern Australian
Poetry

Hart-Smith (1911): The Unceasing Ground V

Howarth (1906): Literary Particles E

'James, Brian' (1892): Cookabundy Ridge S

Macartney, F. T. (1887): Gaily the Troubadour
V

McAuley (1917): Under Aldebaran V

McCuaig (1908): Quod Ronald McCuaig V

Mackaness (1882) (ed.): Poets of Australia

McKellar (d. 1932): Collected Poems

Madigan (1889): Crossing the Dead Heart P
[publd 1947]

Manifold (1915): Selected Verse

Marshall, Alan (1902): Tell Us About the
Turkey, Jo S

Mitchell, A. G. (1911): The Pronunciation of
English in Australia P [rev. edn 1965]

Prichard (1883): The Roaring Nineties N
[goldfields trilogy, vol. 1; cf. 1948, 1950]

Rees (1905): Karrawingi the Emu Y

Rees (1905) (ed.): Australian Radio Plays

Rivett (1917): Behind Bamboo A

Stead (1902): Letty Fox, Her Luck N

Stewart, Douglas (1913): The Dosser in
Springtime V

Stivens (1911): The Courtship of Uncle Henry S

Tennant (1912): Lost Haven N

Trist (1914): What Else is There? S

Turnbull (1906): Eureka B [of Peter Lalor;
cf. 1965]
Bonanza B [of G. F. Train; cf. 1965]

Wright, Judith (1915): The Moving Image V

1947

Anderson, Ethel (1883): Sunday at Yarralumla V

Boyd, Robin (1919): Victorian Modern C

Casey, Gavin (1907): The Wits Are Out N

Cleary (1917): You Can't See Round Corners N

Cox (1873): The Missing Angel N

Cusack (1904) & **James, Florence** (1904): Four Winds and a Family Y

Daley (d. 1905): Creeve Roe V [ed. by M. Holburn & M. Pizer]

Drake-Brockman (1901): The Fatal Days N

Dunn (1895): Time of Arrival V

'Eldershaw, M. Barnard': Tomorrow and Tomorrow N

Elliott (1910): Singing to the Cattle C

Ellis, M. H. (1890): Lachlan Macquarie B

Fenton, Clyde (1901): Flying Doctor A

Finnin (1906): Alms for Oblivion V

Franklin, Miles (1879): Sydney Royal Y

'Grahame, Jim' (1874): Under Wide Skies V

Hetherington (1907): The Winds Are Still N

Hopegood (1891): Circus at World's End V

Hughes, W. M. (1864): Crusts and Crusades A

Kershaw (1921): Defeat by Time Past V

Lindsay, Norman (1879): Halfway to Anywhere N

Macartney, F. T. (1887): Tripod for Homeward Incense V

McDonald (1921): Pacific Sea V

Mann, Cecil (1896): Light in the Valley N

Mitchell, Elyne (1913): Images in Water E

Moll (1900): Beware the Cuckoo V

Morris, Myra (1893): The Township S

Morrison, John (1904): Sailors Belong Ships S

Murdoch (1874): 72 Essays [selection of earlier vols]

Neilson (d. 1942): Unpublished Poems [ed. by James Devaney]

R. H. Croll d.

Lennie Lower d.

C. T. Madigan d.

Twentieth Century begins

C. Hartley Grattan (ed.), Australia

David Martin, The Shoes Men Walk In S [in U.K.]

Esther Landolt, Namenlos

Biblionews, ed. by Walter Stone, begins

1947 (*contd*)

Palmer, Vance (1885): Hail Tomorrow   D
Cyclone   N
Roderick (1911) (ed.): Twenty Australian
Novelists   C
Stewart, Douglas (1913): Glencoe   V
Shipwreck   D   [cf. 1958]
Trist (1914): Daddy   N
Vallis (1916): Songs of the East Coast   V

1948

Anderson, Ethel (1883): Indian Tales
Bridges (1885): That Yesterday Was Home   H
Chauncy (1900): They Found a Cave   Y
Close (1903): Morn of Youth   A
Dark (1901): Storm of Time   N
Dobson (1920): The Ship of Ice   V
Drake-Brockman (1901): Sydney or the Bush
S
The Lion-Tamer   D
Edwards, Don (1905): The Woman at Jingera
N
Ewers (1904): For Heroes to Live In   N
Farwell (1911): Down Argent Street   H
Fu. ~hy (d. 1912): The Buln-Buln and the
Brolga   N   ['by Tom Collins']
Gilmore (1865): Selected Verse [enlarged 1969]
Harpur (d. 1868): Rosa: Love Sonnets to
Mary Doyle [ed. by C. W. Salier; publd
1949]
Hart-Smith (1911): Christopher Columbus   V
Howarth (1906): Involuntaries   V   ['by R.G.
H.']
Hurley (1890): Shackleton's Argonauts   Y
Ingamells (1913): Come Walkabout   V
Lowe, Eric (1889): Beyond the Nineteen
Counties   N
McCrae, Hugh (1876): Story Book Only   S
McGuire (1903) *et al.*: The Australian Theatre   H

R. J. Cassidy ('Gil-
rooney') *d.*
R. H. Long d.
Marie Pitt d.
S. Locke Elliott, Rusty
Bugles, *produced* [*cf.*
Hanger 1968]
J. Le Gay Brereton,
Writings on the
Elizabethan Drama
[*ed. by R. G.*
Howarth]
Geoffrey Rawson, Aus-
tralia *and* Desert
Journeys

Marshall, Alan (1902): Ourselves Writ Strange
A [republd as These Were My Tribesmen
1965]

Moll (1900): The Waterhole V

Mountford (1890): Brown Men and Red
Sand A

Palmer, Nettie (1885): Fourteen Years A

Palmer, Vance (1885): Golconda N [cf.
1957, 1959]
Louis Esson and the Australian Theatre C

Park (   ): The Harp in the South N

Prichard (1883): Golden Miles N [goldfields
trilogy, vol. 2; cf. 1946, 1950]

Reynolds (1899): Edmund Barton B

'Richardson, Henry Handel' (d. 1946): Myself
When Young A

Riddell (1909): Poems

Roderick (1911): In Mortal Bondage: the
Strange Life of Rosa Praed B

'Roland, Esther' (1918): I Camp Here N

Shave (1888): Five Proven One-Act Plays

Stead (1902): A Little Tea, A Little Chat N

Stewart, Douglas (1913): The Flesh and the
Spirit C

Stewart, Harold (1916): Phoenix Wings V

Turnbull (1906): Black War: the Extermination
of the Tasmanian Aborigines H

Uren (1900): Land Looking West H
Glint of Gold H

Villiers (1903): Whalers of the Midnight Sun Y

Webb (1925): A Drum for Ben Boyd V

White, Patrick (1912): The Aunt's Story N

1949

Badham, H. E. (1899): A Study of Australian
Art C

'Boake, Capel' (d. 1944): Selected Poems [ed.
by Myra Morris]

Boyd, Martin (1893): Such Pleasure N

H. E. Boote d.
'Jim Grahame' d.
Roderic Quinn d.
Marcie Muir, Anthony
Trollope in Australia

69

F

Campbell, David (1915): Speak With the Sun V

Christesen (1912) (ed.): Australian Heritage

Cleary (1917): The Long Shadow N

Clift (1923) & **Johnston, George** (1912): High Valley N

Dwyer (1874): Leg-irons On Wings A

Ellis, M. H. (1890): Francis Greenway B

Ewers (1904): Harvest S

FitzGerald (1902): Heemskerck Shoals V

Fitzpatrick, Kathleen (1905): Sir John Franklin in Tasmania H

Glassop (1913): Lucky Palmer N

Ingamells (1913): Handbook of Australian Literature C

Kiddle (1914): West of Sunset Y

La Nauze (1911): Political Economy in Australia H

Lett (1878): Sir Hubert Murray of Papua B

Marshall, Alan (1902): How Beautiful Are Thy Feet N
Pull Down the Blind S

Moodie Heddle (1904): Australian Literature Now C

Morrison, John (1904): The Creeping City N

Park ( ): Poor Man's Orange N

Porteous (1897): Sailing Orders N ['by Standby']

Robinson, Roland (1912): Language of the Sand V [inc. in Deep Well 1962]

Roderick (1911) (ed.): Wanderers in Australia

Russell (1881): William James Farrer B

Serle, P. (1871): Dictionary of Australian Biography

Turnbull (1906): These Tears of Fire B [of Francis Adams, q.v.; cf. 1965]
Frontier B [of Paddy Hannan; cf. 1965]

Willis ( ): By Their Fruits B [of Ferdinand von Mueller]

Wright, Judith (1915): Woman to Man V

David Martin, The Stones of Bombay N [*in U.K.*]

Abbott, C. L. A. (1886): Australia's Frontier Province H

Casey, Gavin (1907): City of Men N

Cato (1917): The Darkened Window V

Clark, C. M. H. (ed.): Select Documents in Australian History 1788-1850

Cleary (1917): Just Let Me Be N

Cusack (1904): Three Australian Three-Act Plays ['Comets Soon Pass', 'Morning Sacrifice', 'Shoulder the Sky']

Dennis (d. 1938): Selected Verse [ed. A. H. Chisholm]

Devaney (1890): Poems

Dutton (1922): The Mortal and the Marble N

Farwell (1911): Surf Music S

Franklin, Miles (1879): Prelude to Waking N ['by Brent of Bin Bin']

Hardy (1917): Power Without Glory N

Hart-Smith (1911): On the Level S

Heney, Helen (1907): The Chinese Camellia N

Hughes, W. M. (1864): Policies and Potentates A

'James, Brian' (1892): The Advancement of Spencer Button N

Kiddle (1914): Caroline Chisholm B

Lindsay, Norman (1879): Dust or Polish? N

Mackaness (1882) (ed.): Fourteen Journeys Over the Blue Mountains [3 parts 1950-51]

Marshall, Alan (1902): Bumping into Friends S

Morrison, John (1904): Port of Call N

Murphy, Arthur ( ): Contemporary Australian Poets C

Palmer, Nettie (1885): Henry Handel Richardson C

Prichard (1883): Winged Seeds N [goldfields trilogy, vol. 3; cf. 1946, 1948]

Roderick (1911): An Introduction to Australian Fiction C

Slessor (1901): Portrait of Sydney P [text; ed. by G. M. Spencer & S. Ure Smith]

Erle Cox d.
W. J. Dakin d.
W. S. Fairbridge d.
Austrovert, *ed. by B. W. Muirden, 1950-53*
'Nevil Shute', A Town Like Alice

Southall (1921): The Weaver From Meltham B
Meet Simon Black Y
Tennant (1912): John o' the Forest Y
Wells, H. C. (1908): The Earth Cries Out N
Williams, Ruth (1897): Verity of Sydney Town Y

1951

Banning (1921): Everyman His Own Hamlet V
Cumpston (1880): Charles Sturt B
Cusack (1904) & **James, Florence** (1904): Come In Spinner N
Dunn (1895): Portrait of a Country V
Ferguson (1881): Bibliography of Australia iii [1839-45]
Gilchrist (   ) (ed.): John Dunmore Lang P
Green, H. M. (1881): Australian Literature 1900-1950 [rev. edn 1963]
Hardy (1917): The Man From Clinkapella S
Heney, Helen (1907): The Proud Lady N
Ingamells (1913): The Great South Land V
Keesing (1923): Imminent Summer V
Lambert (1921): Twenty Thousand Thieves N
Lowe, Eric (1889): O Willing Hearts N
McCrae, Hugh (1876): The Ship of Heaven D
Mackaness (1882): Annotated Bibliography of Henry Lawson
Mackenzie, Kenneth (1913): Dead Men Rising N ['by Seaforth Mackenzie']
Mathew (1929): With Cypress Pine V
Murdoch (1874) & **Drake-Brockman** (1901) (edd.): Australian Short Stories
Palmer, Vance (1885) (ed.): Old Australian Bush Songs
Park (   ): The Witch's Thorn N
Pearce (1870): Carpenter to Cabinet A
Simpson, Colin (1908): Adam in Ochre P
Stivens (1911): Jimmy Brockett N
Thiele (1920): The Golden Lightning V

Daisy Bates d.
Arthur Gask d.
J. J. Hardie d.
W. R. Humphries d.
S. W. Jephcott d.
Brian Penton d.
Percival Serle d.
Charles Higham, A Distant Star V [in U.K.]
Frances J. Woodward, Portrait of Jane [about Lady Franklin]

Adams, David (1908) (ed.): The Letters of Rachel Henning

Banning (1921): The Instant's Clarity V

Bowden (1908): George Bass B

Boyd, Martin (1893): The Cardboard Crown N [Langton series, vol. 1; cf. 1955, 1957, 1962]

Boyd, Robin (1919): Australia's Home C

Braddon (1921): The Naked Island A

Cleary (1917): The Sundowners N

Crawford, R. M. (1906): Australia H

De Boissiere (1907): Crown Jewel N

Devaney (1890): Poetry in Our Time C

Durack, Mary (1913): Child Artists of the Australian Bush [with Florence Rutter]

FitzGerald (1902): Between Two Tides V

Hasluck, Paul (1905): ¶The Government and the People 1939-41 H

Hawdon (d. 1871): The Journal of a Journey from N.S.W. to Adelaide

Hungerford (1915): The Ridge and the River N

Ingamells (1913): Aranda Boy N
Of Us Now Living N
William Gay C

Ingleton (1908) (ed.): True Patriots All [early broadsides]

Long, Gavin (1901): ¶To Benghazi H

Marshall, Alan (1902): People of the Dreamtime L [publd 1951]

Miller (1881): Pressmen and Governors H

'O'Brien, John' (1879): On Darlinghurst Hill H

Phipson (1912): Christmas in the Sun Y

Robinson, Roland (1912): Legend and Dreaming L

Roderick (1911) (ed.): Ralph Rashleigh N [attributed to James Tucker, 1808-88?; another edn 1968]

Stead (1902): The People With the Dogs N

Stewart, Douglas (1913): Sun Orchids V

C. H. Bertie d.
E. J. Brady d.
Roy Bridges d.
J. F. Dwyer d.
W. M. Hughes d.
Victor Kennedy d.
R. C. Mills d.
'John O'Brien' d.
Sir George Pearce d.
Ern Malley's Journal, ed. by Max Harris et al., 1952-55
The Realist Writer, ed. by Bill Wannan, later by S. Murray-Smith, 1952-54
Chester Wilmot, The Struggle for Europe
'Nevil Shute', The Far Country
H. C. Cameron, Sir Joseph Banks

Tennant (1912): Tether a Dragon   D
Tyrrell (1875): Old Books, Old Friends, Old
   Sydney   A
Waten (1911): Alien Son   S
Webb (1925): Leichhardt in Theatre   V

1953

Anderson, Hugh (1927): A Guide to Ten
   Australian Poets [biblio.]
Aughterson (1903) (ed.): Taking Stock   C
Bladen (1922): The Old Ladies at Newington   V
Brennan, C. J. (d. 1932): The Burden of Tyre
   V
Butlin (1910): Foundations of the Australian
   Monetary System   H
Dark (1901): No Barrier   N
Drake-Brockman (1901): Australian Legendary
   Tales [sel. from Mrs K. Langloh Parker
   (later Stow) 1896, 1898, 1918, 1930, qq.v.]
Eggleston (1875): Reflections of an Australian
   Liberal   A
Ewers (1904): With the Sun on My Back   A
Fairbridge (d. 1950): Poems
FitzGerald (1902): This Night's Orbit   V
Ford (1902): The Life and Work of William
   Redfern   B
Heney, Helen (1907): Dark Moon   N
Hornibrook (1898): Bibliography of Queens-
   land Verse
Hungerford (1915): Riverslake   N
Levy (1889): Governor George Arthur   B
Long, Gavin (1901): ¶Greece, Crete and Syria
   H
McKie (1909): Proud Echo   H
Martin, David (1915): From Life   V
Moll (1900): The Lifted Spear   V
Moore, T. Inglis (1901) (ed.): Australia Writes
Moorehead (1910): Rum Jungle   H

J. H. M. Abbott d.
Kate Baker d.
A. Dorrington d.
Louis Lavater d.
Bernard O'Dowd d.
J. H. Ross d.
*'Nevil Shute', In the
   Wet*
*Charles Higham, Spring
   and Death   V   [in
   U.K.]*
*Geoffrey   Dutton,   A
   Long Way South*
*Geoffrey Rawson, The
   Count [about P. E.
   de Strzelecki, q.v.]*

1953 (contd)

Murray-Smith (1922) (ed.): The Tracks We Travel S [first collection; 2nd, ed. by J. Beasley, 1961; 3rd, ed. by L. C. Haylen, 1965]

Park (   ): A Power of Roses N

Picot (d. 1944): With a Hawk's Quill V

Portus (1883): Happy Highways A

Rees (1905): Towards an Australian Drama C

Robinson, Roland (1912): Tumult of the Swans V [inc. in Deep Well 1962]

Roderick (1911): Australian Round-up S

Stivens (1911): The Gambling Ghost S

Tennant (1912): The Joyful Condemned N [abridged version of Tell Morning This 1967] Australia H

Travers (1919): The Captain-General B [of L. Macquarie]

Webb (1925): Birthday V

Wilkes (1927): New Perspectives on Brennan's Poetry C

Wilson, Erle (1898): Coorinna N

Wright, Judith (1915): The Gateway V

Young, G. F. (1872): Under the Coolibah Tree A

1954

Bassett (1889): The Hentys H

Bedford, Ruth (1882): Think of Stephen B

Blainey, Geoffrey (1930): The Peaks of Lyell H

Blight (1913): The Two Suns Met V

Buckley (1925): The World's Flesh V

Cleary (1917): The Climate of Courage N

Clune (1893) & **Stephensen** (1901): The Viking of Van Diemen's Land B [of J. Jorgenson, q.v.]

Craig (1923): Far-Back Country V

Max Afford d.
J. S. Battye d.
J. H. L. Cumpston d.
Sir Frederick Eggleston d.
Miles Franklin d.
'Sydney de Loghe' d.
Jack McLaren d.
E. E. Pescott d.
G. V. Portus d.
Lionel Shave d.
Chester Wilmot d.

Crossland (1913): Wainewright in Tasmania H

Crowley (1924): The Records of Western Australia H

Cumpston (1880): Thomas Mitchell B

Currey (1890): The Irish at Eureka H

Dunn (1895): The Mirror and the Rose V

Franklin, Miles (1879): Cockatoos N ['by Brent of Bin Bin']

Gibson, L. J. (1924): Henry Handel Richardson and Some of Her Sources C

Gilmore (1865): Fourteen Men V

Hancock (1898): Country and Calling A

Herington (1916): ¶Air War Against Germany and Italy 1939-43 H

Herman (1907): The Early Australian Architects and Their Work H

Hetherington (1907): Blamey B

Hungerford (1915): Sowers of the Wind N

Kennedy, Victor (d. 1952) & **Palmer, Nettie** (1885): Bernard O'Dowd B

Lambert (1921): The Veterans N
The Five Bright Stars N

Langley (1908): White Topee N

McDonald (1921): The Lonely Fire V

Mackenzie, Kenneth (1913): The Refuge N ['by Seaforth Mackenzie']

'O'Brien, John' (d. 1952): The Parish of St Mel's V

Palmer, Vance (1885): The Legend of the Nineties C

Ronan (1907): Vision Splendid N

Rowbotham (1924): Ploughman and Poet V

Stephensen (1901): Kookaburras and Satyrs A

Stone, Walter (1910): Henry Lawson: a Chronological Checklist of his Contributions to the *Bulletin*

Tennant (1912): Long John Silver Y

Thompson, John (1907): Thirty Poems

Tindale (1900) & **Lindsay, H. A.** (1900): The First Walkabout Y

Waten (1911): The Unbending N

G. F. Young d.

Overland, ed. by S. Murray-Smith, begins

Filippo Sacchi, La Casa in Oceania

Anderson, Hugh (1927): Frank Wilmot
('Furnley Maurice') C [with biblio.]

Anderson, Hugh (1927) (ed.): Colonial Ballads
[rev. edn 1962]

Boyd, Martin (1893): A Difficult Young Man
N [Langton series, vol. 2; cf. 1952, 1957,
1962]

Brown, E. T. (1889): Not Without Prejudice E

Butlin (1910): ¶ War Economy 1939-42 H

Clark, C. M. H. (1915) (ed.): Select Documents
in Australian History 1851-1900

Cleary (1917): Justin Bayard N [republd 1961
as Dust in the Sun]

Clune (1893): Martin Cash B

Dobson (1920): Child With a Cockatoo V

Drake-Brockman (1901): Men Without Wives
and Other Plays

Durack, Mary (1913): Keep Him My Country
N

Ellis, M. H. (1890): John Macarthur B

Ferguson (1881): Bibliography of Australia iv
[1846-50]

Glaskin (1923): A World of Our Own N

Greenwood (1913) (ed.): Australia: a Social
and Political History

Harris, Max (1921): The Coorong V

Hasluck, Alexandra (1908): Portrait With
Background B [of Georgiana Molloy]

Hope (1907): The Wandering Islands V

Jury (1894): Icarius D

Keesing (1923): Three Men and Sydney V

Macartney, F. T. (1887): Furnley Maurice B

Mackaness (1882) & Stone, Walter (1910):
The Books of the *Bulletin* C

Marshall, Alan (1902): I Can Jump Puddles A

Morphett, G. C. (1901): Sir James Hurtle
Fisher B

Morrison, John (1904): Black Cargo S

Niland (1917): The Shiralee N

Palmer, Vance (1885): Let the Birds Fly S

Park ( ): Pink Flannel N

Robert Crossland d.
Rex Ingamells d.
S. S. Mackenzie d.
Charles Shaw d.
M. L. Skinner d.
'Brian Vrepont' d.
Jeanne Young d.

1955 (contd)

Porteous (1897): Close To the Wind N
['by Standby']
Tambai Island N
Roderick (1911): The Lady and the Lawyer N
Roderick (1911) (ed.): Jemmy Green in
Australia D [attributed to James Tucker,
1808–88?]
Schlunke (1906): The Man in the Silo S
Shaw, A. G. L. (1916): The Story of Australia
H
Stewart, Douglas (1913): The Birdsville
Track V
Stewart, Douglas (1913) & **Keesing** (1923)
(edd.): Australian Bush Ballads
Stivens (1911): Ironbark Bill S
Stone, Walter (1910): Joseph Furphy [biblio.]
Tennant (1912): The Bells of the City Y
Vickers (1903): The Mirage N
White, M. R. (1888): Beyond the Western
Rivers A
White, Patrick (1912): The Tree of Man N
Wright, Judith (1915): The Two Fires V
Wrightson (1921): The Crooked Snake Y

1956

Anderson, Ethel (1883): At Parramatta S
Anderson, Hugh (1927): Shaw Neilson [biblio.;
rev. edn 1964]
Banning (1921): Apocalypse in Springtime V
Barnard, Marjorie (1897): Sydney: the Story
of a City H
Braddon (1921): Nancy Wake B
Out of the Storm N
Brown, Cyril (   ): Writing for Australia C
Burke, Keast (1896): T. A. Browne ('Rolf
Boldrewood') [biblio.]
Campbell, David (1915): The Miracle of
Mullion Hill V
Charlwood (1915): No Moon Tonight A
Clark, Mavis Thorpe (   ): The Brown Land
Was Green Y
De Boissiere (1907): Rum and Coca-Cola N

Flora Eldershaw d.
F. S. Hibble d.
Randolph Hughes d.
Nathan Spielvogel d.
Quadrant *begins* [*ed.*
by James McAuley
1956– , with Donald
Horne 1964-66, with
Peter Coleman 1967-]
Westerly *begins*
'*Nevil Shute*', Beyond
the Black Stump
Geoffrey Dutton, Africa
in Black and White

Ewers (1904): Who Rides on the River? N
[based on the life of Charles Sturt, q.v.]

Franklin, Miles (d. 1954): Laughter, Not For a
Cage A
Gentlemen at Gyang Gyang N ['by Brent
of Bin Bin']

Friend (1914): A Collection of Hillendiana H

Gross (1893): Charles Joseph La Trobe B

Heney, Helen (1907): This Quiet Dust N

Herman (1907): The Architecture of Victorian
Sydney H

Hungerford (1915)(ed.): Australian Signpost M

'James, Brian' (1892): The Bunyip of Barney's
Elbow S

Lambert (1921): Watermen N

McAuley (1917): A Vision of Ceremony V

MacCallum (1913): A Voyage in Love N

Marshall, Alan (1902): How's Andy Going? S

Mathew (1929): Song and Dance V

Miller (1881) & **Macartney, F. T.** (1887):
Australian Literature [based on Miller 1940]

Moorehead (1910): Gallipoli H

Niland (1917) & **Park** (   ): The Drums Go
Bang A

Porter, Hal (1911): The Hexagon V

Robinson, Roland (1912): The Feathered
Serpent L

Ronan (1907): Moleskin Midas N

Rowbotham (1924): Town and City S

Smith, Vivian (1933): The Other Meaning V

Southall (1921): They Shall Not Pass Unseen H

Spielvogel (1874): Selected Short Stories

Stewart, Harold (1916): Orpheus V

Stow, Randolph (1935): A Haunted Land N

Taylor, Geoff. (1920): Piece of Cake A

Tennant (1912): The Honey Flow N

Vickers (1903): First Place to the Stranger N

West, Morris (1916): Gallows on the Sand N

Wright, Judith (1915) (ed.): A Book of
Australian Verse [rev. edn 1968]

1957

Anderson, Ethel (1883): The Song of Hagar V

Anderson, Hugh (1927): Australian Song Index [biblio.]

Atkinson, Hugh (1925): The Pink and the Brown N

Bean (1879): Two Men I Knew B

Blainey, Geoffrey (1930): A Centenary History of the University of Melbourne

Boyd, Martin (1893): Outbreak of Love N [Langton series, vol. 3; cf. 1952, 1955, 1962]

Buckley (1925): Essays in Poetry, Mainly Australian C

Cato (1917): The Dancing Bough V

Clark, C. M. H. (1915) (ed.): Sources of Australian History

Cleary (1917): The Green Helmet N

Collinson (1925): The Moods of Love V

Deakin (d. 1919): The Crisis in Victorian Politics 1879-1881 [ed. by J. A. La Nauze & R. M. Crawford]

Drake-Brockman (1901): The Wicked and the Fair N

Finnin (1906): The Shield of Place V

Fitzpatrick, Brian (1905): The Australian Commonwealth H

Gill (1895): ¶Royal Australian Navy 1939-42 H

Harrington (1896): The Swagless Swaggie V

Harrower (1928): Down in the City N

Kendall (d. 1882): Selected Poems [ed. by T. Inglis Moore]

La Nauze (1911): The Hopetoun Blunder H

Law (1912) & **Béchervaise** (1910): ANARE: Australia's Antarctic Outposts P

Lawler (1921): The Summer of the Seventeenth Doll D

Macartney, F. T. (1887): Australian Literary Essays C

E. T. Brown d.
V. G. Childe d.
Dorothy Cottrell d.
Sir Robert Garran d.
W. G. Henderson d.
Bertha Lawson (Mrs Henry Lawson) d.
Will Lawson d.
Gilbert Murray d.
Australian Letters
1957-68 [ed. by G. Dutton 1957-68, Max Harris 1957-68, Rosemary Wighton 1963-68, M. B. Davies 1957-64, see The Vital Decade, *sel. by Dutton & Harris 1968]*
'Nevil Shute', On the Beach
Edna Purdie & Olga M. Roncoroni (edd.), Henry Handel Richardson

Macmillan (1925): A Squatter Went to Sea   B
[of Sir William Macleay]

Mann, Leonard (1895): Elegiac and Other
Poems

Moll (1900): Poems 1940-1955
Below These Hills   H

Moore, T. Inglis (1901): Bayonet and Grass   V

Nadel (1923): Australia's Colonial Culture   H

Niland (1917): Call Me When the Cross Turns
Over   N

Odgers (1916): ¶Air War Against Japan 1943-45
H

O'Grady (1907): They're a Weird Mob   N
['by Nino Culotta']

Palmer, Vance (1885): Seedtime   N   [sequel
to Golconda 1948; cf. also 1959]
The Rainbow Bird   S   [sel. by A. Edwards]

Park ( ): One-a-pecker, Two-a-pecker   N

Pike (1908): Paradise of Dissent   H

Porteous (1897): Brigalow   N

Ruhen (1911): Land of Dahori   S

Slessor (1901): Poems

Stewart, Douglas (1913) & **Keesing** (1923)
(edd.): Old Bush Songs and Rhymes of
Colonial Times [based on A. B. Paterson
1905]

Stivens (1911): The Scholarly Mouse   S

Stow, Randolph (1935): Act One   V
The Bystander   N

Waten (1911): Shares in Murder   N

West, Morris (1916): Kundu   N
Children of the Sun   P
The Big Story   N

White, Patrick (1912): Voss   N

Whyte (1879): William Morris Hughes   B

Wigmore (1899): ¶The Japanese Thrust   H

Wright, Judith (1915) (ed.): New Land, New
Language   V

1958

Anderson, Hugh (1927) (ed.): Goldrush Songster [Charles Thatcher, q.v.]

Astley (1925): Girl With a Monkey N

Austin, A. G. (1918): George William Rusden B

Barry, J. V. (1903): Alexander Maconochie of Norfolk Island B

Blainey, Geoffrey (1930): Gold and Paper H

Bolton (1931): Alexander Forrest B

Boyd, Martin (1893): Much Else in Italy A

Braddon (1921): End of a Hate A

Casey, Gavin (1907): Snowball N

Cato (1917): All the Rivers Run N

Chisholm, A. H. (1890) (ed.): Australian Encyclopedia

Chisholm, A. R. (1888): Men Were My Milestones A

Clift (1923): Mermaid Singing A

Cowan (1914): The Unploughed Land S

Derham (d. 1941): Poems

Dutton (1922): Antipodes in Shoes V

Elliott (1910): Marcus Clarke B

Fitzpatrick, Kathleen (1905) (ed.): Australian Explorers

Garran (d. 1957): Prosper the Commonwealth A

Gunn, John (1925): Sea Menace Y

Hardy (1917): The Four-Legged Lottery N

Harney (1895): Content to Lie in the Sun A

Harrower (1928): The Long Prospect N

Hyde (1902): Gregory Blaxland X

Inglis (1929): Hospital and Community H

Kennedy, Donald (1928): Charles Sturt X

Koch (1932): The Boys in the Island N

Lambert (1921): The Dark Backward N

Lindsay, Jack (1900): Life Rarely Tells A

Martin, David (1915): Poems 1938-1958

Mawson, Paquita (1891): Vision of Steel B [of G. D. Delprat, her father]

Mellor (1903): ¶The Role of Science and Industry H

Ethel Anderson d.
A. A. Bayldon d.
Mary Grant Bruce d.
C. R. Jury d.
Margaret Kiddle d.
Philip Lindsay d.
Hugh McCrae d.
Sir Douglas Mawson d.
J. K. Moir d.
Ethel Turner d.
W. F. Whyte d.
Melbourne Critical Review *begins* [*since 1965 titled* The Critical Review]
Nation *begins*
Observer, *ed. by Donald Horne, 1958-61*
J. D. Pringle, Australian Accent
Geoffrey Dutton, States of the Union
Geoffrey Rawson, Sea Prelude

Menzies (1894): Speech is of Time P
'O'Conner, Elizabeth' (1913): Steak for
Breakfast A
Paull (1906): Retreat from Kokoda H
Pearl (1906): Wild Men of Sydney H
Phillips, A. A. (1900): The Australian Tradition
C [enlarged edn 1966]
Pike (1908): John McDouall Stuart X
Porteous (1897): Tambai Treasure N
Porter, Hal (1911): A Handful of Pennies N
Robinson, Roland (1912): Black-feller, White-
feller S
Ronan (1907): The Pearling Master N
Rowbotham (1924): Inland V
Ruhen (1911): Naked Under Capricorn N
Schlunke (1906): The Village Hampden S
Southall (1921): Bluey Truscott B
Spence, Eleanor (1928): Patterson's Track Y
Stewart, Douglas (1913): Four Plays [those
publd in 1943, 1944, 1947]
Stivens (1911): The Wide Arch N
Stow, Randolph (1935): To the Islands N
Taylor, Geoff. (1920): The Hollow Square N
Taylor, T. Griffith (1880): Journeyman Taylor
A
Thompson, John (1907), **Slessor** (1901) &
Howarth (1906) (edd.): The Penguin Book
of Australian Verse [later titled The Penguin
Book of Modern Australian Verse]
Trist (1914): Morning in Queensland N
Vickers (1903): Though Poppies Grow N
Ward, J. M. (1919): Earl Grey and the Aus-
tralian Colonies H
Ward, Russel (1914): The Australian Legend H
Webster (1900): John McDouall Stuart B
West, Morris (1916): The Second Victory N
McCreary Moves In N ['by Michael East']
Wigmore (1899) (ed.): Span M [Australian
and Asian writing]
Wright, Judith (1915): Kings of the Dingoes Y

1959

Anderson, Ethel (d. 1958): The Little Ghosts S

Bateson (1903): The Convict Ships 1787-1868 H [enlarged edn 1969]

Béchervaise (1910): Antarctica X

Burns (1925): Mr Brain Knows Best N

Byrnes (1899) & **Vallis** (1916) (edd.): The Queensland Centenary Anthology

Campbell, David (1915): Evening Under Lamplight S

Cato (1917): Time, Flow Softly N

Clark, C. M. H. (1915): Abel Tasman X

Cleary (1917): Back of Sunset N

Crowley (1924): A Short History of Western Australia

Dark (1901): Lantana Lane N

Drake-Brockman (1901) (ed.): West Coast Stories S

Durack, Mary (1913): Kings in Grass Castles H

FitzGerald (1902): The Wind at Your Door V

'Forrest, David' (1924): The Last Blue Sea N

Greenwood (1913): Brisbane 1859-1959 [with J. Laverty]

Hadgraft (1904): Queensland and its Writers C

Hart-Smith (1911): Poems of Discovery

Hasluck, Alexandra (1908): Unwilling Emigrants H

Herbert (1901): Seven Emus N

Hewett (1923): Bobbin Up N

Higham (1931): The Earthbound V

Howarth (1906): Nardoo and Pituri V ['by R.G.H.']

Hudson (1913): Pools of the Cinnabar Range V

'James, Brian' (1892) (ed.): Selected Australian Stories

Lockwood (1918): Crocodiles and Other People P

McAuley (1917): The End of Modernity C

McCarthy (1911): ¶South West Pacific Area— First Year: Kokoda to Wau H

McDonald (1921): The Lighthouse V

Mann, Leonard (1895): Andrea Caslin N

Lance Fallaw d.
V. W. Hyde d.
Vance Palmer d.
Vincent Buckley, Poetry and Morality
H. C. Allen, Bush and Backwoods

84

Mudie, Ian (1911): The Blue Crane V
Niland (1917): The Big Smoke N
  Gold in the Streets N
Palmer, Vance (1885): The Big Fellow N
  [sequel to Golconda 1948 and Seedtime 1957]
Pownall (   ): Mary of Maranoa B
Price (1892) (ed.): The Humanities in Australia
  C
Prichard (1883): N'Goola S
Roderick (1911) (ed.): A Companion to Henry
  Lawson
Rowlands (1925): Why Can't the English? A
Ryan (1923): Fear Drive My Feet A
'Sidney, Neilma' (1922): Saturday Afternoon S
Spencer, A. H. (1886): The Hill of Content A
Stone, Walter (1910) & **Anderson, Hugh**
  (1927): Christopher Brennan [biblio.]
Stuart, Donald (1913): Yandy N
Tennant (1912): Speak You So Gently B
  All the Proud Tribesmen Y
  The Bushrangers' Christmas Eve Y
Turner, George R. (1916): Young Man of
  Talent N
Wallace-Crabbe (1934): The Music of Division
  V
West, Morris (1916): The Devil's Advocate N
Wright, Judith (1915): The Generations of
  Men B

1960

Anderson, Hugh (1927): The Colonial Minstrel
  B [of Charles Thatcher, q.v.]
Astley (1925): A Descant for Gossips N
Beynon (1928): The Shifting Heart D
Blainey, Geoffrey (1930): Mines in the Spini-
  fex H
Boyd, Robin (1919): The Australian Ugliness
  C
Brennan, C. J. (d. 1932): Verse [ed. by A. R.
  Chisholm & J. J. Quinn]

E. J. R. Atkinson d.
Sir Frank Fox d.
Archer Russell d.
E. O. Schlunke d.
E. V. Timms d.
Southern Festival
  [*South Australian writing*]
Hugh Hunt, The
  Making of the Aus-
  tralian Theatre

Cato (1917): Green Grows the Vine   N
Cleary (1917): North From Thursday   N
Crawford, R. M. (1906): An Australian Perspective   H
Crowley (1924): Australia's Western Third   H
Dow, Hume (1916) & **Barnes** (1931) (edd.): World Unknown   P
Dunlop (1910): John Oxley   X
Dutton (1922): Founder of a City   B   [of William Light, q.v.]
Foster (1914): The Exiles   N
Hadgraft (1904): Australian Literature   C
Harrower (1928): The Catherine Wheel   N
Hetherington (1907): Australians: Nine Profiles   B
Hope (1907): Poems
Iggulden (1917): Breakthrough   N
   Storms of Summer   N
Jones, Evan (1931): Inside the Whale   V
Joyce, R. B. (1924): New Guinea   X
Kellaway (1922): A Straight Furrow   N
Keon (1918): The Durian Tree   N
Lindsay, Jack (1900): The Roaring Twenties   A
McKie (1909): The Heroes   H
McLean (1905): The Roaring Days   N
Meredith, John (1920): The Wild Colonial Boy   H
Mossenson (1917): John Forrest   X
Murphy, R. D. (1910): Speak to Strangers   V
'O'Conner, Elizabeth' (1913): The Irishman   N
Parkin (1910): Out of the Smoke   A
Pearl (1906): Always Morning   B   [of R. H. Horne, q.v.]
Porteous (1897): Cattleman   N
Reed (1902): Henry Kendall   C
Roderick (1911): Henry Lawson's Formative Years   B
Ruhen (1911): White Man's Shoes   N
Simpson, R. A. (1929): The Walk Along the Beach   V

Eric Partridge, A Charm of Words
Gilbert Murray, An Unfinished Autobiography

Slessor (1901): Australian Profile   P   [text]
Smith, Bernard (1916): European Vision and the South Pacific   C
Southall (1921): Softly Tread the Brave   H
Stewart, Douglas (1913): Fisher's Ghost   D
Stewart, Douglas (1913) (ed.): Voyager Poems
Stewart, Harold (1916): A Net of Fireflies   M
Taylor, Geoff. (1920): The Crop Dusters   N
   Blueberg   Y
Thiele (1920): Man in a Landscape   V
Tullipan (1917): Follow the Sun   N
West, Morris (1916): The Naked Country   N
   ['by Michael East']
Wright, Judith (1915): The Day the Mountains Played   Y

1961

Adams, Nancy (1890): Saxon Sheep   N
Atkinson, Hugh (1925): Low Company   N
Austin, A. G. (1918): Australian Education 1788-1900   H
Barnard, Alan (1928): Visions and Profits   B
   [of T. S. Mort]
'Baylebridge, William' (d. 1942): This Vital Flesh   V   [ed. by P. R. Stephensen; memorial edn, vol. 1; cf. 1939]
Beaver (1928): Under the Bridge   V
Béchervaise (1910): The Far South   P
Blake (1913): Shaw Neilson in the Wimmera   B
Brissenden, Alan (1932) & **Higham** (1931) (edd.): They Came To Australia   P
Buckley (1925): Masters in Israel   V
   Henry Handel Richardson   W
Calthorpe (1905): The Dyehouse   N
Crisp (1917): Ben Chifley   B
Davies, A. F. (1924): A Sunday Kind of Love   S
Dexter (1917): ¶The New Guinea Offensives   H
Dutton (1922): Patrick White   W
Evers (1926): The Racketty Street Gang   Y

H. E. Badham d.
Mrs Æneas Gunn d.
Sir Lionel Lindsay d.
G. D. Mitchell d.
Sir Earle Page d.
James Tyrrell d.
Myrtle Rose White d.
Australian Book Review *begins* [*ed. by* G. Dutton *1961-64,* M. Harris *1961-* , R. Wighton *1962-*]
Australian National Bibliography (*National Library*) *begins*
Jeanne MacKenzie, Australian Paradox
Geoffrey Dutton, Walt Whitman
Critic *begins*

Gare (1919): The Fringe Dwellers N

Green, H. M. (1881): A History of Australian Literature

Hall (1935): Penniless Till Doomsday V

Hardy (1917): The Hard Way A

Harris, Max (1921) (ed.): Ern Malley's Poems [cf. 1944]

Heney, Helen (1907): In a Dark Glass B [of P. E. de Strzelecki, q.v.]

Herbert (1901): Soldiers' Women N

Hetherington (1907): Norman Lindsay W [rev. edn 1969]

Jury (d. 1958): The Sun in Servitude D

Kelly (1922): There is No Refuge N

Kiddle (d. 1958): Men of Yesterday H

Lawler (1921): The Piccadilly Bushman D

Macartney, F. T. (1887): Selected Poems

McCrae, Hugh (d. 1958): The Best Poems [ed. by R. G. Howarth]

McCuaig (1908): The Ballad of Bloodthirsty Bessie V [inc. the titles of 1938, 1941, 1946]

Mackenzie, Kenneth (d. 1955): Selected Poems [ed. by Douglas Stewart]

McLaren, Ian (1912): C. J. Dennis B

McLeod, A. L. (1928) (ed.): The Commonwealth Pen C [inc. articles on Australian literature by the editor and by H. J. Oliver]

Manifold (1915): Nightmares and Sunhorses V

Marshall, Alan (1902): The Gay Provider H

Martin, David (1915): Spiegel the Cat V

Mathew (1929): South of the Equator V
A Bohemian Affair S
A Spring Song D [intro. by E. Hanger; CAP, vol. 1]

Mattingley (1922): Matthew Flinders and George Bass X

Moore, T. Inglis (1901) (ed.): A Book of Australia M

Mudie, Ian (1911): Riverboats H

Newman (1898): The Spirit of Wharf House H
[the Campbell family 1788-1830]

Niland (1917): Logan's Girl S
The Ballad of the Fat Bushranger S

Osborne (1927) (ed.): Australian Stories of Today

Park (   ): The Good-Looking Women N

Porter, Hal (1911): The Tilted Cross N

Porter, Peter (1929): Once Bitten, Twice Bitten V

Riddell (1909): Forbears V

Roderick (1911): The Later Life of Henry Lawson B

Ronan (1907): Only a Short Walk N

Rowlands (1925): On Top of the World A

Shapcott (1935): Time on Fire V

Stuart, Donald (1913): The Driven N

Thiele (1920): The Sun on the Stubble N

Turner, George R. (1916): A Stranger and Afraid N

Vallis (1916): Dark Wind Blowing V

Waten (1911): Time of Conflict N

Webb (1925): Socrates and Other Poems

West, Morris (1916): Daughter of Silence N
[as a play 1962]

White, M. R. (1888): From That Day to This A

White, Patrick (1912): Riders in the Chariot N

Woodberry (1921): Rafferty Rides a Winner Y

1962

Anderson, Hugh (1927): Out of the Shadow B
[of John Pascoe Fawkner]

Astley (1925): The Well Dressed Explorer N

Baker, S. J. (1912): My Own Destroyer B
[of Matthew Flinders, q.v.]

Barnard, Alan (1928): Thomas Sutcliffe Mort G

Barnard, Marjorie (1897): A History of Australia

Jean Devanny d.
Dame Mary Gilmore d.
H. M. Green d.
W. E. Harney d.
Frank Hurley d.
Joseph Jones (ed.),
'Image of Australia',
Texas Quarterly
(Summer)

1962 (contd)

Bassett (1889): Realms and Islands   H

Bate (1924): A History of Brighton

'Baylebridge, William' (d. 1942): An Anzac Muster S [ed. by P. R. Stephensen; memorial edn, vol. 2; cf. Blocksidge 1921]

Bladen (1922): Masque for a Modern Minstrel V

Boyd, Martin (1893): When Blackbirds Sing   V [Langton series, vol. 4; cf. 1952, 1955, 1957]

Braddon (1921): Joan Sutherland   B

Brennan, C. J. (d. 1932): Prose [ed. by A. R. Chisholm & J. J. Quinn]

Brennan, Niall (1918): A Hoax Called Jones   A

Buckley (1925): The Campion Paintings [text and notes to paintings by Leonard French]

Campbell, David (1915): Poems

Campbell, Ross (1910): Daddy, Are You Married?   S

Casey, Gavin (1907): Amid the Plenty   N

Casey, Maie (   ): An Australian Story   H

Casey, R. G. (1890): Personal Experience   A

Cato (1917): But Still the Stream   N

Chisholm, A. H. (1890): Ferdinand von Mueller   G

Clark, C. M. H. (1915): A History of Australia [vol. i; vol. ii 1968]

Clark, Robert (1911): The Dogman   V

Cleary (1917): The Country of Marriage   N

Cobley (1914) (ed.): Sydney Cove 1788   H

Coleman (1928) (ed.): Australian Civilisation   C

Cowen (1919): Isaac Isaacs   G

Crowley (1924): Westralian Suburb   H

Cutlack (1886): Breaker Morant   B

Dawe, Bruce (1930): No Fixed Address   V

Donath (1906): William Farrer   G

Dutton (1922): Flowers and Fury   V
The Paintings of S. T. Gill   C

Edwards, Hugh (1933): Gods and Little Fishes   P

FitzGerald (1902): Southmost Twelve   V

Charles Osborne (ed.) London Magazine, Australian issue (September)

J. P. Matthews, Tradition in Exile [Australian and Canadian writing]

S. B. Liljegren, Aspects of Australia in Contemporary Literature

Sir Joseph Banks, The Endeavour Journal 1768-71 (ed. by J. C. Beaglehole)

'Forrest, David' (1924): The Hollow Woodheap N

Gardiner (1927): Thomas Mitchell X

Gillison (1899): ¶Royal Australian Air Force
1939-42 H

Heney, Helen (1907): The Leaping Blaze N

Hetherington (1907): Forty-two Faces B
John Monash G

Howard (1904): Charles Kingsford Smith G

Hutton (1909): Melba G

Johnston, Grahame (1929) (ed.): Australian
Literary Criticism [publd 1963]

Kellaway (1922): The Quest for Golden Dan Y

Kramer (1924): A Companion to Australia
Felix C

Lambert (1921): Ballarat N

La Nauze (1911): Alfred Deakin G

Latham (   ): John Batman G

Law (1912): Australia and the Antarctic P

Lindsay, Jack (1900): Fanfrolico and After A

Lindsay, Joan (1896): Time Without Clocks A

McLean (1905): The World Turned Upside
Down N

Macmillan (1925): John Dunmore Lang G

Malouf (1934), Maynard (1937), Hall (1935) &
Green, Judith (1936): Four Poets V

Marshall, A. J. (1911) & Drysdale (1912):
Journey Among Men P

Marshall, Alan (1902): This is the Grass A

Martin, David (1915): The Young Wife N

Moll (1900): The Rainbow Serpent V

Morrison, John (1904): Twenty-three S

Morrison, W. A. (1877): Ernest Morrison G

Murray-Smith (1922): Henry Lawson W

Normington-Rawling (1898): Charles Harpur
B

Phelan (1913): The River and the Brook N

Pike (1908): Australia, the Quiet Continent H

Porter, Hal (1911): A Bachelor's Children S

1962 (contd)

Pryor (1881): Australia's Little Cornwall   H
Robinson, Roland (1912): Deep Well   V
  [inc. 1949 and 1953 titles]
Rohan (1928): The Delinquents   N
Ronan (1907): Deep of the Sky   H
Seymour (1927): The One Day of the Year   D
  [repr. 1963 in Three Australian Plays, intro.
  by H. G. Kippax; as a novel 1967]
Smith, Bernard (1916): Australian Painting   H
Southall (1921): Hills End   Y
Steven, Margaret (1933): Arthur Phillip   G
Stewart, Douglas (1913): Rutherford   V
  The Garden of Ships   V
Stow, Randolph (1935): Outrider   V
Stuart, Donald (1913): Yaralie   N
Taylor, Geoff. (1920): Dreamboat   N
Taylor, T. Griffith (1880): Douglas Mawson   G
Thiele (1920): Gloop the Gloomy Bunyip   Y
Tullipan (1917): March into Morning   N
Turner, George R. (1916): The Cupboard
  Under the Stairs   N
West, Francis (1927): Hubert Murray   G
Wright, Judith (1915): Birds   V
  Range the Mountains High   Y

1963

Alexander, Fred. (1899): Campus at Crawley
  H
Anderson, Hugh (1927): Bernard O'Dowd
  [biblio.]
Barnes (1931): Joseph Furphy   W
Barry, Clive (1922): The Spear Grinner   N
Bateson (1903): Gold Fleet for California   H
Batty (   ): Namatjira   B
'Baylebridge, William' (d. 1942): The Growth
  of Love   V   [ed. by P. R. Stephensen;
  memorial edn, vol. 3]
Béchervaise (1910): Blizzard and Fire   A

Ruth Bedford d.
Herbert Brookes d.
Max Dunn d.
Don Edwards d.
Eric Lowe d.
G. C. Morphett d.
W. H. Ogilvie d.
R. S. Porteous
  ('Standby') d.
H. W. Pryce d.
W. S. Robinson d.
Criena Rohan d.
Arnold Shore d.

Blainey, Geoffrey (1930): The Rush That Never Ended H [enlarged 1969]

Blight (1913): A Beachcomber's Diary V

Bolton (1931): A Thousand Miles Away H

Borchardt (1916): Australian Bibliography

Buckley (1925), **Collinson** (1925), **Craig** (1923), **Dunn** (1895), **Macainsh** (1926), **Martin, David** (1915), **Simpson, R. A.** (1929) & **Wallace-Crabbe** (1934): Eight by Eight V

Casey, Gavin (1907): The Man Whose Name Was Mud N

Clark, C. M. H. (1915): A Short History of Australia

Cleary (1917): Forests of the Night N
A Flight of Chariots N
Pillar of Salt S

Cobley (1914) (ed.): Sydney Cove 1789-90 H

Cunnington (1923): Big Fat Tuesday S

Currey (1890): The Transportation, Escape and Pardoning of Mary Bryant H

Daley (d. 1905): Victor Daley AP [sel. by H. J. Oliver]

Dobson (1920): Rosemary Dobson AP [sel. by author]

Drake-Brockman (1901): Voyage to Disaster H

Durack, Mary (1913): To Ride a Fine Horse H [condensation of 1959 title; illustrations by E. Durack]
Kookanoo and Kangaroo Y [text; illustrations by E. Durack]

Erdos (1911): Ludwig Leichhardt X

Ferguson (1881): Bibliography of Australia v [1851-1900, A-G]

FitzGerald (1902): The Elements of Poetry C
Robert D. FitzGerald AP [sel. by author]

Fitzpatrick, Kathleen (1905): Martin Boyd W

Franklin, Miles (d. 1954): Childhood at Brindabella A

Gare (1919): Green Gold N

Gilmore (d. 1962): Mary Gilmore AP [sel. by R. D. FitzGerald]

T. Griffith Taylor d.
Australian Literary Studies, *ed. by L. T. Hergenhan, begins*
Southern Review *begins*
James McAuley, Edmund Spenser and George Eliot
J. D. Pringle, Australian Painting Today
The Literary Review, *Australia number* (*Winter*)
Louise E. Rorabacher (*ed.*), Two Ways Meet [*migrant stories*]
Elizabeth Odeen, Maurice Guest: A Study
Ray Lawler, The Unshaven Cheek *produced*
Geoffrey Rawson, Pandora's Last Voyage

Green, Louis (1929): Ernest Giles   X

Hadgraft (1904) (ed.): A Century of Australian Short Stories [with R. Wilson]

Hague (1907): Sir John Jeffcott   B

Hall (1935): Forty Beads on a Hangman's Rope   V

Hardy (1917): Legends from Benson's Valley   S

Harpur (d. 1868): Charles Harpur   AP   [sel. by Donovan Clarke]

Harris, Max (1921): Kenneth Slessor   W

Harwood (1920): Poems

Hasluck, Alexandra (1908): James Stirling   G Remembered With Affection   B   [of Lady Mary Anne Barker, later Lady Broome, 1831-1911, with an edn of her Letters to Guy]

Hazzard (1931): Cliffs of Fall   S

Herbert (1901): Larger than Life   S Disturbing Element   A

Herington (1916): ¶Air Power over Europe 1944-45   H

Herman (1907): The Blackets   B Early Colonial Architecture   H

Heseltine (1931) (ed.): Australian Idiom   P

Hetherington (1907): Australian Painters   B

Hope (1907): Australian Literature 1950-62   C A. D. Hope   AP   [intro. and notes by author; sel. by D. Stewart]

Hungerford (1915): Shake the Golden Bough   N

'James, Brian' (1892): Hopeton High   N

'James, Brian' (1892) (ed.): Australian Short Stories

Keesing (1923): By Gravel and Gun   Y

Kendall (d. 1882): Henry Kendall   AP   [sel. by T. Inglis Moore]

King, Hazel (   ): Richard Bourke   G

Locke Elliott (1917): Careful, He Might Hear You   N

Long, Gavin (1901): ¶The Final Campaigns   H

McAuley (1917): James McAuley   AP   [sel. by author]
C. J. Brennan   W

MacCallum (1913): Son of Mars   N

Mackerras (1899): The Hebrew Melodist   B [of Isaac Nathan]

McLeod, A. L. (1928) (ed.): The Pattern of Australian Culture   C

McPheat (1929): John Flynn, Apostle to the Inland   B

Mann, Cecil (1896): Three Stories

Mann, Leonard (1895): Venus Half-Caste   N

Marshall, Alan (1902): In Mine Own Heart   A

Mathew (1929): Miles Franklin   W

Mitchell, Mary (1892): Uncharted Country   A

Moorehead (1910): Cooper's Creek   H

Mudie, Ian (1911): The Northbound Rider   V

Neilson (d. 1942): Shaw Neilson   AP   [sel. by Judith Wright]

Niland (1917): Dadda Jumped Over Two Elephants   S

'O'Conner, Elizabeth' (1913): Find a Woman   N

O'Dowd (d. 1953): Bernard O'Dowd   AP [sel. by A. A. Phillips]

Page (d. 1961): Truant Surgeon   A

Parkin (1910): Into the Smother   A

Paull (1906): Old Walhalla   H

Pearl (1906) (ed.): The Best of Lennie Lower   S

Perry (1927): Australia's First Frontier   H

Porteous (1897): Salvage   S
The Silent Isles   N

Porter, Hal (1911): The Watcher on the Cast-Iron Balcony   A
The Tower   D   [in Three Australian Plays, intro. by H. G. Kippax]

Prest (1930): Hamilton Hume and William Hovell   X

Prichard (1883): Child of the Hurricane   A

'Prout, Denton' (1910): Henry Lawson, the Grey Dreamer   B

Rienits, Rex (1909) & **Thea** (1919): Early Artists of Australia   B

Roderick (1911): John Knatchbull   B

Roe (1931): Philip Gidley King   G

Rohan (1928): Down by the Dockside   N

Semmler (1914): For the Uncanny Man   E

Serle, Geoffrey (1922): The Golden Age   H

Slessor (1901): The Grapes Are Growing   P

Souter, Gavin (1929): New Guinea, the Last Unknown   P

Stewart, Douglas (1913): Douglas Stewart AP   [sel. by author]

Stow, Randolph (1935): Tourmaline   N

Taylor, Geoff. (1920): Sir   N

Thiele (1920): Storm Boy   Y

Turnbull (1906): Essington Lewis   G

Wallace-Crabbe (1934): In Light and Darkness V   [publd 1964]

Wallace-Crabbe (1934) (ed.): Six Voices   V [poems of FitzGerald, Hope, McAuley, Slessor, Douglas Stewart and Judith Wright]

Wannan (1915) (ed.): A Marcus Clarke Reader

West, Morris (1916): The Shoes of the Fisherman   N

Wighton (1925): Early Australian Children's Literature   W

Wighton (1925) (ed.): Kangaroo Tales   Y

Wigmore (1899): The Long View   H

Wright, Judith (1915): Five Senses   V
Charles Harpur   W
Country Towns   Y
Judith Wright   AP   [sel. by author]

Aitchison (1923): The Illegitimates N

Anderson, Hugh (1927): Farewell to Old England H

Austin, K. A. (1911): The Voyage of the Investigator H

Barnard, Marjorie (1897): Lachlan Macquarie G

Barry, J. V. (1903): The Life and Death of John Price B

'Baylebridge, William' (d. 1942): Salvage V [ed. by P. R. Stephensen; memorial edn, vol. 4]

Beasley (1926): The Rage for Life: the Work of Katharine Susannah Prichard C

Beaver (1928): Seawall and Shoreline V

Berndt, R. M. (1916): The World of the First Australians P [with C. Berndt]

Birrell (1928): Walter Burley Griffin B

Blainey, Geoffrey (1930): A History of Camberwell

Bowden (1908): Captain James Kelly of Hobart Town B

Braddon (1921): The Year of the Angry Rabbit N

Brennan, Niall (1918): Dr Mannix B

Brinsmead (1922): Pastures of the Blue Crane Y

Brissenden, R. F. (1928) (ed.): Southern Harvest S

Campbell, Ross (1910): Mummy, Who is Your Husband? S

Casey, Gavin (1907): The Mile That Midas Touched H [with T. Mayman]

Casson (1889): George Cockburn Henderson B

Cato (1917): The Sea Ants S

Chaplin (1896): A Neilson Collection [biblio.]

Cleary (1917): The Fall of an Eagle N

Cowan (1914): Summer N

Cowan (1914) (ed.): Short Story Landscape

Craig (1923): The Living Sky V

Cumpston (d. 1954): The Inland Sea and the Great River H

L. H. Allen d.
Gavin Casey d.
Zora Cross d.
E. Morris Miller d.
Nettie Palmer d.
Tarlton Rayment d.
Arthur Upfield d.
The Australian begins
C. D. Narasimhaiah (ed.), An Introduction to Australian Literature
A. L. McLeod (ed.), Walt Whitman in Australia and New Zealand
S. B. Liljegren, Ballarat and the Great Gold Rush

Davison (1893): The Road to Yesterday S

De Boissiere (1907): No Saddles for Kangaroos N

Dow, Gwyneth (1920): George Higinbotham B

Durack, Mary (1913): The Courteous Savage Y [text; illustrations by E. Durack]

Dutton (1922): Russell Drysdale C

Dutton (1922) (ed.): The Literature of Australia C

Fitzhardinge (1908): William Morris Hughes B [vol. i]

Forward (1936): Samuel Griffith G

Herman (1907): Francis Greenway G

Hetherington (1907): Witness to Things Past H

Hopegood (1891): Snake's-eye View of a Serial Story V

Horne, Donald (1921): The Lucky Country C

Howell (1938): Thomas Arnold the Younger in Van Diemen's Land B

Iggulden (1917): The Clouded Sky N

Ireland (1927): Image in the Clay D [CAP, vol. 2; intro. by N. McVicker]

Johnston, George (1912): My Brother Jack N

Jones, Suzanne Holly (1944): Harry's Child N

Keneally (1935): The Place at Whitton N

Legg (1906): War Correspondent A

Lindsay, Joan (1896): Facts Soft and Hard A

Lindsay, Rose (1881): Ma and Pa A

McAuley (1917): Captain Quiros V

McPheat (1929): John Flynn G

Manifold (1915): Who Wrote the Ballads? C

Manifold (1915) (ed.): The Penguin Australian Song Book

Martin, A. W. (1928): Henry Parkes G

Mawson, Paquita (1891): Mawson of Antarctica B

Moore, T. Inglis (1901) (ed.): Poetry in Australia, vol. I: From the Ballads to Brennan

1964 *(contd)*

Morphett, Tony (1938): Mayor's Nest   N
Patrick (   ): Weave a Circle   N
Ronan (1907): Packhorse and Pearling Boat   A
Rowbotham (1924): All the Room   V
The Man in the Jungle   N
Shapcott (1935): The Mankind Thing   V
Sonnets 1960-63
Shore (d. 1963): Tom Roberts   G
Simpson, R. A. (1929): This Real Pompeii   V
Smith, Patsy Adam (1926): Hear the Train Blow   A
Southall (1921): Lawrence Hargrave   G
Stewart, Douglas (1913) (ed.): Poetry in Australia, vol. II: Modern Australian Verse [cf. Moore above]
Tennant (1912) (ed.): Summer's Tales 1   S
Thompson, John (1907): I Hate and I Love   V
Tregenza (1931): Australian Little Magazines 1923-54   C   [with biblio.]
Tritton (1886): Time Means Tucker   A
Uren (1900): Edward John Eyre   X
Walker, Kath (1920): We are Going   V
Ward, Russel (1914) (ed.): The Penguin Book of Australian Ballads
Waten (1911): Distant Land   N
Webb (1925): The Ghost of the Cock   V
White, Patrick (1912): The Burnt Ones   S
Wright, Judith (1915): City Sunrise   V

1965

Abdullah (1930) & **Mathew** (1929): The Time of the Peacock   S
Anderson, Hugh (1927): The Singing Roads [biblio. of Y; part II, 1969]
Astley (1925): The Slow Natives   N
Atkinson, Hugh (1925): The Reckoning   N
Bagot (1893): Coppin the Great   B
Barry, Clive (1922): Crumb Borne   N
Bolton (1931): Richard Daintree   B
Boyd, Martin (1893): Day of My Delight   A

Lex Banning d.
Marjory R. Casson d.
H. V. Evatt d.
Brian Fitzpatrick d.
E. Gerard ('Trooper Gerardy') d.
P. R. Stephensen d.
H. P. Tritton d.
Balcony begins
S. A. Read, Australian Literary Criticism 1939-64

Boyd, Robin (1919): The Puzzle of Architecture
C

Cato (1917): North West By South   N   [about Sir John Franklin, q.v.]

Charlwood (1915): All the Green Year   N

Cobley (1914) (ed.): Sydney Cove 1791-92   H

Collins, J. A. (1899) : As Luck Would Have It   A

Cowan (1914): The Empty Street   S

Davies, A. F. (1924) (ed.): Australian Society   C   [ed. with S. Encel; inc. 'Drama' by H. G. Kippax]

Dawe, Bruce (1930): A Need of Similar Name
V

Dick, William (1937): A Bunch of Ratbags   N

Dobson (1920): Cock Crow   V

Durack, Mary (1913): A Pastoral Emigrant   Y

Dutton (1922): Tisi and the Yabby   Y   [with Dean Hay]

Edwards, Cecil (1903): Bruce of Melbourne   B

Ewers (1904) (ed.): Modern Australian Short Stories

Ferguson (1881): Bibliography of Australia   vi   [1851-1900, H-P; vii, Q-Z, 1969]

FitzGerald (1902): Forty Years' Poems

Fysh (1895): Qantas Rising   A

Gosse (1919): William Gosse Hay   W

Hardy (1917): The Yarns of Billy Borker   S

Hasluck, Alexandra (1908): Thomas Peel of Swan River   B
C. Y. O'Connor   G

Herman (1907) (ed.): Annabella Boswell's Journal   A

Heseltine (1931): John Le Gay Brereton   W

Hetherington (1907): Uncommon Men   B

Heydon (1913): Quiet Decision   B   [of G. F. Pearce, q.v.]

Hope (1907): The Cave and the Spring   C

Horne, Donald (1921): The Permit   N

'James, Brian' (1892): The Big Burn   S

Johnson, Colin (1938): Wild Cat Falling   N

Keesing (1923): Douglas Stewart   W   [rev. edn 1969]

Keneally (1935): The Fear   N

Koch (1932): Across the Sea Wall   N

La Nauze (1911): Alfred Deakin   B

Lawson, Henry (d. 1922): The Stories [3 vols, ed. by Cecil Mann]

Legg (1906): The Gordon Bennett Story   B

Lindsay, Daryl (1890): The Leafy Tree   A

Lindsay, Norman (1879): Bohemians of the *Bulletin*   C

McInnes (1912): The Road to Gundagai   A

Mackaness (1882): Bibliomania   A

Macmillan (1925): Edgeworth David   G

Mansfield (1926): Australian Democrat   B   [of E. W. O'Sullivan]

Martin, David (1915): The Hero of Too   N

Mathew (1929): Charles Blackman   C

Matthews, Harley (1889): Patriot's Progress   V

Moore, T. Inglis (1901) *et al.*: Mary Gilmore: a Tribute

Murray, Les. (1938) & **Lehmann** (1940): The Ilex Tree   V

Murray-Smith (1922) (ed.): An Overland Muster   M

Neilson (d. 1942): Poems [ed. by A. R. Chisholm]

Niland (1917): The Apprentices   N

O'Collins (1931): Patrick McMahon Glynn   B

Ottley (   ): By the Sandhills of Yamboorah   Y

Palmer, Aileen (1915): World Without Strangers?   V

Porter, Hal (1911): The Cats of Venice   S
Stars of Australian Stage and Screen   B

Porter, Peter (1929): Poems Ancient and Modern

Prichard (1883): On Strenuous Wings [sel. by J. Williams]

Rivett (1917): Australian Citizen   B   [of Herbert Brookes, q.v.]

H

Robinson, Roland (1912): The Man Who Sold His Dreaming L

Robson (1931): The Convict Settlers of Australia H

Rolfe (   ): No Love Lost N

Rowland (1925): The Feast of Ancestors V

Rowlands (1925): A Bird in the Hand N

Sayers (1901): David Syme B

Schlunke (d. 1960): Stories of the Riverina [ed. by C. Semmler]

Semmler (1914): Barcroft Boake W
A. B. (Banjo) Paterson W

Slessor (1901): Life at the Cross P [text; photographs by R. Walker]

Smith, Patsy Adam (1926): Moonbird People P

Smith, Vivian (1933): James McAuley W

Souter, Gavin (1920): Sydney P [text; photographs by Q. Davis; another edn 1968 titled Sydney Observed, with drawings by G. Molnar]

Steven, Margaret (1933): Merchant Campbell H

Stow, Randolph (1935): The Merry-go-round in the Sea N

Tennant (1912): Trail Blazers of the Air Y

Tennant (1912) (ed.): Summer's Tales 2 S

Thiele (1920): February Dragon Y

Tolchard (1908): The Humble Adventurer B [of James Ruse]

Turnbull (1906): Australian Lives B [of Stephens, Whitehead, Train, Lalor, Adams and Hannan, cf. 1945, 1946, 1949]
A Concise History of Australia

Turner, George R. (1916): A Waste of Shame N

Ward, Russel (1914): Australia H

West, Morris (1916): The Ambassador N

White, Patrick (1912): Four Plays ['The Ham Funeral', 'The Season at Sarsaparilla', 'A Cheery Soul', 'Night on Bald Mountain']

Wright, Judith (1915): Preoccupations in Australian Poetry C

Adams, Nancy (1890): Family Fresco B

Aitchison (1923): Contillo N

Bassett (1889): Behind the Picture H [H.M.S. Rattlesnake's Cruise 1846-50]

Bateson (1903): Patrick Logan, Tyrant of Brisbane Town B

Beaver (1928): You Can't Come Back N

Blainey, Geoffrey (1930): The Tyranny of Distance H

Brennan, C. J. (d. 1932): Christopher Brennan AP [sel. by A. R. Chisholm]

Brissenden, R. F. (1928): Patrick White C

Buckley (1925): Arcady and Other Places V

Cannon (1929): The Land Boomers H

Casey, Maie (   ): Tides and Eddies A

Casey, R. G. (1890): Australian Father and Son B

Chaplin (1896): A Brennan Collection [biblio.]

Charlwood (1915): An Afternoon of Time S

Chisholm, A. R. (1888): The Familiar Presence A

Cleary (1917): The High Commissioner N
The Pulse of Danger N

Cowan (1914): Seed N

Crowley (1924): South Australian History [biblio.]

Dick, Margaret (   ): The Novels of Kylie Tennant C

Dutton (1922): Seal Bay Y [with Dean Hay]

Dutton (1922) (ed.): Modern Australian Writing M
Australia and the Monarchy P

Edwards, Hugh (1933): Islands of Angry Ghosts P

Finch (1942): Bibliography of Hal Porter
Bibliography of Patrick White

Gye (1888): Father Clears Out S ['by James Hackston']

Harrison (1932): Points in a Journey V

Harrower (1928): The Watch Tower N

Roy Connolly d.
Douglas Gillison d.
Lawson Glassop d.
E. P. Harrington d.
Eric Lambert d.
Frank Legg d.
Lewis Lett d.
J. P. McKinney d.
Myra Morris d.
J. Normington-Rawling d.
Edward Sweetman d.
James McAuley, A Primer of English Versification
A. Grove Day, Louis Becke
Desmond O'Grady, A Long Way from Home
Once Around the Sun, ed. by Brian Thompson [verse by children]

Hart-Smith (1911): The Talking Clothes V
Hazzard (1931): The Evening of the Holiday N
Hetherington (1907): Pillars of the Faith H
Higham (1931): Noonday Country V
Hope (1907): Collected Poems 1930-65
Iggulden (1917): Dark Stranger N
Iggulden (1917) (ed.): Summer's Tales 3 S
Johnston, George (1912): The Australians P
[text; photographs by R. B. Goodman]
Kendall (d. 1882): Poetical Works [ed. by
T. T. Reed]
Kramer (1924): Myself When Laura C
Lawson, Henry (d. 1922): Best Stories [sel.
by Cecil Mann; another edn 1968 with
intro. by S. Murray-Smith]
Lawson, Sylvia (1932): Mary Gilmore G
[publd 1967]
Legg (1906): Cats on Velvet A
Once More on My Adventure B [of Frank
Hurley, q.v.; with T. Hurley]
Lindsay, Norman (1879): The Scribblings of
an Idle Mind C
Locke Elliott (1917): Some Doves and Pythons
N
Lurie (1938): Rappaport N
McCrae, Hugh (d. 1958): Hugh McCrae AP
[sel. by Douglas Stewart]
McCulloch (1916): George Gipps G [publd
1967]
McGregor (1933): Profile of Australia C
McInnes (1912): Humping My Bluey A
Macmillan (1925): John McDouall Stuart B
Marks (1923): The Heart is Where the Hurt Is N
Martin, David (1915): The Gift V
The King Between N
Mathers (1931): Trap N
Maughan (1912): ¶Tobruk and El Alamein H
Moorehead (1910): The Fatal Impact H
Mudie, Ian (1911): Wreck of the Admella H
Rivers of Australia P

Niland (1917): Pairs and Loners S

'O'Conner, Elizabeth' (1913): The Chinee Bird Y

Patrick (   ): Inapatua N

Pike (1908) (ed.): Australian Dictionary of Biography [vol. 1: 1788-1850, A-H]

Porter, Hal (1911): The Paper Chase A
The Professor D

Powell (1940): A Different Kind of Breathing V

Ramson (1932): Australian English P

Robinson, Roland (1912): Aboriginal Myths and Legends

Roderick (1911): Henry Lawson, Poet and Short Story Writer C

Ronan (1907): Once There Was a Bagman B

Semmler (1914): The Banjo of the Bush B [of A. B. Paterson]
Kenneth Slessor C

Semmler (1914) & **Whitelock** (1934) (edd.): Literary Australia C

Shaw, A. G. L. (1916): Convicts and the Colonies H

'Sidney, Neilma' (1922): Beyond the Bay N

Sinclair (1928): Behind the Ranges A

Slessor (1901): Canberra P
Sydney Harbour P [text; photographs by L. Le Guay]

Smith, Jan (1935): An Ornament of Grace N

Stead (1902): Dark Places of the Heart N [U.S. title; in U.K. called Cotters' England 1967]

Stephensen (d. 1965): The History and Description of Sydney Harbour

Stewart, Douglas (1913): The Seven Rivers A

Syred (1911): Cocky's Castle Y

Talbot (1936) (ed.): XI Hunter Valley Poets + VII

Taylor, Geoff. (1920): Court of Honour N

Thiele (1920): In Charcoal and Conté V
The Rim of the Morning S

1966 (contd)

Turner, G. W. (1921): The English Language in Australia and New Zealand P

Walker, Kath (1920): The Dawn is at Hand V

Walker, R. B. (1925): Old New England H

Waten (1911): Season of Youth N

Weatherburn (1911): George William Evans, Explorer B

White, Patrick (1912): The Solid Mandala N

Wright, Judith (1915): The Other Half V
The River and the Road Y
The Nature of Love S

1967

Alexander, Fred. (1899): Australia Since Federation H

Atkinson, Hugh (1925): The Games N

Auchterlounie (1915): The Dolphin V

Austin, K. A. (1911): The Lights of Cobb and Co. H

Bach (1923): William Bligh G

Barnard, Marjorie (1897): Miles Franklin B

Barnes (1931): Joseph Furphy G

Beaver (1928): Open at Random V

Béchervaise (1910): Australia, World of Difference P
Australia and Antarctica P

Blainey, Geoffrey (1930): Wesley College H [with J. Morrissey & S. E. K. Hulme]

Bolton (1931): Dick Boyer B

Boyd, Robin (1919): Artificial Australia C

Brookes, Mabel (1894): Riders of Time H

Chaplin (1896): A McCrae Miscellany [biblio.]

Christesen (1912) (ed.): On Native Grounds M [selections from *Meanjin* 1940-66]

Clark, Robert (1911): Segments of the Bowl V [publd 1968]

Cleary (1917): The Long Pursuit N

F. M. Cutlack d.
Hal Gye d.
John Herington d.
Cecil Mann d.
A. J. Marshall d.
D'Arcy Niland d.
A. Grove Day (ed.), South Sea Supercargo [*stories by Louis Becke*]
W. P. Friederich, Australia in Western Imaginative Prose Writings
Barry Argyle, Patrick White
Charles Osborne, Kafka
Elspeth Huxley, Their Shining Eldorado
Ray Lawler, A Breach in the Wall *produced*

Collinson (1925): Who is Wheeling Grandma? V

Couper (1914): East of Living   V

Cowen (1919): Isaac Isaacs   B

Davis, Beatrice (1909) (ed.): Short Stories of Australia: the Moderns [cf. Stewart below]

Dobson (1920) (sel.): Songs for All Seasons   Y

Drake-Brockman (1901): Katharine Susannah Prichard   W

Dutton (1922): Poems Soft and Loud
On My Island   Y
The Hero as Murderer   B   [of E. J. Eyre, q.v.]

Elliott (1910): The Landscape of Australian Poetry   C

Fogarty (1933): George Chaffey   G

Forshaw (1923): An Affair of Clowns   N

Gunton (1943): Catherine Helen Spence [biblio.]

Hall (1935): Eyewitness   V

Hannaford (1897): Index to the *Lone Hand* (1907-13)

Hardy (1917): Billy Borker Yarns Again   S

Harris, Max (1921): A Window at Night   V [sel. by Robert Clark]
The Land That Waited [with Alison Forbes]

Harrison (1932): Variations on a Ground   V

Hazzard (1931): People in Glass Houses   N

Hetherington (1907): Melba   B

Hewett (1923): Hidden Journey   V

Higham (1931) (ed.): Australians Abroad   P [with M. Wilding]

Horne, Donald (1921): The Education of Young Donald   A
Southern Exposure   P   [text; photographs by D. Beal]

Irvin, Margaret (1916): The Rock and the Pool   V

Jones, Evan (1931): Understandings   V

Keesing (1923) (ed.): Gold Fever   H

Keneally (1935): Bring Larks and Heroes   N

Kramer (1924): Henry Handel Richardson   G

Lawson, Henry (d. 1922): Collected Verse [ed. by C. Roderick; vol. i; vol. ii, 1968; vol. iii, 1969]
Humorous Stories [sel. by Cecil Mann]

Lindsay, Joan (1896): Picnic at Hanging Rock   N

Lindsay, Lionel (d. 1961): Comedy of Life   A

Lindsay, Rose (1881): Model Wife   A

Macartney, F. T. (1887): Proof Against Failure   A

McGregor (1933): The High Country   P [text; photographs by H. Gritscher]

McInnes (1912): Finding a Father   A

Mathew (1929): The Joys of Possession   N

Menzies (1894): Afternoon Light   A

Morphett, Tony (1938): Dynasty   N

Pearl (1906): Morrison of Peking   B

Phelan (1913): Serpents in Paradise   N

Pike (1908) (ed.): Australian Dictionary of Biography [vol. 2: 1788-1850, I-Z]

Pothan (1929): A Time to Die   N

Prichard (1883): Happiness   S
Subtle Flame   N
Moggie and Her Circus Pony   Y

Quinlan (1900): Here My Home   B   [of John Stuart Hepburn]

Robinson, Roland (1912): Grendel   V

Robinson, W. S. (d. 1963): If I Remember Rightly   A   [ed. by G. Blainey]

Rolls (1923): Sheaf Tosser   V

Rowbotham (1924): Bungalow and Hurricane   V

Scott, W. N. (1923): Focus on Judith Wright C

Semmler (1914): A. B. Paterson G

Semmler (1914) (ed.): The World of 'Banjo' Paterson M
Twentieth Century Australian Literary Criticism

Shapcott (1935): A Taste of Salt Water V
Focus on Charles Blackman C

Shumack (d. 1940): An Autobiography [ed. by J. E. & S. Shumack]

Smith, Patsy Adam (1926): There Was a Ship P

Smith, Vivian (1933): An Island South V

Stead (1902): The Puzzleheaded Girl S

Stewart, Douglas (1913): Collected Poems

Stewart, Douglas (1913) (ed.): Short Stories of Australia: the Lawson Tradition

Stewart, Douglas (1913) & **Keesing** (1923) (edd.): The Pacific Book of Bush Ballads [another edn 1968 titled Bush Songs, Ballads and Other Verse]

Stow, Randolph (1935): Midnite Y

Sutherland, Wendy (1936): Caroline Chisholm G

Tennant (1912): Tell Morning This N [cf. 1953]
Ma Jones and the Little White Cannibals S

Thiele (1920): Mrs Munch and Puffing Billy Y

Turner, George R. (1916): The Lame Dog Man N

Villiers (1903): Captain Cook B

Wallace-Crabbe (1934): The Rebel General V

Welsby (d. 1941): Collected Works [ed. by A. K. Thomson]

Wright, Judith (1915): Henry Lawson G

Young, Lynette (1894): The Melody Lingers On B [of Tarlton Rayment, q.v.]

Anderson, Hugh (1927): Bernard O'Dowd B [rev. 1969 as The Poet Militant]

Anderson, Hugh (1927) & **Meredith, John** (1920): Folk Songs of Australia

Astley (1925): A Boat Load of Home Folk N

Auchmuty (1909): John Hunter G

Bateson (1903): The War With Japan H

Blainey, Ann (1935): The Farthing Poet B [of R. H. Horne, q.v.]

Blainey, Geoffrey (1930): The Rise of Broken Hill H
Across a Red World A

Blake (1913): Australian Writers C

Blight (1913): My Beachcombing Days V

Blunden (1906): Charco Harbour N [about Captain Cook]

Campbell, David (1915): Selected Poems 1942–1968

Cleary (1917): Season of Doubt N

Crowley (1924): Sir John Forrest B [Macrossan lecture]

Currey (1890): Sir Francis Forbes B
The Brothers Bent B
Mount Wilson H

Davison (1893): The White Thorntree N

Dawe, Bruce (1930): An Eye For a Tooth V

Deakin (d. 1919): Federated Australia H [letters to the *Morning Post* 1900–10 sel. and ed. by J. A. La Nauze]

Dutton (1922): Andy N
Tisi and the Pageant Y [with Dean Hay]

Dutton (1922) & **Harris, Max** (1921): The Vital Decade M [selections from *Australian Letters 1957–68*]

Fysh (1895): Qantas at War H

Gill (1895): ¶Royal Australian Navy 1942–45 H

Nancy Adams d.
Alec Bagot d.
C. E. W. Bean d.
Bernard Cronin d.
Arthur Davies d.
Henrietta Drake-Brockman d.
Alan Gross d.
Gavin Long d.
George Mackaness d.
Dorothea Mackellar d.
Harley Matthews d.
Les. Robinson d.
John Thompson d.
Vincent Buckley, Poetry and the Sacred
Louise E. Rorabacher (ed.), Aliens in their Land [*stories about Aboriginals*]
W. H. Pearson, Henry Lawson Among Maoris
Grant Watson, Journey Under the Southern Stars

---

[1] The entries for 1968 are limited to books by or about writers who have already appeared in a previous year.

Hall (1935): The Autobiography of a Gorgon V
The Law of Karma V
Focus on Andrew Sibley C

Hall (1935) & **Shapcott** (1935) (edd.): New Impulses in Australian Poetry

Hanger (1911) (intro.): Khaki, Bush and Bigotry D [contains 'Rusty Bugles' by Sumner Locke Elliott, cf. 1948; 'We Find the Bunyip' by Ray Mathew; 'The Well' by J. P. McKinney; CAP, vol. 3]

Hardy (1917): The Unlucky Australians P

Harwood (1920): Poems, Volume Two

Hewett (1923): Windmill Country V

Higham (1931) (ed.): Australian Writing Today

Ireland (1927): The Chantic Bird N

Irvin, Eric (1908): A Suit for Everyman V

Keesing (1923): Showground Sketchbook V

Kelly (1922): The Red Boat N

Keneally (1935): Three Cheers for the Paraclete N

Lehmann (1940): A Voyage of Lions V

Leichhardt (d. 1848?): Letters [ed. by M. Aurousseau]

Lindsay, Norman (1879): Rooms and Houses N

Lurie (1938): The London Jungle Adventures of Charlie Hope N

McGregor (1933): People, Politics and Pop C
To Sydney with Love [text; photographs by H. Gritscher]

McInnes (1912): Goodbye, Melbourne Town A

Martin, David (1915): The Idealist V

Moore, T. Inglis (1901): Rolf Boldrewood G

Mudie, Ian (1911): The Heroic Journey of John McDouall Stuart H

Muirden (1928): The Puzzled Patriots H

O'Brien, P. A. (1945): A. D. Hope [biblio.]
Randolph Stow [biblio.]
Judith Wright [biblio.; with E. Robinson]

Oliver (1916): Shaw Neilson W
Louis Stone W

Osborne (1927): Swansong V

Pike (1908): Charles Hawker G

Porter, Hal (1911): The Actors P
Elijah's Ravens V

Powell (1940): I Learn By Going V

Rienits, Rex (1909) & **Thea** (1919): The
Voyages of Captain Cook H

Rivett (1917): Australia P

Robinson, Roland (1917): Wandjina, Children
of the Dreamtime L

Simpson, R. A. (1929): After the Assassination
V

Smith, Patsy Adam (1926): Tiger Country P
Hobart Sketchbook P [text; drawings by
M. Angus]

Souter, Gavin (1929): A Peculiar People H
['New Australia' in Paraguay]

Steven, Margaret (1933): John Macarthur G

Stivens (1911): Three Persons Make a Tiger N

Talbot (1936): Poems for a Female Universe

Taylor, Geoff. (1920): Day of the Republic N

Thiele (1920): Heysen of Hahndorf B
Barossa Valley Sketchbook [text; drawings by
J. McLeod]

Thomson (1901) (sel.): Critical Essays on
Kenneth Slessor
Critical Essays on Judith Wright

Thwaites (1915): Poems of War and Peace

Tregenza (1931): Professor of Democracy B
[of C. H. Pearson, q.v.]

West, Francis (1927): Hubert Murray, Australian Pro-Consul B

West, Morris (1916): The Tower of Babel N

Wigmore (1899): Struggle for the Snowy P

Wilson, Gwendoline (   ): Murray of
Yarralumla B [of Terence Aubrey
Murray, also treats Anna Maria Bunn, q.v.]

INDEX

INDEX

Abbott, Charles Lydiard Aubrey, 1886- .
Australia's Frontier Province 1950.

‡Abbott, John Henry Macartney, 1874-1953. Tommy Cornstalk 1902, Plain and Veldt '03.

Abdullah, Mena, 1930- . *With R. Mathew, q.v.*: The Time of the Peacock 1965.

Adam Smith, Patsy, *see* Smith.

‡Adams, Arthur Henry, 1872-1936. Tussock Land 1904, London Streets '06, Galahad Jones '10, A Touch of Fantasy '11, Collected Verses '13, Three Plays '14, Grocer Greatheart '15, The Australians '20, A Man's Life '29. *Ed.*: *Bulletin* Red Page 1906-09.

Adams, David, 1908- . *Ed.*: The Letters of Rachel Henning 1952.

‡Adams, Francis, 1862-93. Australian Essays 1886, Poetical Works '87, Songs of the Army of the Night '88, Australian Life '92, The Australians '93. *See also C. Turnbull 1949.*

Adams, Nancy, 1890-1968. Saxon Sheep 1961, Family Fresco '66.

Adelaide Observer 1843-1931. *See also 1881.*

Advertiser (Adelaide). *See 1858.*

‡Afford, Max, 1906-54. The Founder 1936, Lady in Danger '44.

Age, The (Melbourne). 1854- .

Aitchison, Raymond, 1923- . The Illegitimates 1964, Contillo '66.

‡Aldridge, James, 1918- . Signed With Their Honour 1942.

‡Alexander, Frederick, 1899- . Campus at Crawley 1963, Australia since Federation '67.

Alexander, Joseph Aloysius, 1892- . The Life of George Chaffey 1928. *Ed.*: Who's Who in Australia 1938-67.

All About Books. 1928-38.

*Allen, Harry Cranbrook, 1917- . Bush and Backwoods 1959.

Allen, Leslie Holdsworth, 1879-1964. Gods and Wood Things 1913, Billy Bubbles '20, Phaedra '21, Araby '24, Patria '41. *See also M. Clarke 1885.*

Anderson, Ethel, 1883-1958. Squatter's Luck 1942, Adventures in Appleshire '44, Timeless Garden '45, Sunday at Yarralumla '47, Indian Tales '48, At Parramatta '56, The Song of Hagar '57, The Little Ghosts '59.

Anderson, Hugh, 1927- . A Guide to Ten Australian Poets 1953, Frank Wilmot ('Furnley Maurice') '55, Shaw Neilson '56, Australian Song Index '57, The Colonial Minstrel '60, Out of the Shadow '62, Bernard O'Dowd [biblio.] '63, Farewell to Old England '64, The Singing Roads '65, Bernard O'Dowd (B) '68. *Ed.*: Colonial Ballads 1955, Goldrush Songster '58. *With J. Meredith*: Folk Songs of Australia 1968. *With W. Stone, q.v.*: Christopher Brennan 1959. *See also A. L. Gordon 1864.*

‡Angas, George French, 1822-86. Savage Life and Scenes in Australia and N.Z. 1847, The Wreck of the Admella '74.

Angry Penguins. 1940-46. Ed. by M. Harris q.v.

Archer, Laura Palmer-, *see* Palmer-Archer.

Archibald, John Feltham (Jules François), 1856-1919. *Sel. with F. J. Broomfield, q.v.*: A Golden Shanty 1890. *Ed.*: *Bulletin* 1886-1902.

Argus, The (Melbourne). 1846-1957.

*Argyle, Barry, 1933- . Patrick White 1967.

*Arnold, Thomas, 1823-1900. *See 1850 and P. A. Howell 1964.*

Art in Australia. 1916-42.

Ashton, Julian, 1851-1942. Now Came Still Evening On 1941.

Astley, Thea, 1925- . Girl With a Monkey 1958, A Descant for Gossips '60, The Well Dressed Explorer '62, The Slow Natives '65, A Boatload of Home Folk '68.

Astley, William, *see* 'Warung, Price'

Athenaeum, The. 1875-76.

Atkinson, Caroline [*Mrs* Calvert], 1834-72. Gertrude the Emigrant 1857, Cowanda '59.

‡Atkinson, Evelyn John Rupert, 1881-1960. The Shrine of Desire 1906, A Nocturne '19.

Atkinson, Hugh, 1925- . The Pink and the Brown 1957, Low Company '61, The Reckoning '65, The Games '67.

Atlas, The. 1844-48. *Ed. by*: Robert Lowe, q.v.

‡Auchmuty, James Johnston, 1909- . John Hunter 1968.

Auchterlounie, Dorothy, 1915- . Kaleidoscope 1940, The Dolphin '67.

'Baylebridge, William'—*contd*
Vital Flesh 1961, An Anzac Muster '62, The Growth of Love '63, Salvage '64.

Baynton, Barbara, 1862-1929. Bush Studies 1902, Human Toll '07, Cobbers '17.

Bean, Charles Edwin Woodrow, 1879-1968. On the Wool Track 1910, The Dreadnought of the Darling '11, the Story of Anzac '21, '24, The A.I.F. in France '29, '33, '37, '42, Anzac to Amiens '46, Two Men I Knew '57. *Ed.*: Official History of Australia in the War of 1914-1918 (1921-43).

Beasley, Jack, 1926- . The Rage for Life: The Work of K. S. Prichard 1964. *See also S. Murray-Smith 1953.*

‡Beaver, Bruce, 1928- . Under the Bridge 1961, Seawall and Shoreline '64, You Can't Come Back '66, Open at Random '67, Letters to Live Poets '69.

Béchervaise, John, 1910- . Antarctica 1959, The Far South '61, Blizzard and Fire '63, Australia, World of Difference '67, Australia and Antarctica '67. *With P. G. Law, q.v.*: ANARE 1957.

‡'Becke, Louis' [George Lewis Becke], 1855-1913. By Reef and Palm 1894. *With W. J. Jeffrey, q.v.*: A First Fleet Family 1895, The Mutineer '98. *See also A. G. Day 1966, '67.*

Bedford, Randolph, 1868-1941. True Eyes and the Whirlwind 1903, The Snare of Strength '05, Billy Pagan '11, The Silver Star '17, Aladdin and the Boss Cockie '19, Naught to Thirty-three '44.

Bedford, Ruth Marjory, 1882-1963. Think of Stephen 1954.

Beeby, *Sir* George Stephenson, 1869-1942. Concerning Ordinary People 1923.

Bennett, George, 1804-93. Wanderings in N.S.W. 1834.

Bennett, Marie Montgomerie, . Christison of Lammermoor 1927.

Bennett, Samuel, 1815-78. History of Australian Discovery and Colonisation 1867.

‡Berndt, Ronald Murray, 1916- . *With C. Berndt*: The World of the First Australians 1964.

‡Bertie, Charles Henry, 1875-1952. Stories of Old Sydney 1912, Isaac Nathan '22.

Beynon, Richard, 1928- . The Shifting Heart 1960.

Biblionews, 1947- .

*Bigge, John Thomas, 1780-1843. *See* 1822, '23.

Biggs, Maurice, 1915- . Poems of War and Peace 1945.

Birnie, Richard, 1808-88. Essays 1879.

Birrell, James, 1928- . Walter Burley Griffin 1964.

Birth. 1916-22.

'Black, Donald', *see* Gray, J. L.

Bladen, Peter, 1922- . The Old Ladies at Newington 1953, Masque for a Modern Minstrel '62. *As 'L. Bladen'*: Selected Poems 1945.

Blainey, Ann, 1935- . The Farthing Poet 1968.

Blainey, Geoffrey, 1930- . The Peaks of Lyell 1954, A Centenary History of the University of Melbourne '57, Gold and Paper '58, Mines in the Spinifex '60, The Rush That Never Ended '63, A History of Camberwell '64, The Tyranny of Distance '66, Across a Red World '68, The Rise of Broken Hill '68. *With J. Morrissey & S. E. K. Hulme*: Wesley College 1967. *See also W. S. Robinson 1967.*

Blair, David, 1820-99. The History of Australasia 1878.

‡Blake, Leslie (Bamford) James, 1913- . Shaw Neilson in the Wimmera 1961, Australian Writers '68.

Bland, William, 1789-1868. Journey of Discovery etc. 1831.

Blaxland, Gregory, 1778-1853. Journal 1823. *See also V. W. Hyde 1958.*

Blight, John, 1913- . The Old Pianist 1945, The Two Suns Met '54, A Beachcomber's Diary '63, My Beachcombing Days '68.

Blocksidge, C. W., *see* 'Baylebridge, William'.

'Bluebush', *see* Bourke, J. P.

‡Blunden, Godfrey, 1906- . No More Reality 1935, Charco Harbour '68.

Boake, Barcroft Henry, 1866-92. Where the Dead Men Lie 1897. *See also C. Semmler 1965.*

'Boake, Capel' [Doris Boake Kerr], 1895-1944. Painted Clay 1917, The Romany Mark '23, The Dark Thread '36, The Twig is Bent '46, Selected Poems '49. *With B. Cronin, q.v.*: Kangaroo Rhymes 1922.

Boissiere, Ralph De, *see* De Boissiere.

‡'Boldrewood, Rolf' [Thomas Alexander Browne], 1826-1915. Ups and Downs 1878, Robbery Under Arms '82-'83, '88, Old Melbourne Memories '84, The Squatter's Dream '90, A Colonial Reformer '90, The Miner's Right '90, A Sydney-side Saxon '91, Nevermore '92, The Sphinx of Eaglehawk '95, Plain Living '98, A Romance of Canvas Town '98, Babes in the Bush 1900, In Bad Company '01, The Ghost Camp

'Boldrewood, Rolf'—*contd*
'02, The Last Chance '05. *See also
K. Burke 1956, T. I. Moore 1968.*

Bolton, Geoffrey Curgenven, 1931- .
Alexander Forrest 1958, A Thousand
Miles Away '63, Richard Daintree '65,
Dick Boyer '67.

‡Bonwick, James, 1817-1906. The Discovery and Settlement of Port Phillip
1856, William Buckley '56, John
Batman '67, The Tasmanian Lily '73,
Australia's First Preacher '98, An
Octogenarian's Reminiscences 1902. *See
also E. E. Pescott 1939.*

Bookfellow, The. 1899-1925. Founded by
A. G. Stephens, q.v.

Boomerang, The. 1887-92. *Ed.* William
Lane, q.v.

‡Boote, Henry Ernest, 1868-1949. A Fool's
Talk 1915, Tea With the Devil '28.

‡Boothby, Guy, 1867-1905. In Strange
Company 1894.

Borchardt, Dietrich Hans, 1916- . Australian Bibliography 1963.

Boswell, Annabella, 1826-1916. Journal
[ed. by M. Herman] 1965.

Bourke, John Phillip ['Bluebush'], 1860-
1914. Off the Bluebush 1915.

Bowden, Keith Macrae, 1908- . George
Bass 1952, Captain James Kelly of
Hobart Town '64.

Boyd, Martin, 1893- . *As 'Martin
Mills'*: Love Gods 1925, Brangane '26,
The Montforts '28. *Under own name*:
Retrospect 1920, Scandal of Spring '34,
The Lemon Farm '35, The Painted
Princess '36, The Picnic '37, Night of
the Party '38, A Single Flame '39, Nuns
in Jeopardy '40, Lucinda Brayford '46,
Such Pleasure '49, The Cardboard
Crown '52, A Difficult Young Man
'55, Outbreak of Love '57, Much Else
in Italy '58, When Blackbirds Sing '62,
Day of My Delight '65, The Tea-Time
of Love '69. *See also K. Fitzpatrick 1963.*

Boyd, Robin, 1919- . Victorian Modern
1947, Australia's Home '52, The Australian Ugliness '60, The Puzzle of
Architecture '65, Artificial Australia '67.

‡Braddon, Russell, 1921- . The Naked
Island 1952, Nancy Wake '56, Out of
the Storm '56, End of a Hate '58,
Joan Sutherland '62, The Year of the
Angry Rabbit '64.

‡Brady, Edwin James, 1869-1952. The
Ways of Many Waters 1899, The
Earthen Floor 1902, Bushland Ballads
'10, Bells and Hobbles '11, The House
of the Winds '19, Wardens of the
Seas '33.

'Breaker, The', *see* Morant, H. H.

Brennan, Christopher John, 1870-1932.
XVIII Poems 1897, XXI Poems '97,
Poems 1913 [1914], A Chant of Doom
'18, Twenty-three Poems '38, The
Burden of Tyre '53, Verse '60, Prose
'62, Selected Poems (AP) '66. *With
J. Le Gay Brereton, q.v.*: A Mask 1913.
*See also H. F. Chaplin 1966, A. R.
Chisholm 1946, H. M. Green 1939,
R. Hughes 1934, J. McAuley 1963,
A. G. Stephens 1933, W. Stone & H.
Anderson 1959, G. A. Wilkes 1953.*

‡Brennan, Niall, 1918- . A Hoax Called
Jones 1962, Dr Mannix '64.

'Brent of Bin Bin', *see* Franklin, Miles.

Brereton, John Le Gay, 1871-1933. The
Song of Brotherhood 1896, Perdita '96,
Sweetheart Mine '97, Landlopers '99,
Oithona 1902, Sea and Sky '08, To-
morrow '10, The Burning Marl '19,
The Carillon Poem '24, Swags Up! '28,
The Temple on the Hill '28, Knocking
Round '30, So Long, Mick '31, Writings
on Elizabethan Drama '48. *Ed. with
Bertha Lawson, q.v.*: Henry Lawson, By
His Mates 1931. *With C. J. Brennan,
q.v.*: A Mask 1913. *See also H. P.
Heseltine 1965.*

‡Brickhill, Paul, 1916- . Escape to
Danger 1946.

‡Bridges, Roy, 1885-1952. The Barb of
an Arrow 1909, From Silver to Steel
'20, That Yesterday Was Home '48.

‡Brinsmead, Hesba Fay, 1922- . Pastures
of the Blue Crane 1964.

Brissenden, Alan, 1932- . *Ed. with
C. Higham, q.v.*: They Came to Australia 1961. *See also 'Rolf Boldrewood'
1882.*

Brissenden, Robert Francis, 1928- . Patrick White 1966. *Ed.*: Southern Harvest 1964.

Brockman, Henrietta Drake-, *see* Drake-
Brockman.

Brookes, Herbert, 1867-1963. *Ed.*: The
Federal Story (Deakin) 1944. *See also
R. Rivett 1965.*

‡Brookes, *Dame* Mabel, 1894- . Riders
of Time 1967.

Broomfield, Frederick John, 1860-1941.
Henry Lawson and His Critics 1930.
Sel. with J. F. Archibald, q.v.: A Golden
Shanty 1890.

Brown, Cyril,   . Writing for
Australia 1956.

Brown, Edwin Tylor, 1889-1957. Excursions and Enquiries 1935, Not
Without Prejudice '55.

Brown, Phillip Lawrence, 1904- . *Ed.*: The Narrative of George Russell of Golf Hill 1935, Clyde Company Papers 1941-68.

Browne, R. Spencer-, *see* Spencer-Browne.

Browne, T. A., *see* 'Boldrewood, Rolf'.

‡Bruce, Mary Grant, 1878-1958. A Little Bush Maid 1910.

‡Buchanan, Alfred Johnson, 1874-1941. The Real Australia 1907, Where Day Begins '11.

Buckley, Vincent, 1925- . The World's Flesh 1954, Essays in Poetry '57, Poetry and Morality '59, Masters in Israel '61, Henry Handel Richardson '61, Arcady and Other Places '66, Poetry and the Sacred '68. *Contrib. to*: The Campion Paintings (L. French) 1962, Eight by Eight '63.

Bull, John Wrathall, 1804-86. Early Experiences of Colonial Life in South Australia 1878, '84.

Bulletin, The. (Sydney). 1880- .

Bunn, Anna Maria [*née* Murray], 1808-89. The Guardian 1838 [anon.]. *See G. Wilson 1968*.

Burke, James Lester, c.1822-79. *Ed.*: Martin Cash 1870, q.v.

‡Burke, Keast, 1896- . T. A. Browne ('Rolf Boldrewood') 1956.

Burn, David, 1799?-1875. Plays and Fugitive Pieces 1842. *See also 1829*.

Burns, Robert, 1925- . Mr Brain Knows Best 1959.

Busby, James, 1801-71. Treatise etc. 1825, Manual '30.

‡Butlin, Sydney James, 1910- . Foundations of the Australian Monetary System 1953, War Economy '55.

Byrne, Desmond, . Australian Writers 1896.

Byrnes, Robert Steel, 1899- . *Ed. with V. Vallis, q.v.*: The Queensland Centenary Anthology 1959.

‡Caffyn, Kathleen Mannington ['Iota'], 1852-1926. A Yellow Aster 1894.

Caffyn, Stephen Mannington, 1850-96. Miss Milne and I 1889, Poppy's Tears '90.

Calthorpe, Mena, 1905- . The Dyehouse 1961, The Defectors '69.

Calvert, Caroline, *see* Atkinson, Caroline.

‡Cambridge, Ada, 1844-1926. The Manor House 1875, Up the Murray '75, Unspoken Thoughts '87, A Marked Man '90, The Three Miss Kings '91, Not All in Vain '92, Fidelis '95, At Midnight '97, Materfamilias '98, Thirty Years in Australia 1903, The Retrospect '12, The Hand in the Dark '13.

★Cameron, Hector Charles, 1878-1958. Sir Joseph Banks 1952.

Campbell, David, 1915- . Speak With the Sun 1949, The Miracle of Mullion Hill '56, Evening Under Lamplight '59, Poems '62, Selected Poems '68.

‡Campbell, Jean, 1906- . Brass and Cymbals 1933.

Campbell, Ross, 1910- . Daddy, Are You Married? 1962, Mummy, Who is Your Husband? '64.

★'Campion, Sarah' [Mary Rose Alpers, *née* Coulton], 1906- . Mo Burdekin 1941, Bonanza '42, The Pommy Cow '44, Dr Golightly '46.

Canberra Times. 1926- .

Cannon, Michael, 1929- . The Land Boomers 1966. *See also J. S. James 1877*.

Carboni, Raffaello, 1820-75. The Eureka Stockade 1855.

Carmichael, (Grace Elizabeth) Jennings, 1868-1904. Poems 1895.

Carnegie, David Wynford, 1871-1900. Spinifex and Sand 1898.

Casey, Gavin, 1907-64. It's Harder for Girls 1942, Birds of a Feather '43, Downhill is Easier '45, The Wits Are Out '47, City of Men '50, Snowball '58, Amid the Plenty '62. The Man Whose Name Was Mud '63. *With T. Mayman*: The Mile That Midas Touched '64.

Casey, Maie [*Lady* Casey], . An Australian Story 1962, Tides and Eddies '66.

‡Casey, Richard Gardiner [Baron Casey of Berwick], 1890- . Personal Experience 1962, Australian Father and Son '66.

Cash, Martin, 1808-77. The Adventures of Martin Cash 1870. *See also F. Clune 1955*.

Cassidy, Robert John ['Gilrooney'], 1880-1948. The Land of the Starry Cross 1911.

Casson, Marjory Rose, 1889-1965. G. C. Henderson 1964.

Cato, Nancy, 1917- . The Darkened Window 1950, The Dancing Bough '57, All the Rivers Run '58, Time, Flow Softly '59, Green Grows the Vine '60, But Still the Stream '62, The Sea Ants '64, North West by South '65.

★Cecil, *Lord* Robert, 1830-1903. Gold Fields Diary 1852, publ. 1935 ed. E. Scott, q.v.

Centennial Magazine. 1888-90.

Champion, Ivan Francis, 1904- . Across New Guinea 1932.

Chaplin, Henry Floyd, 1896- . A Neilson Collection 1964, A Brennan Collection '66, A McCrae Miscellany '67.

Chapman, Ernest, see 'Hatfield, William'.

Charlwood, Donald Ernest, 1915- . No Moon Tonight 1956, All the Green Year '65, An Afternoon of Time '66.

‡Chauncy, Nan, 1900- . They Found a Cave 1948.

‡Childe, Vere Gordon, 1892-1957. How Labour Governs 1923.

‡Chisholm, Alan Rowland, 1888- . Christopher Brennan 1946, Men Were My Milestones '58, The Familiar Presence '66. Ed.: Shaw Neilson 1965, Brennan (AP) '66. Ed. with J. J. Quinn: Brennan's Verse 1960, Prose '62.

‡Chisholm, Alexander Hugh, 1890- . Strange New World 1941, The Making of a Sentimental Bloke '46, Ferdinand von Mueller '62, The Joy of the Earth '69. Ed.: Who's Who in Australia 1947, Selected Verse of C. J. Dennis '50, Australian Encyclopedia '58. See also E. J. Banfield 1908, 1925, J. White 1790.

Chisholm, Caroline, 1808-77. Female Immigration 1842. See also G. L. Dann 1943, M. Kiddle 1950, W. Sutherland 1967.

Christesen, Clement Byrne, 1912- . North Coast 1943, South Coast '44, Dirge and Lyrics '45. Ed.: Meanjin 1940- , Australian Heritage '49, On Native Grounds '67.

Christie, William Harvey, 1808-73. A Love Story 1841.

Clark, Charles Manning Hope, 1915- . Abel Tasman 1959, A History of Australia '62, '68, A Short History of Australia '63, Disquiet '69. Ed.: Select Documents in Australian History 1950, '55, Sources of Australian History '57. See also A. Harris 1847.

‡Clark, Mavis Thorpe, . See Latham, Mavis.

Clark, Robert, 1911- . The Dogman 1962, Segments of the Bowl '67. See also M. Harris 1967.

Clarke, Donovan, 1907- . Ritual Dance 1940, Blue Prints '42. Sel.: Charles Harpur 1963.

Clarke, Marcus, 1846-81. Long Odds 1869, The Peripatetic Philosopher '69, His Natural Life '70, '74, '85, Old Tales of a Young Country '71, Holiday Peak '73, 'Twixt Shadow and Shine '75, Four Stories High '77, The Future Australian Race '77, The Conscientious Stranger '81, The Mystery of Major Molineux and Human Repetends '81, Memorial Volume '84, Sensational Tales '86, Austral Edition '90, Chidiock Tichbourne '93. Ed.: Colonial Monthly 1867-70. See also B. Elliott 1958, 1969, B. Wannan 1963.

Cleary, Jon, 1917- . These Small Glories 1946, You Can't See Round Corners '47, The Long Shadow '49, Just Let Me Be '50, The Sundowners '52, The Climate of Courage '54, Justin Bayard (Dust in the Sun) '55, '61, The Green Helmet '57, Back of Sunset '59, North From Thursday '60, The Country of Marriage '62, Forests of the Night '63, Pillar of Salt '63, A Flight of Chariots '63, The Fall of an Eagle '64, The Pulse of Danger '66, The High Commissioner '66, The Long Pursuit '67, Season of Doubt '68, Remember Jack Hoxie '69.

‡Clift, Charmian, 1923-69. Mermaid Singing 1958. With George Johnston, q.v.: High Valley 1949.

‡Close, Robert, 1903- . Love Me Sailor 1945, Morn of Youth '48.

*Clowes, Evelyn Mary, c. 1872-1942. On the Wallaby Through Victoria 1911. As 'Elinor Mordaunt': Sinabada 1937.

‡Clune, Frank, 1893- . Try Anything Once 1933, Martin Cash '55. With P. R. Stephensen, q.v.: The Viking of Van Diemen's Land 1954.

Coast to Coast. 1941- .

Cobb, Chester, 1899-1943. Mr Moffatt 1925, Days of Disillusion '26.

§Cobbold, Richard, 1797-1877. The History of Margaret Catchpole 1845. See also G. B. Barton 1924.

Cobley, John, 1914- . Ed.: Sydney Cove (1788) 1962, (1789-90) '63, (1791-92) '65.

Coghlan, Sir Timothy Augustine, 1856-1926. Labour and Industry in Australia 1918.

Coleman, Peter, 1928- . Ed.: Australian Civilization 1962, Quadrant 1967- , Bulletin 1964-67.

Collier, James, 1846-1925. Sir George Grey 1909, The Pastoral Age in Australasia '11. See also D. Collins 1798.

Collins, David, 1756-1810. An Account of the English Colony etc. 1798, 1802. See also R. Rienits 1969.

'Collins, Tom', see Furphy, Joseph.

Collins, Sir John Augustine, 1899- . As Luck Would Have It 1965.

Collinson, Laurence, 1925- . The Moods of Love 1957, Who is Wheeling

Collinson, Laurence—*contd*
Grandma? '67. *Contrib. to*: Eight by
Eight (*see* Buckley) 1963.
Colonial Monthly, The. Ed. Marcus Clarke,
q.v. 1867-70.
Colonial Times (Hobart). 1825-57. *See also*
1829.
Colonist, The. 1835-40. Ed. J. D. Lang, q.v.
Comment, A. 1940-47.
Commonwealth, The. 1901-03.
Connolly, Roy, 1896-1966. Southern Saga
1940.
*Conrad, Joseph, 1857-1924. See *1879.*
Coombes, Archie James,   . Some
· Australian Poets 1938.
‡Copland, *Sir* Douglas Berry, 1894-   .
W. E. Hearn 1935.
‡Cottrell, Dorothy, 1902-57. The Singing
Gold 1928.
Couper, John Mill, 1914- . East of
Living 1967, The Book of Bligh '69.
Courier-Mail (Brisbane). 1933- .
Couvreur, Jessie, *see* 'Tasma'.
Cowan, Peter, 1914- . Drift 1944, The
Unploughed Land '58, Summer '64, The
Empty Street '65, Seed '66. *Ed.*: Short
Story Landscape 1964.
‡Cowen, Zelman, 1919- . Isaac Isaacs (G)
1962, Isaac Isaacs '67.
‡Cowling, George Herbert, 1881-1946.
Ed. with 'Furnley Maurice', q.v.: Aus-
tralian Essays 1935.
Cox, Erle, 1873-1950. Out of the Silence
1925, Fools' Harvest '39, The Missing
Angel '47.
Cozens, Charles [unidentified]. Adventures
of a Guardsman 1848.
Crabbe, Chris. Wallace-, *see* Wallace-
Crabbe.
Craig, Alexander, 1923- . Far-Back
Country 1954, The Living Sky '64.
Contrib. to: Eight by Eight (*see* Buckley)
1963.
Crawford, Raymond Maxwell, 1906- .
The Study of History 1939, Ourselves
and the Pacific '41, The Renaissance '45,
Australia '52, An Australian Perspective
'60. *Ed. with J. A. La Nauze, q.v.*: The
Crisis in Victorian Politics (Deakin)
1957.
Crawford, Robert James, 1868-1930. Lyric
Moods 1904, The Leafy Bliss '21.
‡Crisp, Leslie Finlay, 1917- . Ben Chifley
1961.
Critic, The. 1961- .
Critical Review. See 1958.
‡Croll, Robert Henderson, 1869-1947.
Tom Roberts 1935, I Recall '39. *Ed.*:
Neilson's Collected Poems 1934.

‡Cronin, Bernard, 1884-1968. The Coast-
landers 1918. *With 'Capel Boake', q.v.*:
Kangaroo Rhymes 1922.
Cross, Zora, 1890-1964. Songs of Love
and Life 1917, The Lilt of Life '18,
The City of Riddle-me-ree '18, Elegy
'21, Introduction to the Study of
Australian Literature '22.
Crossland, Robert, 1913-55. Wainewright
in Tasmania 1954.
Crowley, E. M., *see* 'Roland, Esther'.
Crowley, Francis Keble, 1924- . The
Records of Western Australia 1954,
A Short History of W.A. '59, Aus-
tralia's Western Third '60, Westralian
Suburb '62, South Australian History
'66, Sir John Forrest '68.
'Culotta, Nino', *see* O'Grady, John.
‡Cumpston, John Howard Lidgett, 1880-
1954. Charles Sturt 1951, Thomas
Mitchell '54, The Inland Sea and the
Great River '64.
Cunningham, Peter Miller, 1789-1864.
Two Years in N.S.W. 1827.
Cunnington, Vivian, 1923- . Big Fat
Tuesday 1963.
Curr, Edward Micklethwaite, 1820-89.
Recollections of Squatting in Victoria
1883, The Australian Race 1886-87.
‡Currey, Charles Herbert, 1890- . The
Irish at Eureka 1954, The Trans-
portation, Escape and Pardoning of
Mary Bryant '63, Sir Francis Forbes '68,
The Brothers Bent '68, Mount Wilson
'68.
‡Cusack, Dymphna, 1904- . Jungfrau
1936, Three Australian Three-Act Plays
'50. *With M. Franklin, q.v.*: Pioneers on
Parade 1939. *With Florence James, q.v.*:
Four Winds and a Family 1947, Come
in Spinner '51.
Cuthbertson, James Lister, 1851-1910.
Barwon Ballads 1912.
‡Cutlack, Frederic Morley, 1886-1967.
The Australian Flying Corps in the
Western and Eastern Theatres of War
1923, Breaker Morant '62.

Daily Mail (Brisbane). 1903-33.
Daily Mirror (Sydney). 1941- .
Daily News (Perth). 1882- .
Daily Telegraph (Melbourne). 1869-92.
Daily Telegraph (Sydney). 1879- . *See*
also 1930.
‡Dakin, William John, 1883-1950. Whale-
men Adventurers 1934.
Daley, Victor, 1858-1905. At Dawn and
Dusk 1898, Poems 1908, Wine and
Roses '11, Creeve Roe '47, Selected

Daley, Victor—*contd*
Poems (AP) '63. *See also A. G. Stephens 1905.*
Dalley, John Bede, 1876-1935. No Armour 1928, Max Flambard '29, Only the Morning '30.
'Daly, Rann', *see* Palmer, Vance.
Dalziel, Kathleen, 1881-   . Known and Not Held 1941.
Dann, George Landen, 1904-   . Caroline Chisholm 1943, Fountains Beyond '44.
'Dare, Ishmael', *see* Jose, A. W.
Dark, Eleanor, 1901-   . Slow Dawning 1932, Prelude to Christopher '34, Return to Coolami '36, Sun Across the Sky '37, Waterway '38, The Timeless Land '41, The Little Company '45, Storm of Time '48, No Barrier '53, Lantana Lane '59.
*Darwin, Charles, 1809-82. *See 1836.*
§Darwin, Erasmus, 1731-1802. *See 1789.*
‡Davies, Alan Fraser, 1924-   . A Sunday Kind of Love 1961. *Ed. with S. Encel*: Australian Society 1965.
Davies, Arthur, 1907-68. The Fiddlers of Drummond 1945.
Davis, Arthur Hoey, *see* 'Rudd, Steele'.
Davis, Beatrice, 1909-   . *Ed.*: Short Stories of Australia: the Moderns 1967.
Davis, Norma, 1905-45. Earth Cry 1943, I, the Thief '44.
Davison, Frank Dalby, 1893-   . Forever Morning 1931, Man-Shy '31, The Wells of Beersheba '33, Children of the Dark People '36, The Woman at the Mill '40, Dusty '46, The Road to Yesterday '64, The White Thorntree '68.
Dawbin, Annie Maria [*née* Hadden, m. (1) Andrew Baxter, (2) Robert Dawbin], 1816-1905. Memories of the Past By a Lady in Australia 1873.
Dawe, Bruce, 1930-   . No Fixed Address 1962, A Need of Similar Name '65, An Eye for a Tooth '68, Beyond the Subdivisions '69.
‡Dawe, Carlton, 1865-1935. The Golden Lake 1891.
*Dawson, Alec John, 1872-1951. The Record of Nicholas Freydon 1914.
Dawson, Robert, 1782-1866. The Present State of Australia 1830.
*Day, Arthur Grove, 1904-   . Louis Becke 1966. *Ed.*: South Sea Supercargo (Becke) 1967.
Deakin, Alfred, 1856-1919. Quentin Massys 1875, The Federal Story 1944, The Crisis in Victorian Politics '57, Federated Australia '68. *See also J. A. La Nauze 1962, '65, W. Murdoch 1923.*

‡Deamer, Dulcie, 1890-   . In the Beginning 1909.
De Boissiere, Ralph, 1907-   . Crown Jewel 1952, Rum and Coca-Cola '56, No Saddles for Kangaroos '64.
'De Loghe, Sydney', *see* Loghe.
Denholm, David, *see* 'Forrest, David'.
Deniehy, Daniel Henry, 1828-65. How I Became Attorney-General of New Barataria 1860, Life and Speeches '84.
Dennis, Clarence (Michael) James, 1876-1938. Backblock Ballads 1913, The Songs of a Sentimental Bloke '15, The Moods of Ginger Mick '16, Doreen '17, The Glugs of Gosh '17, Digger Smith '18, Jim of the Hills '19, A Book for Kids '21, Rose of Spadgers '24, The Singing Garden '35, Selected Verse (Chisholm) '50. *See also A. H. Chisholm 1946, M. Herron, Down the Years 1953, I. McLaren 1961.*
Derham, Enid, 1882-1941. The Mountain Road 1912, Poems '58.
Derwent Star and Van Diemen's Land Intelligencer. 1810.
Desiderata. 1929-39.
‡Devaney, James, 1890-   . The Currency Lass 1927, Shaw Neilson '44, Poems '50, Poetry in Our Time '52. *Ed.*: Unpublished Poems (Neilson) 1947.
‡Devanny, Jean, 1894-1962. Sugar Heaven 1936.
Dexter, David, 1917-   . The New Guinea Offensives 1961.
Dick, Margaret,   . The Novels of Kylie Tennant 1966.
Dick, William, 1937-   . A Bunch of Ratbags 1965, Naked Prodigal '69.
§Dickens, Charles, 1812-70. David Copperfield 1849-50, Great Expectations 1860-61.
Dobson, Rosemary, 1920-   . In a Convex Mirror 1944, The Ship of Ice '48, Child with a Cockatoo '55, Selected Poems (AP) '63, Cock Crow '65. *Sel.*: Songs for All Seasons 1967.
Donath, Egon Joseph, 1906-   . William Farrer 1962.
‡Dorrington, Albert, 1871-1953. Castro's Last Sacrament 1900, And the Day Came '08, Our Lady of the Leopards '11, Children of the Cloven Hoof '11. *With A. G. Stephens, q.v.*: The Lady Calphurnia Royal 1909.
Dow, Gwyneth Maude, 1920-   . George Higinbotham 1964.
Dow, Hume, 1916-   . *Ed.*: Trollope's Australia 1966 (*see 1873*). *Ed. with J. Barnes, q.v.*: World Unknown 1960.

Drake-Brockman, Henrietta, 1901-68. Blue North 1934, Sheba Lane '36, Younger Sons '37, Men Without Wives '38, The Fatal Days '47, The Lion-Tamer '48, Sydney or the Bush '48, Men Without Wives and Other Plays '55, The Wicked and the Fair '57, Voyage to Disaster '63, K. S. Prichard '67. *Ed.*: West Coast Stories 1959. *Sel.*: Australian Legendary Tales 1953. *Ed. with W. Murdoch, q.v.*: Australian Short Stories 1951.

'Dryblower', *see* Murphy, E. G.

Drysdale, *Sir* Russell, 1912- . *With A. J. Marshall, q.v.*: Journey Among Men 1962. *See also* G. Dutton *1964.*

Duffy, *Sir* Charles Gavan, 1816-1903. My Life in Two Hemispheres 1898.

Dunlop, Eric, 1910- . John Oxley 1960.

‡Dunn, Max, 1895-1963. Random Elements 1942, No Asterisks '44, Time of Arrival '47, Portrait of a Country '51, The Mirror and the Rose '54. *Contrib. to*: Eight by Eight (*see* Buckley) 1963.

Durack, Mary, 1913- . Little Poems of Sunshine 1923, All-About '35, Chunuma '36, Son of Djaro '37, Piccaninnies '40, The Way of the Whirlwind '44, The Magic Trumpet '46, Keep Him My Country '55, Kings in Grass Castles '59, To Ride a Fine Horse '63, Kookanoo and Kangaroo '63, The Courteous Savage '64, A Pastoral Emigrant '65, The Rock and the Sand '69. *With F. Rutter*: Child Artists of the Australian Bush 1952.

Dutton, Geoffrey, 1922- . Night Flight and Sunrise 1944, The Mortal and the Marble '50, A Long Way South '53, Africa in Black and White '56, States of the Union '58, Antipodes in Shoes '58, Founder of a City '60, Patrick White '61, Walt Whitman '61, Flowers and Fury '62, The Paintings of S. T. Gill '62, Russell Drysdale '64, Tisi and the Yabby '65, Seal Bay '66, The Hero as Murderer '67, Poems Soft and Loud '67, On My Island '67, Tisi and the Pageant '68, Andy '68. *Ed.*: The Literature of Australia 1964, Modern Australian Writing '66, Australia and the Monarchy '66. *Ed. with others*: Australian Letters 1957-68, *Australian Book Review* 1961-64. *Sel. with M. Harris, q.v.*: The Vital Decade 1968.

‡Dwyer, James Francis, 1874-1952. Leg-irons On Wings 1949.

‡Dyson, Edward George, 1865-1931. Rhymes from the Mines 1896, Below

and On Top '98, The Gold Stealers 1901, Fact'ry 'Ands '06, In the Roaring Fifties '06, Benno and Some of the Push '11, Spats' Fact'ry '14, The Golden Shanty '29.

'E', *see* Fullerton, Mary.

'East, Michael', *see* West, Morris.

Edmond, James, 1859-1933. A Journalist and Two Bears 1913.

Edwards, Allan, 1909- . *Sel.*: The Rainbow Bird (Palmer) 1957.

Edwards, Cecil, 1903- . Bruce of Melbourne 1965.

Edwards, Don, 1905-63. High Hill at Midnight 1944, The Woman at Jingera '48.

*Edwards, Edward, 1812-86. See J. Macarthur 1837.

Edwards, Hugh, 1933- . Gods and Little Fishes 1962, Islands of Angry Ghosts '66.

Edwards, Peter David, 1931- . *Ed. with R. B. Joyce, q.v.*: Australia (Trollope) 1967 (*see 1873*).

Eggleston, *Sir* Frederick William, 1875-1954. State Socialism in Victoria 1932, Reflections of an Australian Liberal '53. *With E. H. Sugden, q.v.*: George Swinburne 1931.

Eldershaw, Flora, 1897-1956. *See next*.

'Eldershaw, M. Barnard' [Marjorie Barnard, q.v., & Flora Eldershaw, q.v.]. A House is Built 1929, Green Memory '31, The Glasshouse '36, Plaque With Laurel '37, Essays in Australian Fiction '38, Phillip of Australia '38, My Australia '39, Captain John Piper '39, Tomorrow and Tomorrow '47.

‡Elkin, Adolphus Peter, 1891- . The Australian Aborigines 1938.

Elliott, Brian, 1910- . James Hardy Vaux 1944, Leviathan's Inch '46, Singing to the Cattle '47, Marcus Clarke (B) '58, (G) '69, The Landscape of Australian Poetry '67.

Elliott, Sumner Locke, *see* Locke-Elliott.

*Ellis, Havelock, 1859-1939. Kanga Creek 1922, My Life '40. *See 1875*.

‡Ellis, Malcolm Henry, 1890-1969. Lachlan Macquarie 1947, Francis Greenway '49, John Macarthur '55.

Empire, The. Conducted by Henry Parkes, q.v., 1850-58; by others 1859-75.

Erdos, Renée, 1911- . Ludwig Leichhardt 1963.

‡Ercole, Velia, . No Escape 1932, Dark Windows '34.

'Ern Malley' [James McAuley & Harold Stewart, qq.v.]. The Darkening Ecliptic 1944, Poems '61.

Ern Malley's Journal. 1952-55. Ed. by M. Harris, q.v.

Esson, Louis, 1879-1943. Bells and Bees 1910, Three Short Plays '12, Red Gums '12, The Time is Not Yet Ripe '12, Dead Timber '20, The Southern Cross '46. *Contrib. to*: Six Australian One-Act Plays 1944. *See also V. Palmer 1948.*

‡Evans, George Essex, 1863-1909. The Repentance of Magdalen Despar 1891, Loraine '98, The Secret Key 1906, Collected Verse '28. *See also H. A. Tardent 1913.*

‡Evatt, Herbert Vere, 1894-1965. Rum Rebellion 1938, Australian Labour Leader '40. *See also R. Carboni 1855.*

Evening News (Sydney). 1867-1931.

‡Evers, Leonard Herbert, 1926- . The Racketty Street Gang 1961.

Express (Adelaide). 1863-1951.

‡Ewers, John Keith, 1904- . Boy and Silver 1929, Money Street '33, Fire on the Wind '35, Tales from the Dead Heart '44, Tell the People '44, Creative Writing in Australia '45, Men Against the Earth '46, For Heroes to Live In '48, Harvest '49, With the Sun on My Back '53, Who Rides on the River? '56. *Ed.*: Modern Australian Short Stories 1965.

Eyre, Edward John, 1815-1901. Journals 1845. *See also G. Dutton 1967, H. Kingsley 1872, M. Uren 1964.*

Fairbridge, Wolfe Seymour, 1918-50. Poems 1953.

Fallaw, Lance, 1876-1959. Unending Ways 1926, Hostage and Survival '39.

*Farjeon, Benjamin Leopold, 1838-1903. Grif 1870.

Farmer, Francis Rhodes, 1899- . Thirsty Earth 1934.

Farrell, John, 1851-1904. Ephemera 1878, Two Stories '82, How He Died '87, Australia to England '97, My Sundowner 1904.

‡Farwell, George, 1911- . Down Argent Street 1948, Surf Music '50.

Favenc, Ernest, 1845-1908. The History of Australian Exploration 1888, The Last of Six '93, The Secret of the Australian Desert '95, Marooned on Australia '96, The Moccasins of Silence '96, My Only Murder '99, Voices of the Desert 1905, The Explorers of Australia '08.

Fenton, Clyde, 1901- . Flying Doctor 1947.

Fenton, James, 1819-1901. A History of Tasmania 1884.

Ferguson, *Sir* John Alexander, 1881-1969. Bibliography of Australia 1941, '45, '51, '55, '63, '65, '69. *With H. M. Green*, q.v. *& Mrs A. G. Foster*: The Howes and their Press 1936.

Fetherstonhaugh, Cuthbert, 1837-1925. After Many Days 1918.

Field, Barron, 1786-1846. First Fruits of Australian Poetry 1819, '23. *Ed.*: Geographical Memoirs on N.S.W. 1825.

Fielding, Sydney Glanville, 1856-1930. The New Vicar of Wakefield 1902.

Finch, Janette, 1942- . *Ed.*: Bibliographies of Hal Porter, Patrick White 1966.

Finlayson, Hedley Herbert, 1895- . The Red Centre 1935.

Finn, Edmund ['Garryowen'], 1819-98. The Garryowen Sketches 1880, The Chronicles of Early Melbourne '88.

Finnin, Mary, 1906- . A Beggar's Opera 1938, Look Down, Olympians '39, Poems '40, Royal '41, Alms for Oblivion '47, The Shield of Place '57.

Finniss, Boyle Travers, 1807-93. The Constitutional History of South Australia 1886.

Fisher, Lala, 1872-1929. Earth Spiritual 1918.

Fison, Lorimer, 1832-1907. *With A. W. Howitt, q.v.*: Kamilaroi and Kurnai 1880.

FitzGerald, Robert David, 1902- . The Greater Apollo 1927, To Meet the Sun '29, Moonlight Acre '38, Heemskerck Shoals '49, Between Two Tides '52, This Night's Orbit '53, The Wind at Your Door '59, Southmost Twelve '62, The Elements of Poetry '63, Selected Poems (AP) '63, Forty Years' Poems '65. *Sel.*: Mary Gilmore (AP) 1963.

Fitzhardinge, Laurence Frederic, 1908- . William Morris Hughes 1964. *See also W. Tench 1793.*

Fitzpatrick, Brian, 1905-65. British Imperialism and Australia 1939, A Short History of the Australian Labour Movement '40, The British Empire in Australia '41, The Australian People '46, The Australian Commonwealth '57. *See also R. Carboni 1855.*

Fitzpatrick, Kathleen, 1905- . Sir John Franklin in Tasmania 1949, Martin Boyd '63. *Ed.*: Australian Explorers 1958.

Flanagan, Roderick, 1828-61. The History of N.S.W. 1862.

Flinders, Matthew, 1774-1814. A Voyage to Terra Australis 1814. *See also K. A. Austin 1964, S. J. Baker 1962, E. Hill 1941, D. Mattingley 1961, E. Scott 1914 and James Mack Matthew Flinders 1967.*

Fogarty, John Philip, 1933- . George Chaffey 1967.

Foott, Mary Hannay, 1846-1918. Where the Pelican Builds 1885, Morna Lee '90.

‡Ford, *Sir* Edward, 1902- . The Life and Work of William Redfern 1953.

Forrest, Alexander, 1849-1901. Journal of Expedition from De Grey to Darwin 1880. *See also G. C. Bolton 1958.*

'Forrest, David' [David Denholm], 1924- . The Last Blue Sea 1959, The Hollow Woodheap '62.

Forrest, *Sir* John, 1847-1918. Explorations in Australia 1875. *See also F. K. Crowley 1968, D. Mossenson 1960.*

‡Forrest, Mabel, 1872-1935. The Rose of Forgiveness 1904, Alpha Centauri '09.

Forshaw, Thelma, 1923- . An Affair of Clowns 1967.

Forster, William, 1818-82. The Weirwolf 1876, The Brothers '77, Midas '84.

Forsyth, William Douglass, 1909- . Governor Arthur's Convict System 1935.

Forward, Roy Kenneth, 1936- . Samuel Griffith 1964.

Foster, Lynn, 1914- . There is No Armour 1945, The Exiles '60.

Fowler, Frank, 1833-63. Southern Lights and Shadows 1859. *Ed.: Month 1857-58.*

‡Fox, *Sir* Frank, 1874-1960. *As 'Frank Renar':* Bushman and Buccaneer 1902.

Franklin, *Sir* John, 1786-1847. Narrative of Some Passages in the History of Van Diemen's Land 1845. *See also N. Cato 1965, K. Fitzpatrick 1949, F. J. Woodward 1951.*

Franklin, Miles, 1879-1954. My Brilliant Career 1901, Some Everyday Folk and Dawn '09, Old Blastus of Bandicoot '31, Bring the Monkey '33, All That Swagger '36, My Career Goes Bung '46, Sydney Royal '47, Laughter, Not For a Cage '56, Childhood at Brindabella '63. *With D. Cusack, q.v.:* Pioneers on Parade 1939. *With Kate Baker, q.v.:* Joseph Furphy 1944. *As 'Brent of Bin Bin':* Up the Country 1928, Ten Creeks Run '30, Back to Bool Bool '31, Prelude to Waking '50, Cockatoos '54, Gentlemen at Gyang Gyang '56. *See also M. Barnard 1967, R. Mathew 1963.*

Fremantle Journal and General Advertiser. 1830.

Fremantle Observer. 1831.

*Friederich, Werner Paul, 1905- . Australia in Western Imaginative Prose Writings 1967.

Friend, Donald, 1914- . A Collection of Hillendiana 1956.

*Froude, James Anthony, 1818-94. Oceana 1886.

‡Fullerton, Mary, 1868-1946. Moods and Melodies 1908, The Breaking Furrow '21, Bark House Days '21. *As 'E':* Moles Do So Little With Their Privacy 1942, The Wonder and the Apple '46.

Furphy, Joseph ['Tom Collins'], 1843-1912. Such is Life 1903, Rigby's Romance '05, Poems '16, The Buln-Buln and the Brolga '48. *See also J. Barnes 1963, 1967, M. Franklin & K. Baker 1944, E. E. Pescott 1938, W. Stone 1955.*

‡Fysh, *Sir* Hudson, 1895- . Taming the North 1934, Qantas Rising '65, Qantas at War '68.

Gantner, Neilma, *see* 'Sidney, Neilma'.

Gardiner, Lyndsay, 1927- . Thomas Mitchell 1962.

Gare, Nene, 1919- . The Fringe Dwellers 1961, Green Gold '63.

Garran, *Sir* Robert, 1867-1957. Prosper the Commonwealth 1958.

'Garryowen', *see* Finn, Edmund.

‡Gask, Arthur, 1872-1951. The Mystery of the Sandhills 1922.

‡Gaskin, Catherine, 1929- . This Other Eden 1946.

‡Gaunt, Mary, c.1862-1942. Dave's Sweetheart 1894.

Gavan Duffy, *see* Duffy.

Gay, William, 1865-97. Complete Poetical Works 1911. *See also R. Ingamells 1952.*

Gellert, Leon, 1892- . Songs of a Campaign 1917, The Isle of San '19, Desperate Measures '28.

Gerard, Edwin ['Trooper Gerardy'], 1891-1965. The Road to Palestine 1918, Australian Light Horse Ballads and Rhymes '19.

‡Gibbs, May [Cecilia May Ossoli Kelly], 1876-1969. Snugglepot and Cuddlepie 1918.

Giblin, Ronald Worthy, 1863-1936. The Early History of Tasmania 1928, '39.

Gibson, George Herbert ['Ironbark'], 1846-1921. Southerly Busters 1878, Ironbark Chips and Stockwhip Cracks '93, Ironbark Splinters from the Australian Bush 1912.

Gibson, Leonie Judith, *see* Kramer.

Gilchrist, Archibald, . *Ed.:* John Dunmore Lang 1951.

Giles, Ernest, 1835-97. Australia Twice Traversed 1889. *See also L. Green 1963.*

‡Gill, George Hermon, 1895- . Royal Australian Navy (1939-42) 1957, (1942-45) '68.

Gillen, Francis James, 1855-1912. *With W. B. Spencer, q.v.*: The Native Tribes of Central Australia 1899, The Northern Tribes of Central Australia 1904, The Arunta '27.

Gillison, Douglas, 1899-1966. Royal Australian Air Force 1962.

Gilmore, *Dame* Mary, 1865-1962. Marri'd 1910, The Tale of Tiddley Winks '17, The Passionate Heart '18, Hound of the Road '22, The Tilted Cart '25, The Wild Swan '30, The Rue Tree '31, Under the Wilgas '32, Old Days: Old Ways '34, More Recollections '35, Battlefields '39, The Disinherited '41, Pro Patria Australia '45, Selected Verse '48, Fourteen Men '54, Selected Poems (AP) '63. *See also T. I. Moore 1965, S. Lawson 1966, G. Souter 1968, W. H. Wilde*, Three Radicals *1969*.

'Gilrooney', *see* Cassidy, R. J.

‡Glaskin, Gerald Marcus, 1923- . A World of Our Own 1955.

Glassop, Lawson, 1913-66. We Were the Rats 1944, Lucky Palmer '49.

Goodge, William Thomas, 1862-1909. Hits! Skits! and Jingles! 1899.

Gordon, Adam Lindsay, 1833-70. The Feud 1864, Sea Spray and Smoke Drift '67, Ashtaroth '67, Bush Ballads and Galloping Rhymes '70, Poems 1912. *See also E. Humphris 1933, E. Humphris & D. Sladen 1912, A. P. Martin 1882, S. Neilson 1943, J. H. Ross 1888, D. Sladen 1934, E. A. Vidler 1926*.

Gordon, James William, *see* 'Grahame, Jim'.

Gosse, Fayette, 1919- . William Gosse Hay 1965.

*Gould, Nat(haniel), 1857-1919. The Double Event 1891.

'Grahame, Jim' [James William Gordon], 1874-1949. Under Wide Skies 1947.

Grano, Paul, 1894- . Poems New and Old 1945.

Grant, Alexander Charles, 1843-1930. Bush Life in Queensland 1881.

*Grattan, Clinton Hartley, 1902- . Australian Literature 1929, Introducing Australia '42. *Ed.*: Australia 1947.

Gray, John Lyons, . *As 'Donald Black*': Red Dust 1931.

Green, Henry Mackenzie, 1881-1962. An Outline of Australian Literature 1930, Christopher Brennan '39, Fourteen Minutes '44, Australian Literature '51, A History of Australian Literature '61. *Ed.*: Modern Australian Poetry 1946. *With J. A. Ferguson, q.v. & Mrs A. G. Foster*: The Howes and their Press 1936.

Green, Judith, 1936- . *Contrib. to*: Four Poets (*see* Malouf) 1962.

Green, Louis, 1929- . Ernest Giles 1963.

‡Greenwood, Gordon, 1913- . *Ed.*: Australia 1955. *With J. Laverty*: Brisbane 1959.

Gregory, *Sir* Augustus Charles, 1819-1905. *With F. T. Gregory, q.v.*: Journals of Australian Explorations 1884.

Gregory, Francis Thomas, 1821-88. *With A. C. Gregory, q.v.*: Journals of Australian Explorations 1884.

Grey, *Sir* George, 1812-98. Journals 1841. *See also J. Collier 1909, G. C. Henderson 1907, and J. Rutherford*, Sir George Grey *1961*.

Gross, Alan, 1893-1968. Charles Joseph La Trobe 1956.

Grover, Montague MacGregor, 1870-1943. The Minus Quantity 1914.

Gullett, *Sir* Henry Somer, 1878-1940. The A.I.F. in Sinai and Palestine 1923.

Gunn, *Mrs* Æneas [*née* Jeannie Taylor], 1870-1961. The Little Black Princess 1905, We of the Never Never '08.

‡Gunn, John, 1925- . Sea Menace 1958.

Gunton, Elizabeth Joan, 1943- . *Ed.*: Bibliography of C. H. Spence 1967.

Gye, Hal ['James Hackston'], 1888-1967. Father Clears Out 1966, The Hole in the Bedroom Floor '69.

'Hackston, James', *see* Gye, Hal.

Hadgraft, Cecil, 1904- . Queensland and its Writers 1959, Australian Literature '60, J. B. Stephens '69. *Ed. with R. Wilson*: A Century of Australian Short Stories 1963. *See also H. Savery 1829, 1830, F. Sinnett 1856, 'Tasma' 1889*.

Hague, Ralph Meyrick, 1907- . Sir John Jeffcott 1963.

‡Hales, Alfred Arthur Greenwood, 1860-1936. The Wanderings of a Simple Child 1890.

*Hall, James, 1887-1951. *With C. Nordhoff, q.v.*: Botany Bay 1941.

Hall, Rodney, 1935- . Penniless Till Doomsday 1961, Forty Beads on a Hangman's Rope '63, Eyewitness '67, The Autobiography of a Gorgon '68, The Law of Karma '68, Focus on Andrew Sibley '68. *Contrib. to*: Four Poets (*see* Malouf) 1962. *Ed. with T. Shapcott, q.v.*: New Impulses in Australian Poetry 1968.

Halloran, Henry, 1811-93. Poems, Odes, Songs 1887, A Few Love Rhymes of a Married Life '90, In Memoriam '90.

Hamilton, George, c. 1812-83. Experiences of a Colonist 1879.

‡Hancock, *Sir* (William) Keith, 1898- .
Australia 1930, Country and Calling '54.

Hanger, Eunice, 1911- . *Intro.*: A Spring
Song (Mathew) 1961, Khaki, Bush and
Bigotry '68.

Hannaford, Cyril Harry, 1897- . Index
to the *Lone Hand* 1967.

Harcourt, John Mewton, 1902- . The
Pearlers 1933, Upsurge '34, It Never
Fails '37.

‡Hardie, John Jackson, 1894-1951. Pastoral
Symphony 1939.

Hardy, Frank, 1917- . Power Without
Glory 1950, The Man From Clinkapella
'51, The Four-Legged Lottery '58, The
Hard Way '61, Legends from Benson's
Valley '63, The Yarns of Billy Borker
'65, Billy Borker Yarns Again '67, The
Unlucky Australians '68.

Harford, Lesbia, 1891-1927. Poems 1941.

‡Harney, William Edward, 1895-1962.
Content to Lie in the Sun 1958.

Harpur, Charles, 1813-68. Thoughts 1845,
The Bushrangers '53, A Poet's Home
'62, The Tower of the Dream '65,
Poems '83, Rosa 1948, Selected Poems
(AP) 1963. *See also J. Normington-
Rawling 1962, J. Wright 1963.*

Harrington, Edward Phillip, 1896-1966.
Songs of War and Peace 1920, Boundary
Bend '36, My Old Black Billy '40, The
Kerrigan Boys '44, The Swagless
Swaggie '57.

Harris, Alexander, 1805-74. Settlers and
Convicts 1847, Testimony to the Truth
'48, The Emigrant Family (Martin Beck)
'49, '52, Religio Christi '58.

Harris, Max, 1921- . The Gift of Blood
1940, Dramas From the Sky '42, The
Vegetative Eye '43, The Coorong '55,
Kenneth Slessor '63, A Window at Night
'67. *Ed.*: Angry Penguins 1940-46, *Ern
Malley's Journal* '52-'55, *Australian
Letters* '57-'68, Ern Malley's Poems '61,
Australian Book Review '61- . With
Alison Forbes: The Land That Waited
1967. *Sel. with G. Dutton, q.v.*: The
Vital Decade 1968.

Harrison, Keith, 1932- . Points in a
Journey 1966, Two Variations on a
Ground '67.

Harrower, Elizabeth, 1928- . Down in
the City 1957, The Long Prospect '58,
The Catherine Wheel '60, The Watch
Tower '66.

Hartigan, P. J., *see* 'O'Brien, John'.

Hart-Smith, William, 1911- . Columbus
Goes West 1943, Harvest '45, The
Unceasing Ground '46, Christopher
Columbus '48, On the Level '50, Poems

of Discovery '59, The Talking Clothes
'66.

Harwood, Gwen, 1920- . Poems 1963,
Poems, Volume Two '68.

*Haskell, Arnold, 1903- . Waltzing
Matilda 1940.

Hasluck, Alexandra [*Lady* Hasluck], 1908-
. Portrait With Background 1955,
Unwilling Emigrants '59, James Stirling
'63, Remembered With Affection '63,
C. Y. O'Connor '65, Thomas Peel of
Swan River '65.

‡Hasluck, *Sir* Paul, 1905- . Into the
Desert 1939, Black Australians '42, The
Government and the People (1939-41)
'52, Collected Verse '69.

‡'Hatfield, William' [*né* Ernest Chapman],
1892- . Sheepmates 1931.

Hawdon, Joseph, 1813-71. Journal of a
Journey 1952.

Hay, William Gosse, 1875-1945. Stifled
Laughter 1901, Herridge of Reality
Swamp '07, Captain Quadring '12,
The Escape of the Notorious Sir
William Heans '19, An Australian Rip
Van Winkle '21, Strabane of the Mul-
berry Hills '29, The Mystery of Alfred
Doubt '37. *See also F. Gosse 1965.*

Hazzard, Shirley, 1931- . Cliffs of
Fall 1963, The Evening of the Holiday
'66, People in Glass Houses '67.

Heads of the People. 1847-48.

Hearn, William Edward, 1826-88. Plutology 1863, The Government of England
'67. *See also D. B. Copland 1935, J. A. La
Nauze 1949.*

Hebblethwaite, James, 1857-1921. Poems
1920, New Poems '21.

Heddle, Enid Moodie, *see* Moodie Heddle.

Henderson, George Cockburn, 1870-1944.
Sir George Grey 1907. *See also M. R.
Casson 1964.*

‡Henderson, Walter George, 1870-1957.
Midnight's Daughter 1907.

Heney, Helen, 1907- . The Chinese
Camellia 1950, The Proud Lady '51,
Dark Moon '53, This Quiet Dust '56,
In a Dark Glass '61, The Leaping Blaze
'62.

Heney, Thomas William, 1862-1928. In
Middle Harbour 1890.

Henning, Rachel, 1826-1914. Letters (ed.
D. Adams, q.v.) 1952.

Herbert, Xavier, 1901- . Capricornia
1938, Seven Emus '59, Soldiers' Women
'61, Larger Than Life '63, Disturbing
Element '63.

Herington, John, 1916-67. Air War
Against Germany and Italy 1954, Air
Power Over Europe '63.

erman, Morton, 1907- . Early Australian Architects 1954, The Architecture of Victorian Sydney '56, The Blackets '63, Early Colonial Architecture '63, Francis Greenway '64. *Ed.*: Annabella Boswell's Journal 1965.

Heseltine, Harry Payne, 1931- . John Le Gay Brereton 1965. *Ed.*: Australian Idiom 1963, Intimate Portraits (V. Palmer) '69.

Hetherington, John, 1907- . Airborne Invasion 1943, The Australian Soldier '43, The Winds Are Still '47, Blamey '54, Australians '60, Norman Lindsay '61, Forty-two Faces '62, John Monash '62, Australian Painters '63, Witness to Things Past '64, Uncommon Men '65, Pillars of the Faith '66, Melba '67.

Hewett, Dorothy, 1923- . Bobbin Up 1959, Hidden Journey '67, Windmill Country '68.

Heydon, Peter Richard, 1913- . Quiet Decision 1965.

Hibble, Frederick Sydney, 1902-56. Karangi 1934.

Hides, Jack Gordon, 1906-38. Through Wildest Papua 1935, Papuan Wonderland '36, Savages in Serge '38, Beyond the Kubea '39. *See also J. Sinclair 1969.*

Higgins, Bertram, 1901- . Mordecaius' Overture 1933.

Higham, Charles, 1931- . A Distant Star 1951, Spring and Death '53, The Earthbound '59, Noonday Country '66. *Ed.*: Australian Writing Today 1968. *Ed. with A. Brissenden, q.v.*: They Came to Australia 1961. *Ed. with M. Wilding*: Australians Abroad 1967.

‡Hill, Ernestine, 1899- . The Great Australian Loneliness 1937, Water into Gold '37, My Love Must Wait '41.

Hill, Fidelia, 1790?-1854. Poems and Recollections of the Past 1840.

Hill, Samuel Prout, 1821-61. Tarquin the Proud 1843.

Hobart Town Almanack. 1829-37. *See also 1835.*

Hobart Town Gazette. 1816-25.

Hobart Town Magazine. 1833-34. *See also 1834.*

Hobarton Mercury. 1854- .

*Hodder, Edwin, 1837-1904. G. F. Angas 1891, The History of South Australia '93.

‡Hogan, James Francis, 1855-1924. The Convict King 1891, Robert Lowe '93.

Holdsworth, Phillip, 1849-1902. Station Hunting on the Warrego 1885.

Holt, Edgar, 1904- . Lilacs out of the Dead Land 1932.

Holt, Joseph, 1756-1826. Memoirs 1838.

Hope, Alec Derwent, 1907- . The Wandering Islands 1955, Poems '60, Australian Literature '63, Selected Poems (AP) '63, The Cave and the Spring '65, Collected Poems '66, New Poems '69. *See also P. A. O'Brien 1968.*

Hopegood, Peter, 1891- . Austral Pan 1932, Peter Lecky By Himself '35, Thirteen from Oahu '40, Circus at World's End '47, Snake's-eye View of a Serial Story '64.

Horne, Donald, 1921- . The Lucky Country 1964, The Permit '65, The Education of Young Donald '67, Southern Exposure '67, God is an Englishman '69. *Ed.*: *Observer* 1958-61, *Quadrant* '64-'66, *Bulletin* '67- .

‡Horne, Richard Henry (Hengist), 1802-84. Australian Facts and Prospects 1859, Prometheus the Fire-bringer '64, The South Sea Sisters '66. *See also C. Pearl 1960, Ann Blainey 1968.*

Hornibrook, James Harold, 1898- . Bibliography of Queensland Verse 1953.

*Hornung, Ernest William, 1866-1921. A Bride from the Bush 1890, The Amateur Cracksman [Raffles] 1899. *See also W. P. Friederich 1967.*

‡Houlding, John Richard ['Old Boomerang'], 1822-1918. Australian Capers 1867, Rural and City Life '70.

‡Howard, Frederick, 1904- . The Emigrant 1928, Charles Kingsford Smith '62.

Howarth, Robert Guy, 1906- . Spright and Geist 1944, Literary Particles '46, Involuntaries '48, Nardoo and Pituri '59. *Ed.*: *Southerly* 1939-56, Best Poems of Hugh McCrae '61. *Ed. with J. Thompson & K. Slessor, qq.v.*: The Penguin Book of Australian Verse 1958. *See also J. Le G. Brereton 1948, W. G. Hay 1919, H. McCrae 1944.*

Howell, Peter Anthony, 1938- . Thomas Arnold the Younger in Van Diemen's Land 1964.

Howitt, Alfred William, 1830-1908. The Native Tribes of South-East Australia 1904. *With L. Fison, q.v.*: Kamilaroi and Kurnai 1880.

Howitt, William, 1792-1879. A Boy's Adventures in the Wilds of Australia 1854, Land, Labour and Gold '55, Tallangetta '57, The History of Discovery in Australia and N.Z. '65.

‡Hudson, Flexmore, 1913- . As Iron Hills 1944, Pools of the Cinnabar Range '59. *Ed.*: Poetry 1941-47.

Hughes, Randolph, 1890-1956. C. J. Brennan 1934.

Hughes, William Morris, 1864-1952. Crusts and Crusades 1947, Policies and Potentates 1950. *See also L. F. Fitzhardinge 1964, W. F. Whyte 1957.*

‡Hume, Fergus, 1859-1932. The Mystery of a Hansom Cab 1886.

Humphries, Walter Richard, 1890-1951. Patrolling in Papua 1923.

§Humphris, Edith, . Life of Adam Lindsay Gordon 1933. *With D. Sladen, q.v.*: Adam Lindsay Gordon and His Friends 1912.

Hungerford, Thomas Arthur Guy, 1915- . The Ridge and the River 1952, Riverslake '53, Sowers of the Wind '54, Shake the Golden Bough '63, A Million Square '69. *Ed.*: Australian Signpost 1956.

*Hunt, Hugh, 1911- . The Making of the Australian Theatre 1960.

Hunter, John, 1737-1821. Historical Journal 1793. *See also J. J. Auchmuty 1968.*

‡Hurley, Frank, 1890-1962. Shackleton's Argonauts 1948. *See also F. Legg & T. Hurley 1966.*

Hutton, Geoffrey, 1909- . Melba 1962.

*Huxley, Elspeth, 1907- . Their Shining Eldorado 1967.

*Huxley, Thomas Henry, 1825-95. *See 1847.*

Huybers, Jessie, *see* 'Tasma'.

Hyde, Victor Wyalong, 1902-59. Gregory Blaxland 1958.

‡Idriess, Ion, 1890- . Madman's Island 1927, Lasseter's Last Ride '31, Flynn of the Inland '32, The Desert Column '32, The Cattle King '36.

Iggulden, John, 1917- . Breakthrough 1960, Storms of Summer '60, The Clouded Sky '64, Dark Stranger '66. *Ed.*: Summer's Tales '66.

Ingamells, Rex, 1913-55. Gumtops 1935, Forgotten People '36, Sun-Freedom '38, Memory of Hills '40, News of the Sun '42, Content are the Quiet Ranges '43, Unknown Land '43, Selected Poems '44, Yera '45, Come Walkabout '48, Handbook of Australian Literature '49, The Great South Land '51, Aranda Boy '52, Of Us Now Living '52, William Gay '52. *Ed.*: Venture 1937-40, Jindyworobak Anthology 1938-41. *With Ian Tilbrook, q.v.*: Conditional Culture 1938.

Ingleton, Geoffrey Chapman, 1908- . Charting a Continent 1944. *Ed.*: True Patriots All 1952.

‡Inglis, Kenneth Stanley, 1929- . Hospital and Community 1958.

Inglis Moore, *see* Moore.

'Iota', *see* Caffyn, K. M.

Ireland, David, 1927- . Image in the Clay 1964, The Chantic Bird '68.

'Ironbark', *see* Gibson, G. H.

Irvin, Eric, 1908- . A Soldier's Miscellany 1945, A Suit for Everyman '68.

Irvin, Margaret, 1916- . The Rock and the Pool 1967.

‡Jack, Robert Logan, 1845-1921. Northmost Australia 1921.

'James, Brian' [John Tierney], 1892- . First Furrow 1944, Cookabundy Ridge '46, The Advancement of Spencer Button '50, The Bunyip of Barney's Elbow '56, Hopeton High '63, The Big Burn '65. *Ed.*: Selected Australian Stories 1959, Australian Short Stories '63.

James, Florence, 1904- . *With D. Cusack, q.v.*: Four Winds and a Family 1947, Come In Spinner '51.

James, Gwynydd Francis, 1912- . *Ed.*: A Homestead History (A. Joyce, q.v.) 1942.

James, John Stanley ['Julian Thomas', 'The Vagabond'], 1843-96. The Vagabond Papers 1877-78. *Ed.*: The Vagabond Annual 1877.

*Jebb, Richard, 1841-1905. Studies in Colonial Nationalism 1905.

‡Jeffery, Walter James, 1861-1922. *With L. Becke, q.v.*: A First Fleet Family 1895, The Mutineer '98.

Jenks, Edward, 1861-1939. The Government of Victoria 1891, The History of the Australasian Colonies '95.

Jephcott, Sydney Wheeler, 1864-1951. The Secrets of the South 1892, Penetralia 1912.

*Jevons, William Stanley, 1835-82. *See 1854.*

Jindyworobak Anthology. 1938-53.

Johns, Fred, 1868-1932. An Australian Biographical Dictionary 1934. *Ed.*: Johns's Notable Australians 1906-21, Who's Who in Australia 1922-32.

Johnson, Colin, 1938- . Wild Cat Falling 1965.

Johnson, Richard, 1753-1827. Address 1794. *See also J. Bonwick 1898, W. H. Rainey, The Real Richard Johnson 1947.*

‡Johnston, George, 1912- . My Brother Jack 1964, The Australians '66, Clean Straw for Nothing '69. *With C. Clift, q.v.*: High Valley 1949.

Johnston, Grahame, 1929- . *Ed.*: Australian Literary Criticism 1962.

Jones, Evan, 1931-   . Inside the Whale 1960, Understandings '67, Kenneth Mackenzie '69.

*Jones, Joseph, 1908-   . Ed.: Image of Australia 1962.

Jones, Suzanne Holly, 1944-   . Harry's Child 1964.

Jorgenson, Jorgen, 1780-1841. A Shred of Autobiography 1835, '38. See also J. F. Hogan 1891, F. Clune & P. R. Stephensen 1954.

Jose, Arthur Wilberforce, 1863-1934. A Short History of Australasia 1899, The Royal Australian Navy '28, Builders and Pioneers of Australia '28, The Romantic Nineties '33. Ed.: Australian Encyclopedia 1925-26. As 'Ishmael Dare': Sun and Cloud on River and Sea 1888.

Journal of Australasia. 1856-58.

Joyce, Alfred, 1821-1901. A Homestead History (ed. G. F. James, q.v.) 1942.

Joyce, Roger Bilbrough, 1924-   . New Guinea 1960. Ed.: Early Constitutional Development in Australia 1963 (see Melbourne 1934). Ed. with P. D. Edwards, q.v.: Australia 1967 (see Trollope 1873).

Jury, Charles Rischbeith, 1894-1958. Love and the Virgins 1929, Galahad, Selenemia and Poems '39, Icarius '55, The Sun in Servitude '61.

'Keese, Oliné', see Leakey, Caroline.

Keesing, Nancy, 1923-   . Imminent Summer 1951, Three Men and Sydney '55, By Gravel and Gun '63, Douglas Stewart '65, Showground Sketchbook '68. Ed.: Gold Fever '67. Ed. with Douglas Stewart, q.v.: Australian Bush Ballads 1955, Old Bush Songs '57, The Pacific Book of Bush Ballads '67.

Kellaway, Frank, 1922-   . A Straight Furrow 1960, The Quest for Golden Dan '62.

Kellow, Henry Arthur, 1881-1935. Queensland Poets 1930.

Kelly, Gwen, 1922-   . There is No Refuge 1961, The Red Boat '68.

Kendall, Henry, 1839-82. Poems and Songs 1862, Leaves From Australian Forests '69, Songs from the Mountains '80, Orara '81, Poems (Sutherland) '86, Poems (Stevens) 1920, Selected Poems (Moore) '57, (AP) '63, Poetical Works (Reed) '66. See also T. T. Reed 1960, A. G. Stephens 1928.

Keneally, Thomas, 1935-   . The Place at Whitton 1964, The Fear '65, Bring Larks and Heroes '67, Three Cheers for the Paraclete '68, The Survivor '69.

Kennedy, Donald, 1928-   . Charles Sturt 1958.

Kennedy, Edward,   . Blacks and Bushrangers 1889.

Kennedy, Victor, 1895-1952. Flaunted Banners 1941. With N. Palmer, q.v.: Bernard O'Dowd 1954.

Keon, Michael, 1918-   . The Durian Tree 1960.

Kerr, Doris Boake, see 'Boake, Capel'.

Kershaw, Alister, 1921-   . The Lonely Verge 1943, Excellent Stranger '44, Defeat by Time Past '47.

Kiddle, Margaret, 1914-58. Moonbeam Stairs 1945, West of Sunset '49, Caroline Chisholm '50, Men of Yesterday '61.

King, Hazel,   . Richard Bourke 1963.

King, Phillip Parker, 1791-1856. Narrative of a Survey 1826.

‡Kingsley, Henry, 1830-76. The Recollections of Geoffry Hamlyn 1859, The Hillyars and the Burtons '65, Tales of Old Travel Re-narrated '69, The Two Cadets '71, Eyre's March and The March of Charles Sturt '72, Reginald Hetherege '74. See also S. M. Ellis, Henry Kingsley 1931.

*Kipling, Rudyard, 1865-1936. See 1891.

'Kirmess, C. H.' [unidentified]. The Australian Crisis 1909.

Kippax, Harold Gemmell, 1920-   . Intro. to: Three Australian Plays 1963. Contrib. to: Australian Society (Davies & Encel) 1965.

Knowles, Conrad Theodore, 1810-44. Salathiel 1842.

Koch, Christopher, 1932-   . The Boys in the Island 1958, Across the Sea Wall '65.

'Kodak', see O'Ferrall, E. F.

Kramer, Leonie Judith, née Gibson, 1924-   . Under maiden name: Henry Handel Richardson and Some of Her Sources 1954. As L. J. Kramer: A Companion to Australia Felix '62, Myself When Laura '66, Henry Handel Richardson '67. See also H. H. Richardson 1910.

Labillière, Francis Peter, 1840-95. Early History of the Colony of Victoria 1878-79.

‡Lambert, Eric, 1921-66. Twenty Thousand Thieves 1951, The Veterans '54, The Five Bright Stars '54, Watermen '56, The Dark Backward '58, Ballarat '62.

‡Lamond, Henry George, 1885-1969. Tooth and Talon 1934.

La Nauze, John Andrew, 1911-   . Political Economy in Australia 1949, The

La Nauze—*contd*
Hopetoun Blunder '57, Alfred Deakin (G) '62, (B) '65. *Ed.*: The Federal Story (Deakin) 1963 (*see* 1944), Federated Australia (Deakin) '68. *Ed. with R. M. Crawford, q.v.*: The Crisis in Victorian Politics (Deakin) 1957.

*'Lancaster, G. B.' [Edith Joan Lyttleton], 1874-1945. Jim of the Ranges 1910, Pageant '33.

Landolt, Esther, 1893-1943. Ewige Herde 1942, Namenlos '47.

Landor, Edward Willson, 1811-78. The Bushman 1847.

Landsborough, William, 1825-86. Journal of Expedition 1862.

Lane, William, 1861-1917. *Ed.*: The Boomerang 1887-92. As '*John Miller*': The Working Man's Paradise 1892. *See also L. Ross 1937, G. Souter 1968.*

‡Lang, John Dunmore, 1799-1878. A Historical and Statistical Account of N.S.W. 1834, Transportation and Colonisation '37, Freedom and Independence '52, Poems Sacred and Secular '72. *Ed.*: The Colonist 1835-40. *See also A. Gilchrist 1951, D. Macmillan 1962.*

‡Lang, John George, 1816-64. The Forger's Wife 1855, Botany Bay '59.

Langley, Eve, 1908- . The Pea Pickers 1942, White Topee '54.

Langloh Parker, Mrs K., *see* Parker.

‡Latham, Mavis,   . John Batman 1962. As *Mavis Thorpe Clark*: The Brown Land Was Green 1956.

Lavater, Louis, 1867-1953. Blue Days and Grey Days 1915, A Lover's Ephemeris '17, This Green Mortality '22. *Ed.*: The Sonnet in Australasia 1926, *Verse* '29-'33.

Law, Phillip Garth, 1912- . Australia and the Antarctic 1962. *With J. Béchervaise q.v.*: ANARE 1957.

Lawler, Ray, 1921- . The Summer of the Seventeenth Doll 1957, The Piccadilly Bushman '61, The Unshaven Cheek *prod.* '63, A Breach in the Wall *prod.* '67.

*Lawrence, David Herbert, 1885-1930. Kangaroo 1923. *With M. L. Skinner, q.v.*: The Boy in the Bush 1924.

Lawson, Bertha (*née* Bredt), 1876-1957. My Henry Lawson 1943.

Lawson, Bertha, 1900- . *Ed. with J. Le Gay Brereton, q.v.*: Henry Lawson, by His Mates 1931.

Lawson, Henry, 1867-1922. Short Stories in Prose and Verse 1894, While the Billy Boils '96, In the Days When the World Was Wide '96, On the Track 1900, Over the Sliprails 1900, Verses Popular and Humorous 1900, Joe Wilson and His Mates '01, Children of the Bush '02, When I Was King '05, The Rising of the Court '10, Mateship '11, Triangles of Life '13, Poetical Works '25, Stories (Mann) '65, Best Stories (Mann) '66, Humorous Stories (Mann) '67, Collected Verse (Roderick) '67, '68, '69. *See also J. Le G. Brereton & B. Lawson 1931, F. J. Broomfield 1930, B. Lawson 1943, G. Mackaness 1951, S. Murray-Smith 1962, W. H. Pearson 1968, 'Denton Prout' 1963, C. Roderick 1959, '60, '61, '66, '67, W. Stone 1954, J. Wright 1967.*

Lawson, Sylvia, 1932- . Mary Gilmore 1966.

‡Lawson, Will, 1876-1957. When Cobb and Co. Was King 1936, Bill the Whaler '44. *Ed.*: Australian Bush Songs and Ballads 1944. *See also B. Lawson 1943.*

Leakey, Caroline, ['Oliné Keese'], 1827-81. The Broad Arrow 1859.

‡Lee, Ida, c. 1875-1943. The Bush Fire 1897, Early Explorers in Australia 1925.

Legg, Frank, 1906-66. War Correspondent 1964, The Gordon Bennett Story '65, Cats on Velvet '66. *With T. Hurley*: Once More on My Adventure 1966.

Lehmann, Geoffrey, 1940- . A Voyage of Lions 1968. *With Les. Murray, q.v.*: The Ilex Tree 1965.

Leichhardt, Ludwig, 1813-48? Journal 1847, Letters 1968. *See also A. H. Chisholm 1941, R. Erdos 1963.*

‡Lett, Lewis, 1878-1966. Sir Hubert Murray of Papua 1949.

Levy, Michael, 1889- . Governor George Arthur 1953.

Lewis, John, 1842-1923. Fought and Won 1922.

Lhotsky, John, 1800-?. A Journey from Sydney to the Australian Alps 1835.

Light, William, 1786-1839. A Brief Journal 1839. *See also G. Dutton 1960, M. P. Mayo 1937.*

§Liljegren, Sten Bodvar, 1885-   . *See* 1962, 1964.

Lindsay, Sir Daryl, 1890- . The Leafy Tree 1965.

‡Lindsay, Harold Arthur, 1900-69. *With N. B. Tindale, q.v.*: The First Walkabout 1954.

‡Lindsay, Jack, 1900- . Fauns and Ladies 1924, Life Rarely Tells '58, The Roaring Twenties '60, Fanfrolico and After '62. *Ed.*: Poetry in Australia 1923, The *London Aphrodite* '28-'29.

Lindsay, Jane, 1920- . Kurrajong 1945.

Lindsay, Joan [*Lady* Lindsay], 1896- .
Time Without Clocks 1962, Facts Soft
and Hard '64, Picnic at Hanging Rock
'67.

Lindsay, *Sir* Lionel, 1874-1961. Conrad
Martens 1920, Comedy of Life '67.

Lindsay, Norman, 1879-1969. A Curate in
Bohemia 1913, The Magic Pudding '18,
Creative Effort '20, Hyperborea '28,
Madam Life's Lovers '29, Redheap '30,
Miracles By Arrangement '32, The
Cautious Amorist '32, Saturdee '33,
Pan in the Parlour '34, The Flyaway
Highway '36, Age of Consent '38, The
Cousin from Fiji '45, Halfway to Any-
where '47, Dust or Polish? '50, Bohe-
mians of the *Bulletin* '65, The Scribblings
of an Idle Mind '66, Rooms and Houses
'68. *See also J. Hetherington 1961,
D. Lindsay 1965, Jack Lindsay 1958, '60,
'62, L. Lindsay 1967, R. Lindsay 1967.*

‡Lindsay, Philip, 1906-58. I'd Live the
Same Life Over 1941.

Lindsay, Rose, 1881- . Ma and Pa 1964,
Model Wife '67.

Loch, F. S., *see* 'Loghe, Sydney De'.

Locke-Elliott, Sumner, 1917- . Interval
1942. *As Sumner Locke Elliott*: Careful,
He Might Hear You 1963, Some Doves
and Pythons '66, Rusty Bugles (*see
Hanger*) '68. *See also 1948.*

‡Lockwood, Douglas, 1918- . Crocodiles and Other People 1959.

'Loghe, Sydney De' [Frederick Sydney
Loch], 1889-1954. The Straits Impreg-
nable 1916, Pelican Pool '17. *See J. Nan
Kivell Loch, A Fringe of Blue 1968.*

London Aphrodite, The. 1928-29. Ed. Jack
Lindsay & P. R. Stephensen, qq.v.

Lone Hand, The. 1907-21. *See also C. H.
Hannaford 1967.*

Long, Gavin, 1901-68. To Benghazi 1952,
Greece, Crete and Syria '53, The Final
Campaigns '63, Macarthur '69. *Ed.*:
Australia in the War of 1939-1945.

Long, Richard Hoopell, 1874-1948. Verses
1917.

'Lovegood, John', *see* Watson, E. L.
Grant.

Loveless, George, 1797-1874. The Victims
of Whiggery 1837.

Lowe, Eric, 1889-1963. Salute to Freedom
1938, Framed in Hardwood '40,
Beyond the 19 Counties '48, O Willing
Hearts '51.

‡Lowe, Robert, *Viscount* Sherbrooke,
1811-92. Poems of a Life 1885. *Ed.*: The
Atlas 1835-40. *See also J. F. Hogan 1893,
A. P. Martin 1893, and Ruth Knight,
Illiberal Liberal 1966.*

Lower, Lennie, 1903-47. Here's Luck 1930.
See also C. Pearl 1963.

Lurie, Morris, 1938- . Rappaport 1966,
The London Jungle Adventures of
Charlie Hope '68, Happy Times '69,
27th Annual African Hippopotamus
Race '69.

Lyttleton, Edith Joan, *see* 'Lancaster, G. B.'

§Lytton, Edward Bulwer [*Lord* Lytton],
1803-73. The Caxtons 1850.

'M.C.', *see* Martin, Catherine.

Macainsh, Noel, 1926- . *Contrib. to*:
Eight by Eight (*see* Buckley) 1963.

Macarthur, James, 1798-1867. New South
Wales 1837 (*but see comment* ad loc.).

Macartney, Frederick Thomas Bennett,
1887- . Dewed Petals 1912, Earthen
Vessels '13, Commercium '17, In War
Time '18, Poems '20, Something for
Tokens '22, A Sweep of Lute Strings '29,
Hard Light '33, Preferences '41, Ode of
Our Times '44, Gaily the Troubadour
'46, Tripod for Homeward Incense '47,
Furnley Maurice '55, Australian Literary
Essays '57, Selected Poems '61, Proof
Against Failure '67. *With E. Morris
Miller, q.v.*: Australian Literature 1956.
See also L. Lavater 1926.

Macartney, John Arthur, 1834-1917.
Reminiscences of a Pioneer 1909.

McAuley, James, 1917- . Under Aldebaran 1946, A Vision of Ceremony '56,
The End of Modernity '59, C. J.
Brennan '63, Edmund Spenser and
George Eliot '63, Selected Poems (AP)
'63, Captain Quiros '64, A Primer of
English Versification '66, Surprises of
the Sun '69. *Ed.*: Quadrant 1956- . *See
also 'Ern Malley'; V. Smith 1965.*

MacCallum, Mungo, 1913- . A Voyage
in Love 1956, Son of Mars '63.

McCarthy, Dudley, 1911- . South West
Pacific Area 1959.

McCombie, Thomas, 1813?-69. Arabin
1845, The History of the Colony of
Victoria '58, Australian Sketches '61,
Frank Henly '68.

McCrae, George Gordon, 1833-1927.
Mämba 1867, The Story of Balladeädro
'67, The Man in the Iron Mask '73, A
Rosebud from the Garden of the Taj '83,
Fleet and Convoy 1915, John Rous '18.
*See also Hugh McCrae 1935, H. F.
Chaplin 1967.*

McCrae, Georgiana, 1804-90. Journal [ed.
by Hugh McCrae] 1934. *See also H. F.
Chaplin 1967.*

132

McCrae, Hugh, 1876-1958. Satyrs and Sunlight: Silvarum Libri 1909, Colombine '20, Idyllia '22, Satyrs and Sunlight '28, My Father and My Father's Friends '35, The Mimshi Maiden '38, Poems '39, Forests of Pan '44, Voice of the Forest '45, Story Book Only '48, The Ship of Heaven '51, Best Poems (Howarth) '61, Selected Poems (AP) '66. *Ed.*: Georgiana's Journal 1934. *See also A. G. Steven 1925, H. F. Chaplin 1967.*

McCuaig, Ronald, 1908- . Vaudeville 1938, The Wanton Goldfish '41, Tales Out of Bed '44, Quod Ronald McCuaig '46, The Ballad of Bloodthirsty Bessie '61. *See also L. Stone 1911.*

McCulloch, Samuel Clyde, 1916- . George Gipps 1966.

McDonald, Nan, 1921- . Pacific Sea 1947, The Lonely Fire '54, The Lighthouse '59, Selected Poems '69.

‡McGrath, Raymond, 1903- . Seven Songs of Meadow Lane 1924.

McGregor, Craig, 1933- . Profile of Australia 1966, The High Country '67, People, Politics and Pop '68, To Sydney With Love '68.

‡McGuire, Paul, 1903- . *With others*: The Australian Theatre 1948.

McInnes, Graham, 1912- . The Road to Gundagai 1965, Humping My Bluey '66, Finding a Father '67, Goodbye Melbourne Town '68.

‡Mack, Amy Eleanor, c. 1877-1939. Bushland Stories 1910.

‡Mack, Louise, 1874-1935. Teens 1897, Dreams in Flower 1901.

‡Mackaness, George, 1882-1968. Life of Bligh 1931, Banks '36, Phillip '37, Annotated Biblio. of Henry Lawson '51, Bibliomania '65. *Ed.*: Australian Short Stories 1928, Poets of Australia '46, Fourteen Journeys over the Blue Mts 1950-51. *Ed. with B. Stevens, q.v.*: Sels from Australian Poets 1913. *With W. Stone, q.v.*: Books of the *Bulletin* 1955. *See also 'Henry Melville' 1835, M. M. Robinson 1810, R. L. Stevenson 1890.*

McKee Wright, David, *see* Wright.

Mackellar, Dorothea, 1885-1968. The Witch Maid 1914.

McKellar, John Alexander Ross, 1904-32. Twenty-six 1932, Collected Poems '46.

*MacKenzie, Jeanne, 1922- . Australian Paradox 1961.

Mackenzie, Kenneth ['Seaforth Mackenzie'], 1913-55. *Under own name*: Our Earth 1937, The Moonlit Doorway '44, Selected Poems (Stewart) '61. *As 'Sea-forth Mackenzie'*: The Young Desire It 1937, Chosen People '38, Dead Men Rising '51, The Refuge '54. *See also E. Jones 1969.*

Mackenzie, Seaforth Simpson, 1883-1955. The Australians at Rabaul 1927.

Mackerras, Catherine, 1899- . The Hebrew Melodist 1963.

‡McKie, Ronald, 1909- . This Was Singapore 1942, Proud Echo '53, The Heroes '60.

McKinney, John Phillip, 1891-1966. The Crucible 1935, The Well (*see* Hanger) '68.

McLaren, Ian, 1912- . C. J. Dennis 1961.

‡McLaren, Jack, 1887-1954. My Crowded Solitude 1926.

‡McLean, Donald, 1905- . The Roaring Days 1960, The World Turned Upside Down '62.

McLean, Elizabeth, *see* 'Roland, Betty'.

McLennan, Lex, 1909- . The Spirit of the West 1943.

McLeod, Alan Lindsey, 1928- . *Ed.*: The Commonwealth Pen 1961, The Pattern of Australian Culture '63, Walt Whitman in Australia and N.Z. '64.

'McLeod, *Mrs* Alick', *see* Martin, Catherine.

'McLeod, Fiona', *see* Sharp, William.

‡Macmillan, David Stirling, 1925- . A Squatter Went to Sea 1957, John Dunmore Lang '62, Edgeworth David '65, John McDouall Stuart '66, Charles Nicholson '69.

McNamara, Barbara, *see* 'O'Conner, Elizabeth'.

Maconochie, Alexander, 1787-1860. Thoughts on Convict Management 1838. *See also J. V. Barry 1958.*

McPheat, William Scott, 1929- . John Flynn (B) 1963, (G) '64.

Madgwick, *Sir* Robert Bowden, 1905- . Immigration into Eastern Australia 1937.

Madigan, Cecil Thomas, 1889-1947. Central Australia 1936, Crossing the Dead Heart '46.

Malouf, David, 1934- . *Contrib. to*: Four Poets 1962.

'Malley, Ern', *see* 'Ern Malley'.

‡Manifold, John, 1915- . The Death of Ned Kelly 1941, Trident '44, Selected Verse '46, Nightmares and Sunhorses '61, Who Wrote the Ballads? '64. *Ed.*: The Penguin Australian Song Book 1964.

Mann, Cecil, 1896-1967. The River 1945, Light in the Valley '47, Three Stories '63. *Sel.*: The Stories of Henry Lawson 1965, Best Stories '66, Humorous Stories '67.

Mann, David Dickenson, 1775?-?. The Present Picture of N.S.W. 1811.

Mann, Leonard, 1895- . Flesh in Armour 1932, Human Drift '35, A Murder in Sydney '37, The Plumed Voice '38, Mountain Flat '39, Poems from the Mask '41, The Go-Getter '42, The Delectable Mountains '44, Elegiac and Other Poems '57, Andrea Caslin '59, Venus Half-Caste '63.

Manning, Frederic, 1882-1935. As 'Private 19022': The Middle Parts of Fortune: Somme and Ancre (Her Privates We) 1929, '30.

Mansfield, Bruce Edgar, 1926- . Australian Democrat 1965.

Manuscripts. 1931-35.

Marks, Harry, 1923- . The Heart is Where the Hurt Is 1966.

Marshall, Alan, 1902- . These Are My People 1944, Tell Us About the Turkey, Jo '46, Ourselves Writ Strange (These Were My Tribesmen) '48, '65, How Beautiful are Thy Feet '49, Pull Down the Blind '49, Bumping into Friends '50, People of the Dreamtime '52, I Can Jump Puddles '55, How's Andy Going? '56, The Gay Provider '61, This is the Grass '62, In Mine Own Heart '63, Whispering in the Wind '69.

Marshall, Alan John, 1911-67. *With R. Drysdale, q.v.*: Journey Among Men 1962.

Martin, Allan William, 1928- . Henry Parkes 1964.

‡Martin, Arthur Patchett, 1851-1902. Fanshawe 1882, Life and Letters of Lowe '93, The Beginnings of an Australian Literature '98. *Ed.*: An Easter Omelette of Prose and Verse 1879, Oak-Bough and Wattle-Blossom '88.

Martin, Catherine, 1847-1937. The Incredible Journey 1923. *Anon.*: An Australian Girl 1890, The Old Roof-Tree 1906. *As 'Mrs Alick McLeod'*: The Silent Sea 1892. *As 'M.C.'*: The Explorers 1874.

Martin, David [*né* Ludwig Detsinyi], 1915- . Battlefields and Girls 1942, Trident (*see Manifold*) '44, Tiger Bay '46, The Shepherd and the Hunter '46, The Shoes Men Walk In '47, The Stones of Bombay '49, From Life '53, Poems '58, Spiegel the Cat '61, The Young Wife '62, The Hero of Too '65, The Gift '66, The King Between '66, The Idealist '68, Where a Man Belongs '69. *Contrib. to*: Eight by Eight (*see Buckley*) 1963.

Martin, *Sir* James, 1820-86. The Australian Sketch Book 1838.

Martin, Robert Montgomery, c. 1803-68. History of the British Colonies 1834, History of Australasia '36.

Mathers, Peter, 1931- . Trap 1966.

Mathew, Ray, 1929- . With Cypress Pine 1951, Song and Dance '56, South of the Equator '61, A Bohemian Affair '61, A Spring Song '61, Miles Franklin '63, Charles Blackman '65, The Joys of Possession '67, We Find the Bunyip (*see Hanger*) '68. *With M. Abdullah, q.v.*: The Time of the Peacock 1965.

Matthews, Harley, 1889-1968. Under the Open Sky 1912, Saints and Soldiers '18, Two Brothers (*see Slessor*) '31, Vintage '38, The Breaking of the Drought '40, Patriot's Progress '65.

Matthews, John Pengwerne, 1927- . Tradition in Exile 1962.

Mattingley, David, 1922- . Matthew Flinders and George Bass 1961.

Maughan, Barton, 1912- . Tobruk and El Alamein 1966.

'Maurice, Furnley' [Frank Wilmot], 1881-1942. *As Wilmot*: Some Verses 1903, Some More Verses '04. *Anon.*: Unconditioned Songs 1913. *As 'Furnley Maurice'*: To God: From the Weary Nations 1917, The Bay and Padie Book '17, Eyes of Vigilance '20, Ways and Means '20, Arrows of Longing '21, Romance '22, The Gully '29, Melbourne Odes '34, Poems (Serle) '44. *Ed. with G. H. Cowling, q.v.*: Australian Essays 1935. *See also H. Anderson 1955, F. T. Macartney 1955, V. Palmer 1942, W. H. Wilde*, Three Radicals *1969*.

Mawson, *Sir* Douglas, 1882-1958. The Home of the Blizzard 1915. *See next and T. G. Taylor 1962.*

Mawson, Paquita [*Lady* Mawson, *née* Delprat], 1891- . Vision of Steel 1958, Mawson of Antarctica '64.

Maynard, Don, 1937- . *Contrib. to*: Four Poets (*see Malouf*) 1962.

Mayo, Mary Penelope, 1889- . The Life and Letters of Col. William Light 1937.

Meanjin. 1940- . Ed. C. B. Christesen, q.v. *See M. Tipping*, Meanjin Quarterly Index *1969*.

Melbourne, Alexander Clifford Vernon, 1888-1943. W. C. Wentworth 1934, Early Constitutional Development in Australia '34, (ed. Joyce) '63.

Melbourne Advertiser. 1838.

Melbourne Critical Review. 1958-64. Since 1965 titled *Critical Review.*

Melbourne Herald. See 1849, '69.

Melbourne Morning Herald. 1849-69.

Melbourne Review. 1876-85. See also *1883.*
Melbourne University Magazine. 1907- .
Meller, Leslie, 1892-   . Quartette 1932,
A Leaf of Laurel '33.
Mellor, David Paver, 1903- . The Role
of Science and Industry 1958.
'Melville, Henry' [Henry Saxelby Melville
Wintle], 1799-1873. The Bushrangers
1834, The History of the Island of Van
Diemen's Land '35.
Mennell, Philip, d. 1905. *Ed.*: In Aus-
tralian Wilds 1889, Dictionary of Aus-
tralasian Biography '92.
'Menippus', *see* Sealy, Robert.
Menzies, *Sir* Robert Gordon, 1894-   .
Speech is of Time 1958, Afternoon
Light '67.
Mercury (Hobart). *See 1854.*
Meredith, John, 1920-   . The Wild
Colonial Boy 1960. *With H. Anderson,*
q.v.: Folk Songs of Australia 1968.
‡Meredith, Louisa Anne, 1812-95. Notes
and Sketches of N.S.W. 1844, My
Home in Tasmania '52, Phoebe's Mother
'69, Nellie '82.
Michael, James Lionel, 1824-68. Songs
Without Music 1857, Sir Archibald
Yelverton '58, John Cumberland '60.
See J. Sheridan Moore, The Life and
Genius of J. L. Michael *1868.*
Miles, Peter, 1921- . Pacific Moon 1945.
Miller, Edmund Morris, 1881-1964. Aus-
tralian Literature 1940, Pressmen and
Governors '52. *With F. T. Macartney,*
q.v.: Australian Literature 1956. *See also*
W. G. Hay 1919.
'Miller, John', *see* Lane, William.
'Mills, Martin', *see* Boyd, Martin.
‡Mills, Reginald Charles, 1886-1952. The
Colonisation of Australia 1915.
Mitchel, John, 1815-75. Jail Journal 1854.
Mitchell, Alexander George, 1911- . The
Pronunciation of English in Australia
1946. *Ed. with R. G. Howarth, q.v.*:
Southerly 1939-44. *See also J. F. Mortlock*
1864.
‡Mitchell, Elyne, 1913- . Images in
Water 1947.
Mitchell, George Dean, 1894-1961. Backs
to the Wall 1937, The Awakening '37.
‡Mitchell, Mary, 1892-   . A Warning
to Wantons 1934, Uncharted Country
'63.
‡Mitchell, *Sir* Thomas Livingstone, 1792-
1855. Three Expeditions etc. 1838,
Journal etc. '48, The Lusiad of Camoens
'54. *See also J. H. L. Cumpston 1954,*
L. Gardiner 1962.
Moir, John Kinmont, 1893-1958. *Ed.*:
Shaw Neilson 1942.

Moll, Ernest George, 1900- . Sedge Fire
1927, Native Moments '31, Blue
Interval '35, Cut From Mulga '40,
Brief Waters '45, Beware the Cuckoo
'47, The Waterhole '48, The Lifted
Spear '53, Poems '57, Below These
Hills '57, The Rainbow Serpent '62.
Moloney, Patrick, 1843-1904. Sonnets ad
Innuptam 1879.
Monckton, Charles Arthur Whitmore,
1872-1936. Some Experiences of a New
Guinea Resident Magistrate 1921, Last
Days in New Guinea '22, New Guinea
Recollections '34.
§Moncrieff, William Thomas, 1794-1857.
Van Diemen's Land 1830.
Monitor (Sydney).ˑ1826-41.
Montgomery, Alexander, 1847-1922. Five
Skull Island 1897.
Month, The. 1857-58.
‡Moodie Heddle, Enid, 1904- . Solitude
1937, Australian Literature Now '49.
Moore, Tom Inglis, 1901- . The Half
Way Sun 1935, The Third Spring '37,
Adagio in Blue '38, Emu Parade '41,
Six Australian Poets '42, We're Going
Through '45, Bayonet and Grass '57,
Rolf Boldrewood '68. *Ed.*: Australia
Writes 1953, Kendall '57, '63, A Book
of Australia '61, From the Ballads to
Brennan '64. *Introd.*: Mary Gilmore
1965. *Ed. with W. Moore, q.v.*: Best
Australian One-Act Plays 1937.
Moore, William, 1868-1937. City Sketches
1905, Studio Sketches '06, The Story of
Australian Art '34. *Ed. with T. I. Moore,*
q.v.: Best Australian One-Act Plays
1937.
‡Moorehead, Alan, 1910- . Rum Jungle
1953, Gallipoli '56, Cooper's Creek '63,
The Fatal Impact '66, Darwin and the
Beagle '69.
Morant, Harry Harbord ['The Breaker'],
1865-1902. Verse *in F. Fox 1902. See*
also F. M. Cutlack 1962, A. J. Buchanan
1911.
'Mordaunt, Elinor', *see* Clowes, E. M.
Moreton Bay Courier. 1846-1933.
Morgan, John, 1792?-1866. The Life and
Adventures of William Buckley 1852.
Morphett, George Cummins, 1901-63. The
Life and Letters of Sir John Morphett
1936, Sir James Hurtle Fisher '55.
Morphett, Tony, 1938- . Mayor's Nest
1964, Dynasty '67, Thorskald '69.
Morris, Edward Ellis, 1843-1902. A
Memoir of George Higinbotham 1895,
Austral English '98.
'Morris, Julian', *see* West, Morris.

'O'Brien, John' [Patrick Joseph Hartigan], 1879-1952. Around the Boree Log 1921, On Darlinghurst Hill '52, The Parish of St Mel's '54.

O'Brien, Patricia Anne, 1945- . A. D. Hope 1968, Randolph Stow '68. *With E. Robinson*: Judith Wright 1968.

O'Brien, William Smith, 1803-64. Principles of Government 1856.

Observer, The. 1958-61. Ed. D. Horne, q.v.

O'Collins, Gerald, 1931- . Patrick McMahon Glynn 1965.

'O'Conner, Elizabeth' [Barbara McNamara], 1913- . Steak for Breakfast 1958, The Irishman '60, Find a Woman '63, The Chinee Bird '66, A Second Helping '69.

§Odeen, Elizabeth, 1924- . Maurice Guest, a Study 1963.

Odgers, George James, 1916- . Air War Against Japan 1957.

O'Dowd, Bernard, 1866-1953. Dawnward? 1903, The Silent Land '06, Dominions of the Boundary '07, The Seven Deadly Sins '09, Poetry Militant '09, The Bush '12, Alma Venus! '21, Poems '41, Fantasies '42, Selected Poems (AP) '63. *See also H. Anderson 1963, 1968, V. Kennedy & N. Palmer 1954, W. H. Wilde*, Three Radicals *1969*.

O'Dwyer, Joseph Henry, 1912- . Poems 1941, The Turning Year '44.

O'Ferrall, Ernest Francis ['Kodak'], 1881-1925. Bodger and the Boarders 1921, Stories '33.

‡Ogilvie, William Henry, 1869-1963. Fair Girls and Gray Horses 1898, Hearts of Gold 1903, My Life in the Open '08, The Australian '16.

*O'Grady, Desmond, 1929- . A Long Way from Home 1966.

‡O'Grady, John ['Nino Culotta'], 1907- . They're a Weird Mob 1957.

O'Hara, John Bernard, 1862-1927. Poems 1918.

'Old Boomerang', *see* Houlding, J. R.

O'Leary, Shawn, 1916- . Spikenard and Bayonet 1941.

‡Oliver, Harold James, 1916- . Shaw Neilson 1968, Louis Stone '68. *Sel.*: Victor Daley (AP) 1963. *See also A. L. McLeod 1961.*

Once Around the Sun. See 1966.

O'Reilly, Dowell, 1865-1923. Tears and Triumph 1913, Five Corners '20, Prose and Verse '24.

O'Reilly, John Boyle, 1844-90. Songs from the Southern Seas 1873, Moondyne '79, Songs, Legends and Ballads '82, The Golden Secret [anon.] '87. *See*

J. J. Roche, Life of J. B. O'Reilly *1891* [inc. complete poems].

Osborne, Charles, 1927- . Kafka 1967, Swansong '68. *Ed.*: Australian Stories of Today 1961, Australian issue of *London Magazine* '62.

‡Ottley, Reginald Leslie, . By the Sandhills of Yamboorah 1965.

Overland. 1954- . Ed. S. Murray-Smith, q.v.

Oxley, John, 1785?-1828. Journals of Two Expeditions 1820. *See also E. Dunlop 1960.*

Page, *Sir* Earle, 1880-1961. Truant Surgeon 1963.

Palmer, Aileen, 1915- . World Without Strangers? 1965.

Palmer, Nettie, 1885-1964. The South Wind 1914, Shadowy Paths '15, Modern Australian Literature '24, H. B. Higgins '31, Talking it Over '32, Fourteen Years '48, Henry Handel Richardson '50. *Ed.*: An Australian Story Book 1928. *With V. Kennedy, q.v.*: Bernard O'Dowd 1954.

Palmer, Vance, 1885-1959. The Forerunners 1915, The World of Men '15, The Camp '20, The Black Horse '24, Cronulla '24, The Man Hamilton '28, Men Are Human '30, The Passage '30, Separate Lives '31, Daybreak '32, The Swayne Family '34, Sea and Spinifex '34, Hurricane '35, Legend for Sanderson '37, National Portraits '40, A. G. Stephens '41, Frank Wilmot (Furnley Maurice) '42, Hail Tomorrow '47, Cyclone '47, Golconda '48, Louis Esson '48, The Legend of the Nineties '54, Let the Birds Fly '55, The Rainbow Bird '57, Seedtime '57, The Big Fellow '59. *As 'Rann Daly'*: The Shantykeeper's Daughter 1920, The Boss of Killara '22, The Enchanted Island '23, The Outpost '24. *Ed.*: Old Australian Bush Songs 1951. *See also H. P. Heseltine 1969.*

Palmer-Archer, Laura, 1864-1929. A Bush Honeymoon 1904.

‡Park, Ruth, . The Harp in the South 1948, Poor Man's Orange '49, The Witch's Thorn '51, A Power of Roses '53, Pink Flannel '55, One-a-pecker, Two-a-pecker '57, The Good-Looking Women '61. *With D. Niland, q.v.*: The Drums Go Bang 1956.

‡Parker, *Mrs* K. Langloh [*née* Catherine Somerville Field, m. (1) K. Langloh Parker, (2) P. R. Stow], 1855?-1940. Australian Legendary Tales 1896, More Australian Legendary Tales '98. *As Catherine Stow*: The Walkabouts of

Parker, *Mrs* K. Langloh—*contd*
Wur-run-nah 1918, Woggheeguy '30.
See also H. Drake-Brockman 1953.
'Parker, Leslie', *see* Thirkell, Angela.
Parkes, *Sir* Henry, 1815-96. Stolen
Moments 1842, Fifty Years in the
Making of Australian History '92.
Cond.: Empire 1850-58. *See also A. W.
Martin 1964.*
Parkin, Ray, 1910- . Out of the Smoke
1960, Into the Smother '63.
‡Partridge, Eric, 1894- . A Charm of
Words 1960.
Pasco, Crawford Aitcheson Denham,
1818-98. A Roving Commission 1897.
Paterson, Andrew Barton ['The Banjo'],
1864-1941. The Man From Snowy
River 1895, Rio Grande's Last Race
1902, An Outback Marriage '06, Salt-
bush Bill '17, Three Elephant Power '17,
Collected Verse '21, The Animals Noah
Forgot '33, Happy Dispatches '34, The
Shearer's Colt '36. *Ed.*: Old Bush Songs
1905. *See also M. Clarke 1885, C.
Semmler 1965, '66, '67.*
Patrick, John, . Weave a Circle
1964, Inapatua '66.
Paull, Raymond Allan, 1906- . Retreat
From Kokoda 1958, Old Walhalla '63.
Pearce, *Sir* George Foster, 1870-1952.
Carpenter to Cabinet 1951. *See also
P. R. Heydon 1965.*
‡Pearl, Cyril, 1906- . Wild Men of
Sydney 1958, Always Morning '60,
Morrison of Peking '67. *Ed.*: The Best
of Lennie Lower 1963.
‡Pearson, Charles Henry, 1830-94.
National Life and Character 1893,
Reviews and Critical Essays '96. *See
also J. Tregenza 1968.*
*Pearson, William Harrison, 1922- .
Henry Lawson Among Maoris 1968.
Pedley, Ethel, 1860?-98. Dot and the
Kangaroo 1899.
Penn-Smith, Frank, 1863-1935. Hang!
1925, The Unexpected '33.
Penton, Brian, 1904-51. Landtakers 1934,
Inheritors '36.
Perry, Thomas Melville, 1927- . Aus-
tralia's First Frontier 1963.
*Perth Gazette and Western Australian
Journal.* 1833-1847. *See also 1847, '64,
'74, '79.*
Pescott, Edward Edgar, 1872-1954. The
Life Story of Joseph Furphy 1938, James
Bonwick 1939.
Petrie, Thomas, 1831-1910. Reminiscences
of Early Queensland 1904 (*see comment
ad loc.*).
‡Phelan, Nancy, 1913- . The River and

the Brook 1962, Serpents in Paradise '67,
A Kingdom by the Sea '69.
Philip, George Blackmore, 1861-1940.
Sixty Years' Recollections 1939.
Phillip, Arthur, 1738-1814. *See 1789 and
also M. Barnard Eldershaw 1938, G.
Mackaness 1938, M. Steven 1962.*
Phillips, Arthur Angell, 1900- . The
Australian Tradition 1958. *Sel.*: Bernard
O'Dowd (AP) 1963. *See also B. Baynton
1902.*
Phillips, Charles, *see* 'Prout, Denton'.
Phillips, Marion, 1881-1932. A Colonial
Autocracy 1909.
‡Phipson, Joan, 1912- . Christmas in the
Sun 1952.
Picot, James, 1906-44. With a Hawk's
Quill 1953.
‡Piddington, Albert Bathurst, 1862-1945.
Spanish Sketches 1916, Worshipful
Masters '29.
Pike, Douglas, 1908- . Paradise of
Dissent 1957, John McDouall Stuart '58,
Australia: the Quiet Continent '62,
Charles Hawker '68. *Ed.*: Australian
Dictionary of Biography 1966, '67, '69.
'Pindar Juvenal' [unidentified]. The Van
Diemen's Land Warriors 1827.
Pitt, Marie Elizabeth Josephine, 1869-1948.
Poems 1925.
Poetry. 1941-47. Ed. F. Hudson, q.v., et al.
Porteous, Richard Sydney ['Standby'],
1897-1963. *As 'Standby'*: Little Known
of These Waters 1945, Sailing Orders
'49, Close to the Wind '55. *Under own
name*: Tambai Island 1955, Brigalow '57,
Tambai Treasure '58, Cattleman '60,
Salvage '63, The Silent Isles '63.
Porter, Hal, 1911- . Short Stories 1942,
The Hexagon '56, A Handful of Pennies
'58, The Tilted Cross '61, A Bachelor's
Children '62, The Watcher on the Cast-
Iron Balcony '63, The Tower '63, The
Cats of Venice '65, Stars of Australian
Stage and Screen '65, The Paper Chase
'66, The Professor '66, The Actors '68,
Elijah's Ravens '68. *See also J. Finch 1966.*
Porter, Peter, 1929- . Once Bitten, Twice
Bitten 1961, Poems Ancient and Modern
'65, Porter Folio '69.
Port Phillip Gazette. 1838-51.
Port Phillip Herald. 1840-49. *See 1849.*
Port Phillip Magazine. 1843.
Port Phillip Patriot and Melbourne Advertiser.
1839-51.
‡Portus, Garnet Vere, 1883-1954. Happy
Highways 1953.
Pothan, Kap, 1929- . A Time to Die 1967.
Powell, Craig, 1940- . A Different Kind
of Breathing 1966, I Learn By Going '68.

‡Pownall, Eve, Mary of Maranoa 1959.

‡Praed, *Mrs* Campbell [*née* Rosa Murray-Prior], 1851-1935. An Australian Heroine 1880, Policy and Passion '81, The Head Station '85, Australian Life '85, Miss Jacobson's Chance '86, The Romance of a Station '89, Outlaw and Lawmaker '93, Mrs Tregaskiss '95, Nulma '97, Dwellers By the River 1902, My Australian Girlhood '02, Fugitive Anne '03, The Maid of the River '05, The Lost Earl of Ellan '06, The Luck of the Leura '07, A Summer Wreath '09, Opal Fire '10, Lady Bridget in the Never Never Land '15, Sister Sorrow '16. *See also C. Roderick 1948.*

‡Pratt, Ambrose, 1874-1944. David Syme 1908.

Prest, Jean, 1930- . Hamilton Hume and William Hovell 1963.

‡Price, *Sir* Archibald Grenfell, 1892- . The Foundation and Settlement of South Australia 1924, Founders and Pioneers of South Australia '28. *Ed.*: The Humanities in Australia 1959.

Prichard, Katharine Susannah, 1883-1969. Clovelly Verses 1913, The Pioneers '15, Windlestraws '16, Black Opal '21, Working Bullocks '26, The Wild Oats of Han '28, Coonardoo '29, Haxby's Circus '30, Kiss on the Lips '32, The Earth Lover '32, Intimate Strangers '37, Brumby Innes '40, Moon of Desire '41, Potch and Colour '44, The Roaring Nineties '46, Golden Miles '48, Winged Seeds '50, N'Goola '59, Child of the Hurricane '63, On Strenuous Wings '65, Subtle Flame '67, Happiness '67, Moggie and Her Circus Pony '67. *See also J. Beasley 1964, H. Drake-Brockman 1967.*

Pringle, John Martin Douglas, 1912- . Australian Accent 1958, Australian Painting Today '63.

'Private 19022', *see* Manning, Frederic.

'Prout, Denton' [Charles Walter Phillips], 1910- . Henry Lawson: the Grey Dreamer 1963.

Pryce, Henry Weston, 1891-1963. Your Old Battalion 1926.

Pryor, Oswald, 1881- . Australia's Little Cornwall 1962.

Punch (Melbourne). 1855-1925.

§Purdie, Edna, 1894-1968. *Ed. with O. M. Roncoroni*: Henry Handel Richardson 1957.

Quadrant. 1956- . *Ed.* J. McAuley, D. Horne, P. Coleman, qq.v.

Quaife, Barzillai, 1798-1873. The Intellectual Sciences 1872.

Quinlan, Lucille Mary, 1900- . Here My Home 1967.

Quinn, John, 1915- . Battle Stations 1944.

Quinn, Roderic, 1867-1949. Mostyn Stayne 1897, The Hidden Tide '99, The Circling Hearths 1901, Poems '20.

Ramson, William Stanley, 1933- . Australian English 1966. *See also A. Harris 1849.*

‡Ranken, George, 1827-95. Windabyne 1878-79, '95.

Ranken, William Logan, 1839-1902. The Dominion of Australia 1874.

Ratcliffe, Francis Noble, 1904- . Flying Fox and Drifting Sand 1938.

Rawling, James Normington-, *see* Normington-Rawling.

*Rawson, Geoffrey, . Bligh of the 'Bounty' 1930, The Strange Case of Mary Bryant '38, Desert Journeys '48, Australia '48, The Count '53, Sea Prelude '58, Pandora's Last Voyage '63.

‡Rayment, Tarlton, 1882-1964. The Valley of the Sky 1937. *See also L. Young 1967.*

§Read, Stanley Arnold, . Australian Literary Criticism 1965.

§Reade, Charles, 1814-84. It is Never Too Late to Mend 1856.

Realist Writer, The. 1952-54. Ed. B. Wannan, S. Murray-Smith, qq.v.

Reed, Thomas Thornton, 1902- . Henry Kendall 1960. *Ed.*: Poetical Works of Henry Kendall 1966.

‡Rees, Leslie 1905- . Karrawingi the Emu 1946, Towards an Australian Drama '53. *Ed.*: Australian Radio Plays 1946.

Register (Adelaide). *See 1836.*

Reid, *Sir* George, 1845-1918. My Reminiscences 1917.

'Renar, Frank', *see* Fox, Sir Frank.

Reynolds, John, 1899- . Edmund Barton 1948.

'Richardson, Henry Handel' [*née* Ethel Richardson], 1870-1946. Maurice Guest 1908, The Getting of Wisdom '10, Australia Felix '17, The Way Home '25, Ultima Thule '29, The Fortunes of Richard Mahony '30, The End of a Childhood '34, The Young Cosima '39, Myself When Young '48. *See also V. Buckley 1961, L. J. Kramer 1954, '62, '66, '67, E. Odeen 1963, N. Palmer 1950, E. Purdie & O. M. Roncoroni 1957.*

‡Sandes, John, 1863-1938. Rhymes of the Times 1898, Ballads of Battle 1900, Love and the Aeroplane '10.

Savery, Henry, 1791-1842. The Hermit in Van Diemen's Land 1829, Quintus Servinton 1830-31.

‡Sayers, Charles Edward, 1901- . David Syme 1965. *See also J. Morgan 1852, 'R. Boldrewood' 1884.*

Schlunke, Eric Otto, 1906-60. The Man in the Silo 1955, The Village Hampden '58, Stories of the Riverina '65.

‡Scott, *Sir* Ernest, 1867-1939. Life of Matthew Flinders 1914, A Short History of Australia '16, A History of the University of Melbourne '36, Australia During the War '36. *Ed.*: Australian Discovery 1929, Cambridge History of the British Empire VII.i '33, Gold Fields Diary (Cecil, *see* 1852) '35.

Scott, William Neville, 1923- . Focus on Judith Wright 1967, Some People '69.

Sealy, Robert ['Menippus'], 1831-61. Scraps 1859.

Semmler, Clement, 1914- . For the Uncanny Man 1963, A. B. (Banjo) Paterson '65, Barcroft Boake '65, Kenneth Slessor '66, The Banjo of the Bush '66, A. B. Paterson '67. *Ed.*: Stories of the Riverina (Schlunke) 1965, The World of Banjo Paterson '67, Twentieth Century Australian Literary Criticism '67. *Ed. with D. Whitelock, q.v.*: Literary Australia 1966.

‡Serle, (Alan) Geoffrey, 1922- . The Golden Age 1963. *See also R. Carboni 1855.*

Serle, Percival, 1871-1951. Bibliography of Australian Poetry and Verse 1925, Dictionary of Australian Biography '49. *Ed.*: An Australasian Anthology 1927, Poems of Furnley Maurice '44.

Seymour, Alan, 1927- . The One Day of the Year (D) 1962, (N) '67.

Shann, Edward Owen Giblin, 1884-1935. Cattle Chosen 1926, Economic History of Australia '30.

Shapcott, Thomas, 1935- . Time on Fire 1961, The Mankind Thing '64, Sonnets '64, A Taste of Salt Water '67, Focus on Charles Blackman '67, Inwards to the Sun '69. *Ed. with R. Hall, q.v.*: New Impulses in Australian Poetry 1968.

*Shapiro, Karl, 1913- . See 1942.

*Sharp, William ['Fiona McLeod'], 1856-1905. See 1876.

Shave, Lionel, 1888-1954. Five Proven One-Act Plays 1948.

‡Shaw, Alan George Lewers, 1916- . The Economic Development of Australia 1944, The Story of Australia '55 Convicts and the Colonies '66.

‡Shaw, Charles, 1900-55. The Warrambungle Mare 1943, Outback Occupations '43, A Sheaf of Shorts '44.

Shaw, Winifred, 1905- . The Aspen Tree 1920, The Yellow Cloak '22, Babylon '24.

Shillinglaw, John Joseph, 1830-1905. *Ed.*: Historical Records of Port Phillip 1879.

Shore, Arnold, 1897-1963. Tom Roberts 1964.

Shumack, Samuel, 1850-1940. An Autobiography 1967.

*'Shute, Nevil' [Nevil Shute Norway], 1899-1960. A Town Like Alice 1950, The Far Country '52, In the Wet '53, Beyond the Black Stump '56, On the Beach '57.

'Sidney, Neilma' [Neilma Gantner, *née* Myer], 1922- . Saturday Afternoon 1959, Beyond the Bay '66.

§Sidney, Samuel [*né* Samuel Solomon], 1813-83. The Three Colonies of Australia 1852.

‡Simpson, Colin, 1908- . Infidelities (*see* Slessor) 1931, Adam in Ochre '51.

‡Simpson, Helen, 1897-1940. Boomerang 1932, The Woman on the Beast '33, Under Capricorn '37.

Simpson, Ronald Albert, 1929- . The Walk Along the Beach 1960, This Real Pompeii '64, After the Assassination '68. *Contrib. to*: Eight by Eight (*see* Buckley) 1963.

Sinclair, James Patrick, 1928- . Behind the Ranges 1966, The Outside Man '69.

Sinnett, Frederick, 1830-66. The Fiction Fields of Australia 1856.

‡Skinner, Mary Louisa, 1877-1955. Black Swans 1925. *With D. H. Lawrence, q.v.*: The Boy in the Bush 1924.

*Sladen, Douglas, 1856-1947. See 1888, 1912, 1934, 1939.

Slessor, Kenneth, 1901- . Thief of the Moon 1924, Earth-Visitors '26, Five Visions of Captain Cook '31, Cuckooz Contrey '32, Darlinghurst Nights '33, Funny Farmyard '33, Five Bells '39, One Hundred Poems '44, Portrait of Sydney '50, Poems '57, Australian Profile '60, The Grapes are Growing '63, Life at the Cross '65, Sydney Harbour '66, Canberra '66. *Ed.*: Southerly 1956-61. *Ed. with Jack Lindsay, q.v.*: Poetry in Australia 1923. *Ed. with J. Thompson & R. G. Howarth, qq.v.*: The Penguin Book of Australian Verse 1958. *See also M. Harris 1963, J. A. R. McKellar 1932,*

Slessor, Kenneth—*contd*
L. Robinson 1933, C. Semmler 1966, A. K. Thomson 1968.

Smith, Bernard, 1916- . Place, Taste and Tradition 1945, European Vision and the South Pacific '60, Australian Painting '62.

Smith, Frank Penn-, *see* Penn-Smith.

Smith, Jan, 1935- . An Ornament of Grace 1966, The Worshipful Company '69.

‡Smith, James, 1820-1910. From Melbourne to Melrose 1888.

Smith, Patsy Adam, 1926- . Hear the Train Blow 1964, Moonbird People '65, There Was a Ship '67, Tiger Country '68, Hobart Sketchbook '68, Folklore of Australia's Railwaymen '69, The Rails Go Westward '69.

Smith, Stephen Murray-, *see* Murray-Smith.

Smith, Vivian, 1933- . The Other Meaning 1956, James McAuley '65, An Island South '67.

Smith, William Hart-, *see* Hart-Smith.

‡Sorenson, Edward Sylvester, 1869-1939. The Squatter's Ward 1908.

Souter, Charles Henry, 1864-1944. Irish Lords 1912, To Many Ladies '17, The Mallee Fire '23, The Lonely Rose '35.

Souter, Gavin, 1929- . New Guinea 1963, Sydney (Sydney Observed) '65, '67, A Peculiar People '68.

‡Southall, Ivan, 1921- . Out of the Dawn 1942, The Weaver From Meltham '50, Meet Simon Black '50, They Shall Not Pass Unseen '56, Bluey Truscott '58, Softly Tread the Brave '60, Hills End '62, Lawrence Hargrave '64.

South Asian Register. 1827-28.
South Australian Advertiser 1858- .
South Australian Gazette and Colonial Register. 1836-39. *As Register:* 1839-1931.
South Australian Magazine. 1841-43.
Southerly. 1939- .
Southern Australian (Adelaide). 1838-52.
Southern Review. 1963- .

‡Spence, Catherine Helen, 1825-1910. Clara Morison 1854, Tender and True '56, Mr Hogarth's Will '65, The Author's Daughter '68, Gathered In '81-'82, Autobiography 1910. *See also E. J. Gunton 1967, J. Young 1937.*

‡Spence, Eleanor, 1928- . Patterson's Track 1958.

‡Spence, William Guthrie, 1846-1926. Australia's Awakening 1909.

Spencer, Albert Henry, 1886- . The Hill of Content 1959.

‡Spencer, Thomas Edward, 1845-1911.

How McDougall Topped the Score 1906, Budgeree Ballads '08.

Spencer, *Sir* Walter Baldwin, 1860-1929. The Native Tribes of the Northern Territory 1914, Wanderings in Wild Australia '28. *With F. J. Gillen, q.v.:* The Native Tribes of Central Australia 1899, The Northern Tribes of Central Australia 1904, The Arunta '27. *See also R. R. Marett & T. K. Penniman (edd.),* Spencer's Last Journey *1931.*

Spencer-Browne, Reginald, 1856-1943. Shadow and Shine 1874, The Last Ride '75, Romances of the Goldfield and Bush '90, A Journalist's Memories 1927.

‡Spielvogel, Nathan, 1874-1956. A Gumsucker on the Tramp 1905, The Cocky Farmer '07, Old Eko's Note Book '30, The History of Ballarat '35, Selected Short Stories '56.

Spinner, The. 1924-27.

'Standby', *see* Porteous, R. S.

Star (Sydney). *See 1887.*

Stead, Christina, 1902- . The Salzburg Tales 1934, Seven Poor Men of Sydney '34, The Beauties and Furies '36, House of All Nations '38, The Man Who Loved Children '40, For Love Alone '44, Letty Fox, Her Luck '46, A Little Tea, A Little Chat '48, The People With the Dogs '52, Dark Places of the Heart (Cotters' England) '66, The Puzzleheaded Girl '67. *See also R. G. Geering,* Christina Stead *(W) 1969.*

Stephens, Alfred George, 1865-1933. A Queenslander's Travel-Notes 1894, Oblation 1902, The Red Pagan '04, Victor Daley '05, The Pearl and the Octopus '11, Bill's Idees '13, Henry Kendall '28, Chris. Brennan '33. *Ed.: Bulletin* Red Page 1896-1906, Story Book 1901, Reciter '01, Off the Bluebush (Bourke) '15. *Founded:* The *Bookfellow* 1899-1925. *With A. Dorrington, q.v.:* The Lady Calphurnia Royal 1909. *See also V. Palmer 1941, P. R. Stephensen 1940.*

Stephens, James Brunton, 1835-1902. Convict Once 1871, The Godolphin Arabian '73, A Hundred Pounds '76, Poetical Works 1902, My Chinee Cook and Other Humorous Verses '02. *See also A. P. Martin 1882, C. Hadgraft 1969.*

‡Stephensen, Percy Reginald, 1901-65. The Bushwhackers 1929, The Foundations of Culture in Australia '36, The Life and Works of A. G. Stephens '40, Kookaburras and Satyrs '54, The History and Description of Sydney Harbour '66. *Ed.:* Memorial edn of Baylebridge, q.v.

Stephensen, Percy Reginald—*contd*
Ed. with Jack Lindsay, q.v.: London Aphrodite 1928-29. With F. Clune, q.v.: The Viking of Van Diemen's Land 1954.

Steven, Alexander Gordon, 1865-1923. The Witchery of Earth 1911, Wind on the Wold '14, Poems '18, Revolt '19, Lures '23, Collected Poems '25.

Steven, Margaret, 1933- . Arthur Phillip 1962, Merchant Campbell '65, John Macarthur '68, Robert Campbell (G) '69.

Stevens, Bertram, 1872-1922. *Ed.*: My Sundowner (Farrell) 1904, An Anthology of Australian Verse '06, *Bulletin* Red Page '06-'08, Bush Ballads '08, The Golden Treasury of Australian Verse '09, Wine and Roses (Daley) '11, *Lone Hand* '11-'17, *Art in Australia* '16-'22, Poems (Kendall) '20. *Ed. with G. Mackaness, q.v.*: Selections from the Australian Poets 1913.

*Stevenson, Robert Louis, 1850-94. See 1890.

Stewart, Douglas, 1913- . Green Lions 1936, The White Cry '39, Elegy for an Airman '40, Sonnets to the Unknown Soldier '41, Ned Kelly '43, A Girl With Red Hair '44, The Fire on the Snow and The Golden Lover '44, The Dosser in Springtime '46, Glencoe '47, Shipwreck '47, The Flesh and the Spirit '48, Sun Orchids '52, The Birdsville Track '55, Four Plays '58, Fisher's Ghost '60, The Garden of Ships '62, Rutherford '62, Selected Poems (AP) '63, The Seven Rivers '66, Collected Poems '67. *Ed.*: *Bulletin* Red Page 1941-61, Voyager Poems 1960, Kenneth Mackenzie '61, Modern Australian Verse '64, Hugh McCrae (AP) '66, Short Stories of Australia: the Lawson Tradition '67. *Ed. with N. Keesing, q.v.*: Australian Bush Ballads 1955, Old Bush Songs '57, The Pacific Book of Bush Ballads '67. *See also N. Keesing 1965, A. D. Hope 1963.*

Stewart, Harold, 1916- . Phoenix Wings 1948, Orpheus '56, A Net of Fireflies '60, A Chime of Windbells '69. *See also 'Ern Malley'.*

Stivens, Dal, 1911- . The Tramp 1936, The Courtship of Uncle Henry '46, Jimmy Brockett '51, The Gambling Ghost '53, Ironbark Bill '55, The Scholarly Mouse '57, The Wide Arch '58, Three Persons Make a Tiger '68, Selected Stories '69.

Stone, Louis, 1871-1935. Jonah 1911, Betty Wayside '15. *See also H. J. Oliver 1968.*

Stone, Walter, 1910- . Henry Lawson 1954, Joseph Furphy '55. *Ed.*: *Biblionews* 1947- , *Southerly* 1962. *With H. Anderson, q.v.*: C. Brennan 1959. *With G. Mackaness, q.v.*: The Books of the *Bulletin* 1955. *See also J. Mudie 1837.*

Stow, Catherine, *see* Parker, *Mrs* K. Langloh.

Stow, Randolph, 1935- . A Haunted Land 1956, Act One '57, The Bystander '57, To the Islands '58, Outrider '62, Tourmaline '63, The Merry-go-round in the Sea '65, Midnite '67, A Counterfeit Silence '69. *See also Patricia A. O'Brien 1968.*

Stream. 1931.

Strong, *Sir* Archibald Thomas, 1876-1930. Peradventure 1911, Sonnets of the Empire '15, Poems '18, Four Studies '33.

Strzelecki, *Sir* Paul Edmund de, 1797-1873. Physical Description of N.S.W. and Van Diemen's Land 1845. *See also H. Heney 1961, G. Rawson 1953.*

Stuart, Donald, 1913- . Yandy 1959, The Driven '61, Yaralie '62.

Stuart, John McDouall, 1815-66. Explorations in Australia 1864. *See also D. S. Macmillan 1966, Ian Mudie 1968, D. Pike 1958, M. Webster 1958.*

'Stukeley, Simon', *see* Savery 1829.

Sturt, Charles, 1795-1869. Two Expeditions 1833, Narrative of an Expedition '49. *See also J. H. L. Cumpston 1951, J. K. Ewers 1956, D. E. Kennedy 1958, H. Kingsley 1872 and M. Langley, Sturt of the Murray 1969.*

‡Sugden, Edward Holdsworth, 1854-1935. *With F. W. Eggleston, q.v.*: George Swinburne 1931. *See Mary F. Sugden, E. H. Sugden 1941.*

Sun (Sydney). 1910- .

Sun News-Pictorial (Melbourne). 1922- .

Sutherland, Alexander, 1852-1902. *Ed.*: Poems of Kendall 1886. *With G. Sutherland, q.v.*: The History of Australia 1877. *With H. G. Turner, q.v.*: The Development of Australian Literature 1898. *See also H. G. Turner 1908.*

‡Sutherland, George, 1855-1905. *With A. Sutherland, q.v.*: The History of Australia 1877.

Sutherland, Wendy, 1936- . Caroline Chisholm 1967.

Swan, Nathaniel Walter, 1835-84. Tales of Australian Life 1875.

‡Sweetman, Edward, 1875-1966. Australian Constitutional Development 1925.

Sydney Gazette. 1803-42. *See also 1810.*

Sydney Herald. 1831- .

Sydney Mail. 1860-1938.

Sydney Morning Herald. See 1831.
Sydney University Magazine. 1883-92.
Sydney Monthly Review. 1881-83.
Syme, David, 1827-1908. Outlines of an Industrial Science 1876, Representative Government in England '81, On the Modification of Organisms '90. See also A. Pratt 1908, C. E. Sayers 1965.
Syred, Celia, 1911- . Cocky's Castle 1966.

Talbot, Norman, 1936- . Poems for a Female Universe 1968. Ed.: XI Hunter Valley Poets + VII 1966.
‡Tardent, Henri Alexis, 1854-1929. The Life and Poetry of George Essex Evans 1913.
'Tasma' [née Jessie Huybers, m. (1) C. F. Fraser, (2) A. Couvreur], 1848-97. Uncle Piper of Piper's Hill 1889, In Her Earliest Youth '90, A Sydney Sovereign '90, The Penance of Portia James '91, A Knight of the White Feather '92, Not Counting the Cost '95, A Fiery Ordeal '97.
Taylor, Geoff(rey), 1920- . Piece of Cake 1956, The Hollow Square '58, The Crop Dusters '60, Blueberg '60, Dreamboat '62, Sir '63, Court of Honour '66, Day of the Republic '68.
‡Taylor, George Augustine, 1872-1928. Those Were the Days 1918.
‡Taylor, Thomas Griffith, 1880-1963. Journeyman Taylor 1958, Douglas Mawson '62.
Telegraph (Brisbane). 1872- .
Tench, Watkin, 1758?-1833. A Narrative of the Expedition to Botany Bay 1789, A Complete Account of the Settlement at Port Jackson '93.
‡Tenison-Woods, Julian Edmund, 1832-89. A History of the Discovery and Exploration of Australia 1865.
Tennant, Kylie, 1912- . Tiburon 1935, Foveaux '39, The Battlers '41, Ride on Stranger '43, Time Enough Later '43, Lost Haven '46, John o' the Forest '50, Tether a Dragon '52, The Joyful Condemned '53, Australia '53, Long John Silver '54, The Bells of the City '55, The Honey Flow '56, All the Proud Tribesmen '59, Speak You So Gently '59, The Bushrangers' Christmas Eve '59, Trail Blazers of the Air '65, Tell Morning This '67, Ma Jones and the Little White Cannibals '67. Ed.: Summer's Tales 1964, '65. See also M. Dick 1966.
Thatcher, Charles Robert, 1831-78. Colonial Songster 1857, Colonial Minstrel '64. See also H. Anderson 1958, '60.

Therry, Sir Roger, 1800-74. Reminiscences 1863.
‡Thiele, Colin, 1920- . Progress to Denial 1945, Splinters and Shards '45, The Golden Lightning '51, Man in a Landscape '60, The Sun on the Stubble '61, Gloop the Gloomy Bunyip '62, Storm Boy '63, February Dragon '65, In Charcoal and Conté '66, The Rim of the Morning '66, Mrs Munch and Puffing Billy '67, Heysen of Hahndorf '68, Barossa Valley Sketchbook '68, Blue Fin '69, Yellow Jacket Jock '69.
*Thirkell, Angela, 1890-1961. As 'Leslie Parker': Trooper to the Southern Cross 1934.
Thomas, Evan Henry, 1801?-37. The Bandit of the Rhine 1835.
'Thomas, Julian', see James, John Stanley.
Thompson, Brian, 1938- . Ed.: Once Around the Sun 1966.
‡Thompson, John, 1907-68. Three Dawns Ago 1935, Sesame '44, Thirty Poems '54, I Hate and I Love '64. Ed. with K. Slessor & R. G. Howarth, qq.v.: The Penguin Book of Australian Verse 1958.
‡Thomson, Andrew Kilpatrick, 1901- . Ed.: Collected Works of Thomas Welsby 1967. Sel.: Critical Essays on Kenneth Slessor, Judith Wright 1968.
Thwaites, Michael, 1915- . The Jervis Bay 1943, Poems of War and Peace '68.
Tierney, John, see 'James, Brian'.
Tilbrook, Ian, 1907- . Torn Edges 1938, Time-Shadows '45. With R. Ingamells, q.v.: Conditional Culture 1938.
‡Timms, Edward Vivian, 1895-1960. The Hills of Hate 1925.
‡Tindale, Norman Barnett, 1900- . With H. A. Lindsay, q.v.: The First Walkabout 1954.
Tolchard, Clifford, 1908- . The Humble Adventurer 1965.
Tolmer, Alexander, 1815-90. Reminiscences of an Adventurous and Chequered Career 1882.
Tomholt, Sydney, 1884- . Bleak Dawn 1936.
Tompson, Charles, 1807-83. Wild Notes, from the Lyre of a Native Minstrel 1826.
Travers, Basil Holmes, 1919- . The Captain-General 1953.
Tregenza, John, 1931- . Australian Little Magazines 1964, Professor of Democracy '68.
Triad, The. Published in Sydney 1915-27.
Trist, Margaret, 1914- . In the Sun 1943, Now That We're Laughing '45, What Else is There? '46, Daddy '47, Morning in Queensland '58.

Tritton, Harold Percy ['Duke'], 1886-1965. Time Means Tucker 1964.

*Trollope, Anthony, 1815-82. See 1871, '73, '75, '79, and also M. Muir 1949.

'Trooper Gerardy', see Gerard, Edwin.

Truebridge, B. A., see 'Vrepont, Brian'.

Truran, John William, 1897- . Green Mallee 1932, Where the Plain Begins '33.

Tucker, James, 1808-88? See C. Roderick 1952, 1955.

‡Tucker, Thomas George, 1859-1946. Things Worth Thinking About 1890, The Cultivation of Literature in Australia 1902, Platform Monologues '14.

Tuckey, James Hingston, 1776-1816. An Account of a Voyage 1805.

Tullipan, Ron, 1917- . Follow the Sun 1960, March into Morning '62.

‡Turnbull, Clive, 1906- . Outside Looking In 1933, 14 Poems '44, Bluestone '45, Mulberry Leaves '45, Eureka '46, Bonanza '46, Black War '48, Frontier '49, These Tears of Fire '49, Essington Lewis '63, Australian Lives '65, A Concise History of Australia '65.

Turner, Alexander, 1907- . Hester Siding 1937, Australian Stages '44, Royal Mail '44.

‡Turner, Ethel, 1872-1958. Seven Little Australians 1894.

Turner, George Reginald, 1916- . Young Man of Talent 1959, A Stranger and Afraid '61, The Cupboard Under the Stairs '62, A Waste of Shame '65, The Lame Dog Man '67.

Turner, George William, 1921- . The English Language in Australia and N.Z. 1966.

Turner, Henry Gyles, 1831-1920. A History of the Colony of Victoria 1904, Alexander Sutherland '08. With A. Sutherland, q.v.: The Development of Australian Literature 1898.

‡Turner, Walter James, 1889-1946. Blow For Balloons 1935.

*'Twain, Mark' [Samuel Langhorne Clemens], 1835-1910. See 1895.

Twentieth Century. 1947- .

Tyrrell, James, 1875-1961. Old Books, Old Friends, Old Sydney 1952.

‡Upfield, Arthur, 1892-1964. The House of Cain 1928. See J. Hawke, Follow My Dust! 1957.

‡Ullathorne, William Bernard, 1806-89. The Catholic Mission in Australasia 1837, The Horrors of Transportation '38, A Reply to Judge Burton '40, Autobiography '91.

‡Uren, Malcolm, 1900- . Land Looking West 1948, Glint of Gold '48, Edward John Eyre '64. With Robert Stephens: Waterless Horizons 1941.

'Vagabond, The' see James, John Stanley.

Van Diemen's Land Gazette and General Advertiser. 1814.

Vallis, Val, 1916- . Songs of the East Coast 1947, Dark Wind Blowing '61. Ed. with R. S. Byrnes, q.v.: The Queensland Centenary Anthology 1959.

Vaux, James Hardy, 1782-?. Memoirs 1819. See also B. Elliott 1944.

Venture. 1937-40. Ed. R. Ingamells, q.v.

Verse. 1929-33. Ed. L. Lavater, q.v.

Vickers, Frederick Bert, 1903- . The Mirage 1955, First Place to the Stranger '56, Though Poppies Grow '58.

Victorian Review. 1879-86.

‡Vidal, Mary Theresa, 1815-69. Tales for the Bush 1845, The Cabramatta Store '50, Bengala '60. See Faith Compton Mackenzie, As Much As I Dare 1938.

‡Vidler, Edward Alexander, 1863-1942. Ed.: The A. L. Gordon Memorial Volume 1926.

‡Villiers, Alan, 1903- . Whalers of the Midnight Sun 1948, Captain Cook '67.

Vision. 1923-24.

‡'Vrepont, Brian' [Benjamin Arthur Truebridge], 1882-1955. Beyond the Claw 1943.

§Wakefield, Edward Gibbon, 1796-1862. A Letter From Sydney 1829.

‡Walch, Garnet, 1843-1913. Trookulentos 1872.

Walker, Kath, 1920- . We Are Going 1964, The Dawn is At Hand '66.

Walker, Robin Berwick, 1925- . Old New England 1966.

‡Walker, William, 1828-1908. Australian Literature 1864.

Wallace-Crabbe, Chris(topher), 1934- . The Music of Division 1959, In Light and Darkness '63, The Rebel General '67. Contrib. to: Eight by Eight (see Buckley) 1963. Ed.: Six Voices 1963.

‡Wannan, Bill, 1915- . Ed.: The Realist Writer 1952, A Marcus Clarke Reader '63.

Warburton, Peter Egerton, 1813-89. Journey Across the Western Interior of Australia 1875.

‡Ward, John Manning, 1919- . Earl Grey and the Australian Colonies 1958.

‡Ward, Russel, 1914- . The Australian Legend 1958, Australia '65. Ed.: The

Wilmot, Chester, 1911-54. Tobruk 1944, The Struggle for Europe '52.

Wilmot, Frank, see 'Maurice, Furnley'.

‡Wilson, Erle, 1898- . Coorinna 1953.

Wilson, Gwendoline, . Murray of Yarralumla 1968.

Wintle, Henry Saxelby Melville, see 'Melville, Henry'.

Wise, Bernhard Ringrose, 1858-1916. The Commonwealth of Australia 1909, The Making of the Australian Commonwealth '13.

Withers, William Bramwell, 1823-1913. The History of Ballarat 1870.

‡Wood, George Arnold, 1865-1928. The Discovery of Australia 1922.

*Wood, Thomas, 1892-1950. Cobbers 1934. See also 'Rolf Boldrewood' 1882.

‡Woodberry, Joan, 1921- . Rafferty Rides a Winner 1961.

Woods, J. E. Tenison, see Tenison-Woods.

*Woodward, Frances Joyce, 1921- . Portrait of Jane 1951.

Woolls, William, 1814-93. The Voyage 1832, Australia '33, Miscellanies '38, A Short Account of . . . Samuel Marsden '44.

‡Wright, David McKee, 1869-1928. An Irish Heart 1918, Gallipoli '20.

Wright, Judith, 1915- . The Moving Image 1946, Woman to Man '49, The Gateway '53, The Two Fires '55, Kings of the Dingoes '58, The Generations of Men '59, The Day The Mountains Played '60, Range the Mountains High '62, Birds '62, Five Senses '63, Charles Harpur '63, Country Towns '63, Selected Poems (AP) '63, City Sunrise '64, Preoccupations in Australian Poetry '65, The Other Half '66, The Nature of Love '66, The River and the Road '66, Henry Lawson '67. Ed.: A Book of Australian Verse 1956, New Land, New Language '57. Sel.: Shaw Neilson (AP) 1963. See also P. A. O'Brien 1968, W. N. Scott 1967, A. K. Thomson 1968.

‡Wrightson, Patricia, 1921- . The Crooked Snake 1955.

Wrixon, Sir Henry John, 1839-1913. Jacob Shumate 1903, Edward Fairlie Frankfort '12.

Young, Gordon Forbes, 1872-1954. Under the Coolibah Tree 1953.

Young, Jeanne Forster, 1876-1955. Catherine Helen Spence 1937. See also C. Spence 1910.

Young, Lynette, 1894- . The Melody Lingers On 1967.